social research

An International Quarterly of the Social Sciences

Vol 73 : No 3 : Fall 2006

THE NEW SCHOOL
A UNIVERSITY

EDITOR Arien Mack

EDITORIAL BOARD Arjun Appadurai, Elzbieta Matynia, Alan Ryan, Charles Tilly, Jamie Walkup, Yirmiyahu Yovel

MANAGING EDITOR Cara N. Schlesinger

COPY EDITOR Bill Finan

ASSISTANT COPY EDITOR Sarah Fauer

MANAGING EDITORIAL ASSISTANTS Adam Gannaway, Adam Rothstein

WEB ASSISTANTS John Giunta

CONFERENCE COORDINATOR Maria Juliana Byck

COVER Jamie Prokell

BUSINESS & EDITORIAL OFFICE
Social Research, The New School for Social Research, 65 Fifth Avenue–Room 344, New York, NY 10003 <socres@newschool.edu>

SUBSCRIPTIONS

Print + Online: $40 per year individuals, $120 libraries and institutions. Online only: $36 individuals, $100 libraries and institutions. Single print issues available through our office. Agency discounts available. Subscribe online at <www.socres.org> or contact our office.

Social Research is published quarterly by The New School for Social Research, a division of The New School, 65 Fifth Avenue, Room 344, New York, NY 10003. <http://www.socres.org>. E-mail: socres@newschool.edu

Contributions should be no more than 8,000 words and typed double-spaced on 8.5" x 11" paper. Notes and references should be typed as separate documents, double-spaced and according to MLA style. Two copies of the manuscript and a stamped return envelope are required. Articles published in Social Research may not be reprinted without permission.

Reprints of back issues, if still available, may be ordered from Periodicals Service Co., 11 Main St., Germantown, NY 12526. Microfilm or microfiche copies of complete volumes of Social Research may be ordered from Bell & Howell Information and Learning/UMI, P.O. Box 1346, Ann Arbor, MI 48106. Complete volumes may be ordered by regular subscribers and copies of single issues, if out of print, may be ordered by any reader, in either microfilm or in print enlarged from microfilm.

Bernhard DeBoer, Inc., the U.S. bookstore distributor of Social Research, may be contacted at 113 East Centre St., Nutley, New Jersey 07110.

Social Research is indexed in ABC POL SCI, ASSIA, Current Contents / Social & Behavioral Sciences, Public Affairs Information Service (PAIS), Research Alert, Social Sciences Citation Index, Social Scisearch, and United States Political Science Documents.

Copyright 2006 by The New School. All rights reserved. ISSN 0037-783X. ISBN 1-933481-06-4.

Periodicals postage paid at New York, NY and at additional mailing offices.

Postmaster: Send address changes to Social Research, 55 West 13th St., New York, NY 10011

Contents

Politics and Science How Their Interplay
Results in Public Policy

IV. The Environment

V. Energy: Technology and Sources of Power

VI. Roundtable Discussion

Arien Mack
Editor's Introduction

"POLITICS AND SCIENCE" IS THE FIFTEENTH IN THE *SOCIAL RESEARCH*
conference series, which began in 1989. From the beginning, this
series has tried to foster public discussion of matters of grave importance, and has explored those matters both in terms of their immediate import and, whenever possible, within their historical and cultural
contexts. To realize the mission of the conference series, we attempt
with each conference to bring together scholars and practitioners from
a broad array of disciplines so that the topics are viewed from a range of
perspectives. But something has happened to this series in the past few
years that reflects the troubling changes in our society, with the consequence that the conferences have become less scholarly and academic,
and decidedly more political. Despite our efforts, it turned out to be
extremely difficult to get representatives of the current administration to agree to speak at this conference. In fact, the list of people who
declined our invitation to participate is an impressive one.

Current events seem designed to make the subject of "Politics
and Science" increasingly relevant to what is going on between scientists, policymakers, and government officials. However, the initial idea
for the conference grew out of my reading of a Union of Concerned
Scientists (UCS) report, issued in February 2004, on scientific integrity,
in which the group called for immediate steps to be taken to "restore
the integrity of science in the federal policymaking process." This statement was signed by over 8,000 scientists, including 49 Nobel laureates, 63 National Medal of Science recipients, and 171 members of the
National Academies of Sciences. In June 2005, Anthony Romero, direc-

tor of the American Civil Liberties Union, issued a report documenting how recent changes in federal policy have imposed "excessive, unnecessary, and ineffective restrictions on scientists." Unfortunately, things have only continued to get worse.

It is, I hope, our not-too-delusional wish that this issue of *Social Research*, which contains the papers from the "Politics and Science" conference, will help to change the relationship between scientists and policymakers so that the policies enacted will be based on the best scientific research available and will protect our well-being and that of future generations here and around the world.

I am deeply grateful to our funders, the Hewlett Foundation and the Packard Foundation, for their generous support of the conference, and to the many people who did their best to educate me on this subject and to those who worked with me to make the conference happen.

Arien Mack

EDITOR'S NOTE:

Due to the author's oversight, some passages in "The Political 'Participation' of Entrepreneurs: Challenge or Opportunity for the Chinese Communist Party?" by Gilles Guiheux, published in *Social Research* 73:1 (Spring 2006), were not acknowledged as quoted material. The passages in question occurred on page 223, lines 17-22 ("the mere existence . . . varying degrees.") and page 231, lines 22-31 ("The extent . . . their members"). Both passages were quoted from a paper by Kellee S. Tsai, entitled "A Divided Class: The Politics of Private Enterprise and Self-Employment in China," delivered at the 2000 Annual Meeting of the Association for Asian Studies. The first passage also appeared in a revised version of the paper, published as "Capitalists without a Class: Political Diversity Among Private Entrepreneurs in China, " which appeared in *Comparative Political Studies* 38:9 (Nov 2005): 1130-1158. We apologize to our readers and to Professor Tsai for this oversight.

Arien Mack and *Jean-Philippe Beja*

I. Recent History: The Emerging Conflict between Politics and Science

social research

AN INTERNATIONAL QUARTERLY OF THE SOCIAL SCIENCES

POLITICS AND SCIENCE
AN HISTORICAL VIEW

Arien Mack, Editor   **Volume 73, No. 4 (Winter 2006)**

Because "to forget history is to repeat it," the forthcoming issue of *Social Research* looks back over the long and tangled history of the relationship between politics and the science in order to better understand the present situation and the risks that may be incurred by policy decisions which reflect political or religious ideologies more than scientific data. This special issue examines how, throughout history, developments in science have been reacted to and absorbed into policy by the religious and political powers of the time.

Authors include:

Philip Kitcher on the role of science in democracies
Rivka Feldhay on the Tridentine Church and its politics of knowledge
David Cahan on Science and politics in Germany,1840-1900
Mario Biagioli on the political economy of knowledge disclosure
Nikolai Krementsov on the politics, and in, Soviet science and medicine
Theodore Porter on the historical shifting forms of the relationship between social science and politics/the state
Also including papers by **David Kaiser**, **Alan McGowan,** and **Norton Wise**.

1-933481-07-2. Available in Borders and independent bookstores or by order. $14 ind/$30 inst. Annual subscriptions Print + online: $40 ind/$120 inst. Foreign postage: $8/year or $3 for first back issue plus $2.00 each additional issue. Online only: $ 36 ind/$100 inst. Agent/bookseller discounts available. Payment by check (in US$, drawn on a U.S. bank, payable to Social Research), Visa or MasterCard. 65 Fifth Avenue, Rm 344, New York, NY 10003. Phone (212) 229-5776; Fax (212) 229-5476. socres@newschool.edu

VISIT US AT WWW.SOCRES.ORG.

Gerald Holton
Introduction

THE FIRST SECTION OF THIS SPECIAL ISSUE COVERS THE RECENT HISTORY of the emerging conflict between politics and science in the United States. The questions to be explored include: Has the balance of power among the various interests that play a role in determining public policy changed? What are the consequences of these changes? What lessons can be learned from past successes and failures in public policy?

The attempt to answer these questions comes at what may be a tipping point in the relation of politics and science. To understand better the relative radicalism of the present dilemma and its probable results, it will be useful to step back a bit and recall that from the beginning, and until very recently, science and technology were in mutually fruitful embrace of America's politics and policies. We all know of sturdy and benign offspring in recent decades: for example, the culture-changing Internet, much stimulated by DARPA; the triumphs of genome research, many being the results of federal support in the past; or the findings of economists such as Robert Solow and Zvi Grilliches that over a four-decade period in America, the gross output per man-hour doubled, with as much as 87 percent of that increase attributable to advances in science and technology—the kind that the National Science Foundation, the Department of Energy, and other agencies used to support in style.

To be sure, there have also been some bastard offspring of the union of politics and science—for example, the "Star Wars" missile system. But history reveals an underlying benign potential in the American soul that can and must reassert itself.

Even America's birth certificate, its Declaration of Independence, announced in its very first lines that the new nation was "entitled" to its existence by "the laws of nature." The so-called Founding Fathers were well educated in science, and commonly associated the ideal of society with Newton's image of the solar system, and the laws by which it harmoniously sustained itself.

Thomas Jefferson, who confessed himself most happy when he was doing science, saw a double purpose for the pursuit of science: of course, the advancement of knowledge, but also what he termed "the freedom and happiness of man." Thus, Jefferson's launching of the Lewis and Clark expedition had, in his mind, the double purpose: as a scientific survey of interest on its own, but also getting to know the area to which the nation was bound to expand.

Benjamin Franklin, whose anniversary we are celebrating this year, was of course a major scientist, rightly called the Newton of Electricity, and was also remembered for his studies in oceanography and meteorology, and on medical subjects. It was his great renown as a scientist from the New World that assured him access to the courts of Europe, thereby obtaining help and recognition for his nation at its most perilous moments.

When Alexis de Tocqueville visited in the 1830s, he recognized that America's technology, symbolized by Robert Fulton's steamship, was transforming society. At about that time, as Elting Morison pointed out in his ominously titled book, *From Knowledge to Nowhere*, the great Barge Canal, starting in Erie, was a great technological achievement, resulting in hugely accelerated commerce and the growth of cities.

With the start of the scientific approach to medicine in the 1860s, the curve plotting survival took off, and has continued upward, reflecting the longer and healthier lives that millions can enjoy. As a result, access to proper healthcare is considered more and more to be one of the basic human rights.

Among the numerous examples of the beneficent interaction of science, technology, and society, let me just briefly list a few more from which the nation can learn. World War II might well have ended earlier but with a quite different outcome if it had not been for the development by the Allies of radar. Next, President Franklin Delano Roosevelt turned out to have been quite right when he wrote to Vannevar Bush, one of his principal advisers on science and technology, in November 1944, that there was no reason why the scientific and technical advances that helped to win the war should not be "profitably employed in times of peace . . . for the improvement of national health, the creation of new enterprises bringing new jobs, and the betterment of the national standard of living." The chief result of the Vannevar Bush report was the first strong federal commitment to fund science and technology.

In an analogous way, President Jimmy Carter asked his science adviser, Frank Press, to request from every federal agency a list of vexing problems for which scientific research may find solutions. By November 1977, an impressive master list of 92 such problems of science for society had been assembled (see Gerhard Sonnert, *Ivory Bridges*, 2002). Unhappily, the implementation became one of the victims of the national election in 1980. Similarly, in early November 2000, a large conference of leading scientists and administrators was held in Washington to show how cutting-edge basic research could be put in the service of public objectives. This promising initiative also became dormant owing the results of an election a few days later. But both these initiatives illustrate the readiness for success in strengthening fruitful bonding of policy objectives with science and technology. History assures us that is *truly* the tradition in America, an honorable tradition, the very *opposite* of the present, dark dilemmas the papers in this volume portray, with the aim of overcoming them.

After all, willful dogmatism is eventually vulnerable to empirical data. Rationality sooner or later triumphs over ideology. Remember that in Dostoevsky's novel, *The Brothers Karamazov*, the Grand Inquisitor, flaunting his all-too-familiar dogmatism, tells Ivan: "No science will give men bread. . . . There are three powers, three powers alone, able

WHY DOES IT MATTER?

As Gerald Holton eloquently explains in his introduction, most of the issues we care about hinge increasingly on the way we manage science and technology. The enormous gains in economic productivity, communications, entertainment, and health care that we've enjoyed for a century have all been driven by technical advances. Our national security is rooted in technical leadership. While the bulk of the credit for these advances goes to private inventors, public policy has played an important role both in supporting critical research investment and policies shaping use and adoption of innovations. The benefits of technical advances always seem to come with unintended consequences —consequences that scientists are uniquely able to anticipate. Effective, low-cost responses to problems like environmental challenges depend heavily on scientific advice.

Science and technology advice is also essential if only because research and development has grown to be about 13 percent of discretionary expenditures in the federal budget. There is simply no question that science and technology advice is essential to wise management of public policy in the twenty-first century.

THE STATE OF THE ART

While the need for sound science and technology advice has increased, there is real concern that the capacity for delivering this service is in disarray. There are several classes of concern:

▸ Suppression of analysis and data collection (no information, no problems, no regulation)
▸ Secret proceedings
▸ Packing advisory committees
▸ Magnifying (or manufacturing) uncertainty
▸ Punishing whistle-blowers
▸ Equating fringe science with mainstream science

One class is simply the suppression of analysis and data collection. The motives are clear. If there is no data to document a problem, there is no need to solve it, and therefore no need for public intervention. If your original goal is to block public intervention in the marketplace for any reason, suppressing analysis is a very effective strategy. If decisions are made in secret using advice from unknown sources, there is no way to understand the analytical basis for the decision and it is therefore difficult to critique the process. We also have examples where it certainly appears that technical expertise was not the criteria for selecting the people who are selected to provide advice. For example, Dr. Gerald Keusch, former director of the Fogarty International Center at the National Institutes of Health, recently released a lengthy list of examples of individuals he had tried to place on advisory commissions for his National Institutes of Health group but who were repeatedly turned down, including a Nobel prize winner. Instead, people with no obvious qualifications were appointed.

Another complaint has been the cynical manipulation of uncertainty. There is always uncertainty in scientific analysis and a good scientist takes great care in pointing it out. Few public decisions are made with the luxury of complete certainty about costs and benefits. But the risk of inaction is often greater than the risk of taking action. The standards for certainty seem to vary from issue to issue. Official Washington wants to remove any uncertainty in forecasts of climate change before taking action—in spite of the potentially catastrophic consequence of inaction in this area. Yet decisions in other areas are plainly not held to the same test. If James E. Hanson, the top climate scientist at NASA, had simply said that climate change is a "slam dunk," we would not have had the problems we are having.

Another criticism suggests that the nation is increasingly punishing whistle-blowers—inflicting retribution on people trying to bring information to the public that has been suppressed.

Perhaps the most serious concern about the decline in science advice in public affairs is that there is an organized effort to create an alternative universe of phony science that can compete for legitimacy with the mainstream scientific community. The effort to confuse the public on this point is understandable, and dangerous, because the mainstream scientific community is one of the few groups that has maintained its credibility with the public. When there is a political desire to do something that is not consistent with scientific evidence, why not simply create a new science and heavily promote it? The concept of "sound science" has become almost a codeword for this kind of manufactured science. Legitimate science has a well-defined method for testing theories and winnowing fact from fiction. It is a continuous, open, rough and tumble process of publication, attacks, and rebuttals. Everything in science, of course, is a theory. And there is no surer way to gain advancement and fame in science than finding a famous theory and proving that it is wrong.

But this process is finding itself in competition with a completely synthetic science funded by religious or political groups that often succeed in getting equal treatment in the press.

While the scientific community is under attack and external forces may be undermining the process of science and technology advice, this cannot be an excuse for failure to see its own dirty linen. With huge amounts of research funding on the table, the scientific community often looks like simply one more lobbying group. Scientific lobbyists are constantly on the prowl in Washington. Major universities have huge lobbying operations with the result that "earmarking" of bills was up 7 percent in 2005 (n some areas earmarking has reached 40 percent of the research program). And it is unfortunate but true that the scientific community judges all science advisers not by their ability to ensure effective science and technology advice in public policy, but in their ability to bring in more dollars to their favorite research programs.

An even more crucial question is whether the scientific community is betraying its own values and advocating positions supported by their opinions and not analysis. Any good scientist understands that there is a bright line between stating the facts and stating values. Scientists have unique insights into where opportunities and problems lie. They not only have a right, they have a moral responsibility to step forward and say what they think is true. But it is essential that scientists be absolutely clear about when their statements are based on the best scientific analysis, and when they are speaking from personal values.

Wise policy decisions must be based on how to value outcomes. The most effective political process is one that lets people apply their values to hard choices—choices whose consequences are clearly understood. In environmental policy, for example, there is a clear difference between knowing whether a species will go extinct and knowing what value to place on an endangered species. The value is not zero, or infinite. Science can help in decisions but must be clear when its expertise ends. A political debate at its finest has the best technical advice available and invites people from many points of view to enter the debate—the political equivalent to the scientific process for sorting out ideas.

INSTITUTIONS

Congress gets advice from many sources. The three major organizations reporting directly to Congress are: the General Accounting Office (GAO), the Congressional Budget Office (CBO), and the Congressional Research Service (CRS). A fourth organization that focused exclusively on science and technology policy, the Office of Technology Assessment (OTA), was abolished a decade ago. These organizations have been effective in providing evenhanded economic and other analysis even under duress, though none have been able to fill the gap left by the demise of OTA. As can be expected, they face enormous difficulties. The CRS was severely criticized, for example, for its review of the legal basis for the National Security Agency wiretap program in spite of a painstaking effort to be evenhanded. Since most of its members are lawyers, Congress well understands the legal dictum "never ask questions in public unless you already know the answer." One way to encourage legislators to ask questions when the answers might be embarrassing is to keep the analysis secret. This, of course, raises other problems since the public cannot benefit from their work. In fact, CRS reports are not made available to the public, although individual members of Congress are free to make them public if they do not contain classified information.

Congress can also get information from hearings. In the past congressional hearings often treated issues in depth, producing records that were virtual textbooks on the policy being considered. But there is real concern that this tradition has been replaced by one that is used primarily to promote a point of view rather than to gather evidence.

In practical terms, many congressional staff get the bulk of their technical information using a rolodex of people they know. This can be useful but is obviously not a substitute for organizations that can provide detailed analysis of the practical technical, institutional, and political issues raised in a policy decision. Few policy groups in universities or elsewhere are organized to produce this kind of work.

Staff members under 30 seem to be looking increasingly to Google as the source of all wisdom. It's frightening but I'd guess that half the calls the Federation of American Scientists gets from congressional staff occur because a staff member has Googled an issue and our name came up.

A complex set of institutions operates to provide science and technology advice to the executive branch. Systematic science advice for the president began shortly after World War II when President Dwight Eisenhower selected James Killian as a science adviser. This was the heyday of science advice. Killian and Eisenhower worked well together. Eisenhower respected science advice, knowing how valuable it had been in the conduct of the war. But the relationship between the science adviser and the president has varied, dependent on relations between the president and this individual. Under President Richard Nixon a disaster occurred because the members of the advisory group decided that they disagreed with the president and actually testified on an issue that went against the administration's will. Nixon summarily abolished the office of the science adviser and fired the entire staff, giving them two weeks to clean out their desks.

Congress, which then had a Democratic majority in both houses, in effect said, "Oh no you don't! We're going to force you to have a science adviser." It passed a law that actually established a new agency: the Office of Science and Technology Policy (OSTP). Since then most of the OSTP directors have also served as the president's science and technology adviser. The distinction is that the director of OSTP is subject to Senate confirmation as the head of a federal agency. The director can be called to testify. The science and technology adviser, on the other hand, is an assistant to the president who can provide advice protected by executive privilege.

The current administration has chosen to break with precedent and has not appointed a science and technology adviser to play the insider's role. John Marburger is now only the director of OSTP.

Another source of information for the executive branch comes from advisory councils. Some of these report directly to the White House, but most report directly to federal agencies. I have previously mentioned some of the concerns about the way some of these advisers have been chosen.

Several of the groups have been abolished altogether. These include previously prestigious groups such as the President's Information Technology Advisory Council and the Secretary of Energy's Advisory Council. NASA's senior advisory council has lost several key members to resignations.

Policy offices in major agencies are often also a major source of science and technology analysis. But many of these organizations seem to be losing ground. For example, there have been major reductions in funding for the policy office in the Commerce Department's Technology Administration, which administers the National Institute of Science and Technology and directs much of the nation's competitiveness policy.

The national science academies have picked up a big part of the analysis burden that was formerly borne by other organizations that have been either downscaled or are poorly used. As many as 40 people left OTA when it was closed and moved to the academies, and the academies are now performing many of the jobs that were once carried out by the OTA.

The role of nongovernmental science and technology policy analysis has grown as official sources of analysis have declined. Institutions involved include the National Academies of Science, university policy programs, nongovernmental organizations including my own organization, the Federation of American Scientitsts (FAS), funded by foundations and other sources, and think tanks funded to promote corporate or ideological agendas.

The National Academies has been particularly visible in filling the vacuum left by the demise of OTA and organizations in the administration. They have done spectacular work, but their own management insists that they cannot be expected to replace organizations that worked directly for the Congress or the administration.

The academies themselves have been criticized for relying too heavily on extremely senior people (the "fogey factor") and not enough on younger scientists, who bring new ideas and perspectives. Their work can be slow and may be heavily influenced by one or two members of a panel. They also have a problem in financing in that often an agency finances a study of its own operation. The academies are acutely aware of all these concerns. But the key point is that no matter how effective, they cannot substitute for competent, internal staffs working directly for the Congress, the president, and federal agencies.

REMEDIES

It's always far easier to define problems than to propose solutions. It is even harder to propose solutions that have any practical chance of success in the slugfest that Washington policymaking has become. But there are a number of practical paths forward that build on strategies that have proved to be effective in the past and structures already in place. A set of interesting proposals emerged from a recent FAS project that involved talking with people who had played key roles in advising Congress and the administration over the years—including most of the former science advisers to the president. They proposed remedies in three key areas: 1) science and technology advice for the president, 2) science and technology advice for Congress, and 3) ensuring open access to governmental information and decisions.

Advice for the President

As the brief history of the office of science adviser demonstrates, the president needs two kinds of science and technology advice. The president, of course, has a right to private advice and a way to speak candidly with science advisers so that this advice can be combined with advice from economic and political advisors in the usually messy process of forming policy. This process can succeed only if there is a chance to work in candor, without the fear that every syllable of every conversation will be reported in the press.

There is also a crucial need for advice and analysis that is available to the public and used as the basis for open debate over administration proposals. If nothing else, publicly available analysis raises the threshold of pain for any administration that wants to ignore the scientific advice.

The issue at hand is how to create an institutional framework that can meet the needs for both private and public advice that can function regardless of election returns.

One of the first steps would be to give the National Science and Technology Council some of the powers now enjoyed by the National Security Council (NSC). The NSC is established by statute. It has a permanent staff of career professionals, most of whom do not change with administrations. The NSC has the ability to define critical national security decisions and require agencies to evaluate options so that a decision can be made by the president. Science and technology policy issues should enjoy the same power and access.

Presidential decisions, of course, depend on private advice. There's also a need to strengthen the institutions charged with analysis that will be fully available to the public. This requires strengthening the Office of Science and Technology Policy. A strong competent staff is needed and must be given funding for external research. OSTP has little flexibility in obtaining outside consulting or supporting external analysis. The bulk of the funding that might be used for such work goes to an institution originally called the Critical Technologies Institute, originally managed by RAND and now managed by the Institute for Defense Analysis. OSTP should be given the funding needed to contract with competent organizations, including the National Academies of Science and university policy centers.

It is also important to strengthen the role of presidential advisory panels. One interesting idea is to restore the role initially imagined for the National Science Board that advises the National Science Foundation (NSF). This board was established not just to advise NSF but to provide broad guidance on administration science policy. Care was taken to give it considerable independence. Appointees were given six-year terms so that they could overlap administrations. The group could be very useful if given authority to cover a broad range of science and technology policy issues.

The National Academies and other groups have also developed some interesting proposals that would make it much more difficult to create biased federal advisory panels. These include having professional societies or other groups develop proposed lists of qualified individuals. There should be a clear firewall between people selected to give political advice and people selected to provide unbiased technical reviews.

Finally, there is a pressing need for a better research budget process. At present research plans are drawn up in each agency guided by different parts of the Office of Management and Budget. A hurried effort is made to explain research priorities—usually after key decisions have already been made. Congress, of course, is even more Balkanized and research budgets end up in scores of different subcommittees. Any effort to create coherence in research priorities would have a difficult time surviving the fractured decision process.

Advice for Congress

There is legitimate concern that Congress is unable to operate effectively as an independent branch of government without independent sources of expert advice in science and technology and other areas. Absent this resource it is difficult to develop independent approaches to policy backed by sound analysis. By default most ideas originate in the administration and interest groups. But without their own analytical team, Congress lacks critical tools for evaluating these proposals.

The loss of the OTA created many of these problems. The OTA was created to provide Congress with timely science and technology advice tailored to its unique needs. This proves to be an enormously challenging undertaking. One casualty of the demise of OTA was the loss of marrying science and technology skills to the practical problems of politics. Few scientists have experience working in a congressional environment where being effective means not just having technical expertise but a knowledge of legislative and regulatory issues. The ability to communicate effectively requires the scientist to determine the political context, work with key personalities, and know how to time inputs to be most effective in the political calendar.

It's a difficult adjustment. Developing a technically perfect solution is seldom enough. The practical world of politics requires people who can look for second-best and third-best solutions that can survive brutal political tests. It took OTA almost a decade to figure out how to be effective. Yet by the time the agency learned how to do it right, it was abolished.

It's essential that we find some permanent solution to the Congress' need for science and technology advice. The solution depends on an institution that must:

- be unbiased and enjoy a reputation for being unbiased;
- be protected from political bias by a bipartisan board of some kind and a strong advisory council that would be stable regardless of election outcomes;
- have stable funding of at least $20 million a year;
- have a reliable way of choosing topics that support the needs of both senior and junior members;
- have some flexibility to select topics that may not have current congressional sponsors;
- understand the practical needs of congressional clients, including the need for practical policy proposals and an understanding of the timing of congressional decision making;
- be able to draw on expertise from around the country, including university, corporate, government, and NGO experts;

- encourage diverse opinion and encourage opinions from companies and stakeholders;
- explain uncertainties in costs and benefits.

Restoring OTA in its original form is neither practical nor desirable. Moreover, there is little interest in creating any new institution. One possibility would be to create a strong independent group in GAO or the CRS.

One of OTA's achievements was to provide a staff of professional scientists and engineers that could work for a number of different committees and members. They could operate as a shared technical staff. While it isn't possible to have a significant number of technical people in congressional offices, there is no substitute for having some. If nothing else they are needed as bridges between analytical organizations and the immediate needs of members and committees. It is unfortunate but true that given resources for new staff, few congressional organizations would use them to attract technical talent. The congressional fellowships provided by organizations like the American Association for the Advancement of Science, the American Physical Society, the American Chemical Society, and other organizations have been extremely effective in filling this gap. They have been enormously helpful in building links between Congress and the science and engineering community and played an active role in the establishment of OTA.

It is interesting that similar gaps in science and engineering exist in many federal agencies. The State Department, for example, has endured years of criticism about its underinvestment in science. In most years not a single science sttaché in US embassies has a degree in science. Again the gap was filled by private funding. The MacArthur Foundation and Carnegie funded the Jefferson fellowship that has had enormous success in placing talented scientists and engineers in key State Department offices.

Open Government

The third crucial change in building an enduring institutional framework for science policy is finding a way to ensure that information needed for evaluating public policy is in fact available to the public. It is tautological that if critical information and analysis are hidden, it is difficult for outside groups to evaluate government programs or suggest useful alternatives.

Obviously, some information needs to be protected for reasons of national security, and the definition of security has changed as threats of terrorism increase. But this is largely a solved problem. While there's plenty of room for improvement, the system that evolved from over 60 years of experience has given us a sensible, practical way to protect information whose release could harm US security interests while ensuring that most information is available and protecting us from abuse of the process. The basic framework includes:

▸ the AEA Act, National Security Act, Espionage Act, Intelligence Identities Protection Act, and others provide statutory authority;
▸ the Freedom of Information Act (FOIA) ensures a public right to access agency records, subject to applicable exemptions;
▸ the Executive Order 12958 Classified National Security Information 1995 amended by Executive Order 13292, March 2003;
▸ the Electronic Freedom of Information Act 1996 (E-FOIA) frequently requested records made available on the Internet;
▸ the Interagency Security Classification Appeals Panel (ISCAP) established by Executive Order in 1995.

In the past few years, however, we have seen a tidal wave of new restrictions put in place that seem to have learned nothing from this history. While the government itself has trouble keeping count, there are up to 90 separate new regimes for protecting government information that is "sensitive but unclassified"—much of which had been freely available in the past. Among other things, this has hugely increased the number of people who can effectively stamp "secret" on documents.

The consequences of this have been frightening not just for the role of science in policymaking but for the conduct of science itself. In his 2002 presidential address, Bruce Alberts, who recently stepped down as president of the National Academies, noted that: "The possibility of excessive restrictions on scientific publication, motivated by security concerns, [poses] clear threats to science today. . . . Some of the plans being proposed could severely hamper the U.S. research enterprise and decrease national security." A directive from the Reagan administration—National Security Decision Directive 189—states that for basic research results, the burden of proof is on the government, not on the researcher, to show that they should be released. It still provides a solid line of defense for scientific research publication but must be protected with constant vigilance.

The dangerous confusion about what can be made public, and increasing incentives to withhold information from the public, presents a major danger to any effective science and technology policy. It is essential that all new restrictions on release of government information build on the solid foundation established by traditional classification. Any move to limit disclosure should explicitly or implicitly be subject to questions like these:

▸ Is the information otherwise available in public domain? (Or can it be readily deduced from first principles?)
▸ Is there specific reason to believe the information could be used by our enemies—including terrorists? Are there countervailing considerations that would militate in favor of disclosure—that is, could it be used for beneficial purposes?
▸ Is there specific reason to believe the information should be public knowledge to improve public oversight of environmental or other matters?

If these answers point to the need for withholding information, the process used to deny public access must be based on:

▸ a clear set of principles guiding protection of information developed by an open process: presumption of openness;

- clearly defined and transparent procedures for applying these principles;
- a clear appeals process overseen by an organization not under the control of the agency making the original ruling.

The president has actually noticed that there is chaos in this system that is harming coordination between government agencies—including communication with state and local organizations—and issued a directive in December 2005 requiring a review of the new classification network. Unfortunately, the work seems to focus on facilitating communication within the government and not ensuring that the public's right to know is protected. We can hope, however, that any system emerging from this review will adhere to the principles I have just outlined.

I will conclude by observing that one of the greatest barriers to sound science and technology policy is finding people with the combination of skills needed to be effective. Part of the problem, of course, is the absence of a clear, traditional career path for people interested in the field. The loss of OTA was a particularly painful blow since it provided a superb entry point for many scientists interested in science policy. But universities are a major part of the problem. There are painfully few programs that do an effective job of producing people who have solid technical backgrounds, who understand the political, economic, regulatory, and other factors that shape policymaking, and who have the skills needed to communicate complex subjects to highly diverse audiences—including politicians who have the habit of giving you 15 seconds to make your point.

A handful of university environmental programs are beginning to provide people with these skills. It would be hard to name a dozen programs providing people with the skills needed in national security (a place where once again the MacArthur Foundation has stepped in to build university infrastructure in this key area). But in general the landscape is quite bleak. Policy programs tend to focus on abstract instead of practical policy issues.

In the end it is difficult to avoid the conclusion that the state of science and technology advice to Washington policymakers is in a state of major disrepair. While this kind of advice is not sufficient, it is plainly necessary for competent management of public affairs. We are facing a range of unprecedented threats—new threats to national security, threats to the global environment, limits to global resource supplies, growing income inequality—most of which cannot even be understood absent sound science and technology policy. Any effective solution must grasp opportunities that can only be provided by science. The challenge of integrating science with policy is not something we can postpone without grave risk.

Rita R. Colwell
Cholera Outbreaks and Ocean Climate

WHAT I SHALL DO IN THIS BRIEF PAPER, RATHER THAN JUMP INTO THE
ring with gloves to join the debate on science and policy, is put a
human face on one of the most serious issues we are discussing: the
complexity of climate change.* We need to understand very clearly
that when one discusses, for example, climate and infectious disease,
the problem is complicated and the interactions involved are both
multidisciplinary and interdisciplinary. The human perspective must
be included if we are to comprehend fully the global effects of climate
change.

It would be useful to start not by belaboring points of contention but by indicating where there is agreement. Everyone agrees
that global warming is occurring. Over the past few years, the highest
average temperatures in history have been recorded. No one argues
that. The argument, of course, is whether we are undergoing a natural
cycle or anthropogenic-induced change. But, let us look at the fact
that the ocean surface annual temperatures have increased. Warren
Washington speaks eloquently of his research at the National Center
for Atmospheric Research (NCAR) on the dramatic changes such
temperature increases will invoke on sea surface levels (Washington,
in press).

My focus is on one aspect of global warming: human health and
the weather-related effects of climate change on infectious disease.
The United States surgeon general's report in 1950 declared the war

on infectious disease over because of the discoveries of many power-ful antibiotics. It was a premature declaration; infectious diseases are a moving target and remain very serious threats to the human race. Globally, acute respiratory infections, including pneumonia and influ-enza (avian influenza is a looming threat), are the number one killer. However, for children under the age of five, diarrheal disease remains a major killer, especially in developing countries.

Cholera, a diarrheal disease, has been with us for a very long time, even being mentioned in ancient Sanskrit writings. A medical textbook published in 1875 reported cholera to be a global pandemic, consistently appearing in India, Bangladesh, Latin America, and Africa. Today, cholera remains a serious problem. Until the nine-teenth century, cholera was generally confined to the Indian subcon-tinent, but it then began to appear in Europe and the Americas as well. Since 1817, Western medical history describes seven global pandemics of cholera that have spread illness and death around the world. The second of these seven pandemics reached the United States in 1832, traveling from New York to Philadelphia in a couple of weeks, and then cases appeared along the Atlantic coast all the way to the Gulf of Mexico. In fact, Washington, D.C. and New York, until 1900, saw frequent epidemics of fevers, including typhoid, malaria, and cholera.

Cholera arose in epidemic form in London in 1849, at a time when the germ theory of disease was being debated. John Snow, in that year, carried out the first published epidemiological study, charting cases of cholera in London. He concluded that the cholera cases clus-tered around a well in central London when cholera was at its peak during the summer months. The epidemic abated in the September of 1849 but, as I will explain, the decline had to do with natural factors rather than the purported removal of the handle from the pump by John Snow.

In 1977, my coworkers and I reported that *Vibrio cholerae*, the causative agent of cholera, could be cultured from Chesapeake Bay water samples. It was the first report of the isolation of the cholera vibrio from noncholera-endemic geographical areas; cholera had not been reported in Maryland since the 1900s. It was difficult for us to make our case, namely that the cholera vibrio was a native inhabitant of the Chesapeake Bay, since cholera had not occurred in the region. Nevertheless, the bacterium was there. Subsequently, we were able to apply molecular techniques and show that, indeed, the bacterium is naturally occurring in the aquatic environment, with annual peaks in the spring and fall. Furthermore, we were able to determine that the cholera vibrio is associated with plankton. We now know that river, estuary, and coastal waters are reservoirs of these bacteria globally, but our data showing an environmental source of the cholera bacteria implied a paradigm shift for the medical community. It has taken about 20 years for the paradigm change of cholera being transmitted only by person-to-person contact to the recognition that the cholera vibrio exists in the environment as a natural inhabitant. Furthermore, we discovered that the bacterium undergoes a dormant stage between epidemics and, with molecular techniques—that is, gene probes—we could prove its year-round presence in the environment.

The relationship with zooplankton turned out to be especially important. In the spring, when the water warms, phytoplankton become abundant; using sunlight for energy, the population of phytoplankton increases significantly. That population increase is followed by blooms of zooplankton, the miniature "cattle" of the sea, which graze on the phytoplankton. We were able to show a relationship of sea surface temperature increase with onset of cholera epidemics because of the fact that vibrios comprise the natural microbial flora of zooplankton, the populations of which increase spring and fall in annual cycles. The seasonal pattern of cholera follows the seasonal rise and fall in sea surface temperature and height.

In 1991-1992, a massive cholera epidemic occurred in Peru: approximately 200,000 cases and 5,000 deaths were the result of the epidemic. This was unprecedented, since cholera had not been reported in South America for nearly 100 years. Furthermore, the epidemic occurred at the time of a powerful El Niño. Climatologists predicted another Niño in 1997-1998. We hypothesized that there was a linkage of the 1991-1992 cholera epidemic with El Niño and predicted additional cholera outbreaks would occur in 1997-1998. With colleagues from Peru, Chile, Ecuador, Brazil, and Mexico, we conducted a training session on molecular techniques for direct detection of the cholera vibrio in water and plankton. As the sea surface temperatures in these Latin American countries increased in 1997 because of El Niño, the team was able to detect the presence of the cholera bacteria associated with plankton, with numbers of the bacteria increasing from spring to summer (September 1977 to March 1998) and cases of cholera occurring in late November through the summer of 1998.

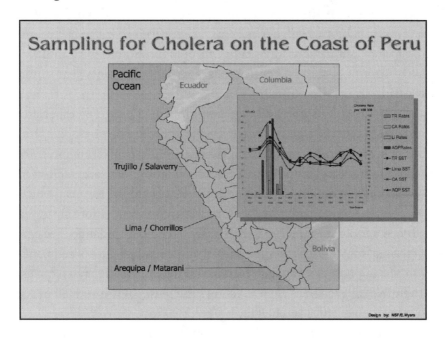

Fig. 1 Cholera Data, Coast of Peru, Related to El Niño, 1997–1998.

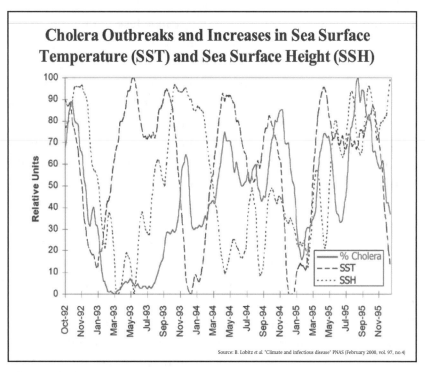

Cholera Outbreaks and Increases in Sea Surface Temperature (SST) and Sea Surface Height (SSH)

Source: B. Lobitz *et al.* "Climate and infectious disease" PNAS (February 2000, vol. 97, no.4)

Fig. 2 Cholera Outbreaks and Increases in Sea Surface Temperature (SST) and Sea Surface Height (SSH).

We were able to conclude that El Niño is another important climate factor related to cholera, notably in cholera-endemic countries. The cases of cholera in Peru in 1997-1998 were directly correlated with sea surface temperature (fig. 1). The relationship of the disease with this climate factor was statistically significant.

In Bangladesh and other countries where severe cholera epidemics occur, such as Peru, Indonesia, and India, the influence of monsoons or severe weather is important. Matlab, near Dhaka, Bangladesh, comprises a "hotspot" of cholera. The villages are constructed around bodies of water, and specific locations of epidemics have been determined. Our research on cholera has been conducted in Matlab, Bangladesh, since 1975.

The influence of the Himalayas on the weather in Bangladesh is significant, because the monsoon rains wash nutrients into the rivers and ponds. Typically, houses in Bangladesh are located at the edge of a pond, from which villagers draw their water for household use.

A definable relationship between sea surface temperature, sea surface height, and cholera epidemics was established and published in the proceedings of the National Academy of Science (Lobitz et al., 2000; see also fig. 2). Taken together, the complex factors of sea surface temperature, sea surface height, and zooplankton populations provide a predictive capacity for cholera epidemics in developing countries that derives from climate monitoring through satellite sensors.

Finally, with the assistance of sociology researchers working in Bangladesh, we were able to test the hypothesis we constructed: that if we could remove zooplankton from the water the villagers used to meet household needs, the incidence of cholera could be reduced. With a very simple filtration technique that we devised using sari cloth folded in 4 layers, we were able to reduce cholera by approximately 50 percent in villages where families had been instructed in the filtration method. The complex of plankton, people, and climate, together with a simple solution based on science (under the electron microscope, the folded sari cloth could be seen to provide a 20 micron filter—and the zooplankton range in size roughly 50 to 200 microns), provides the interrelationship that allows an understanding of a global infectious disease—an understanding that would not otherwise be possible.

Thus, climate change influences a complexity of biological systems of our planet earth and in our models, and the human factor cannot be omitted from climate models, if we care to constrain global infectious disease and protect human health.

THE QUESTION WE RAISED, BASED ON OUR FINDINGS, WAS WHETHER we could predict, using only environmental data, the location, time, and intensity of a cholera epidemic. From satellite observations of sea surface temperature, sea surface height, and chlorophyll, we found that we could, indeed, predict these aspects of a cholera epidemic.

Clearly, global warming can have a profound effect on the pattern of infectious diseases, especially a disease like cholera that is so strongly intertwined with the environment. It can have a profound influence on geographic range and intensity of the disease globally. Similarly, both cholera-related waterborne diseases and vector borne diseases, such as malaria and dengue, will pose enhanced threats in some parts of the world.

In summary, the interaction of humans, cholera bacteria, the zooplankton host of the bacterium (the copepod), and the environment in the case of cholera can be employed to make reasonable predictions about this climate-driven disease. The issues are truly international and represent those that comprise a global scientific enterprise and encompass many other infectious diseases. Our research clearly had to be collaborative and international for a fuller, more nuanced understanding of cholera and, I predict, so it will be for human health and survival on this planet. That is the ultimate exercise for understanding the consequences of global warming and, certainly, for policies addressing societal needs related to global climate change.

NOTES

* I would like to acknowledge colleagues in Bangladesh at the International Center of Diarrheal Diseases Research, and the sociologists, physicians, climatologists, ecologists, students, and postdoctoral colleagues at the University of Maryland, NASA, Ames, NIH, and in universities in those countries cited in my paper. My international community, or rather, my "international village," made possible the research findings presented here.

REFERENCES

Lobitz, Brad, Louisa Beck, Anwar Huq, Byron Wood, George Fuchs, A. S. G. Faruque, and Rita Colwell. "Climate and Infectious Disease:

Use of Remote Sensing for Detection of *Vibrio cholerae* by Indirect Measurement." *Proceedings of the National Academies of Science* 97:4 (2000):1438-1443.

Washington, W. M. "Computer Modeling the 20th- and 21st-Century Climate." *Proceedings of the American Philosophical Society* (In press, 2006).

Daniel J. Kevles
What's New about the Politics of Science?

THIS IS A TIME OF PARADOX IN FEDERAL SCIENCE POLICY. UNDER THE administration of President George W. Bush, the federal government has been providing handsome and steadily increasing dollar support for research and development. In constant 2005 dollars, the federal budget for research and development (R&D) has climbed from some $90 billion in 2000 to $135 billion in 2006, an increase of 50 percent. In his State of the Union speech in January 2006, President George W. Bush drew on an influential report from the National Academy of Sciences to call for an American Competitiveness Initiative that over 10 years would double federal expenditures in critical basic research areas in the physical sciences such as nanotechnology, supercomputing, and alternative energy sources. It would also train an additional 70,000 high school science and mathematics teachers (AASS, 2006; "Transcript of State of the Union Speech," 2006).

Yet the news is not all good, especially in public policymaking for areas related to science and technology. Defense has commanded the preponderant proportion of the increase in the federal R&D budget since 2000 (AASS, 2006). The Bush administration persistently censors, distorts, or manipulates policy-relevant scientific information, ignoring or rejecting the advice of authoritative experts in sensitive areas such as global warming and human stem-cell research. It has reportedly subjected potential scientific advisers to political litmus tests, quashing nominations to advisory committees on partisan grounds (Branscomb, 2004: 54). And the president himself has granted intellectual legitimacy to those who insist, contrary to the settled science of evolutionary biology, that the theory of biological change by intelligent design be given equal time in public-school science classes. At a press conference in February 2004, the Union of Concerned Scientists declared "that the administration of President George W. Bush has disregarded the principle that the contributions of science to public policy decisions must always be weighed from an objective and impartial perspective." The statement went on to say that the Bush administration has politicized science to an egregious degree, sharply departing from the longstanding practices of "presidents and administrators of both parties" (Mooney, 2005: 223).[1]

The chemist James B. Conant knew all about those practices. The president of Harvard University during much of the middle third of the twentieth century, he was a major figure in the mobilization of science during World War II and a key figure in science policymaking afterward. In 1947, in the middle of the postwar construction of the federal scientific system as we know it, he remarked: "You have to get the past straight before you can do much to prepare people for the future" (Hershberg, 1993: 287). The Union of Concerned Scientists' picture of the past is in fact somewhat bent and needs straightening.

After World War II, when the modern era of government science advising began, both presidents and Congress latched onto technical views that suited their political purposes. Who could forget Harry Truman's decision to proceed with the hydrogen bomb, against the advice of his distinguished atomic advisers? Or, in the 1950s, Congress's endorsement of the technologically silly project of a nuclear-powered airplane? Or in the 1980s, President Ronald Reagan's enthusiasm for a national missile defense—Star Wars—in the face of widespread scientific opposition? And the federal dollar commitment to research and development has repeatedly been rocky. In the high-inflation 1970s, the federal R&D budget, measured in constant dollars, actually fell.

During the McCarthy era, political litmus tests were standard operating procedure in the affairs of government science. Under President Truman's loyalty program, some 60,000 scientists were subjected to security reviews. Many scientists then and in the early Eisenhower years were denied clearances—and jobs—and many were not told of the charges against them (Wang, 1999: 88). Even prominent scientists were by no means immune from ostracism on security grounds, as the notorious case of J. Robert Oppenheimer, in 1954, made manifestly clear. In the 1970s, President Richard Nixon included scientists on his "enemies list" and abolished the President's Science Advisory Committee for its members' opposition to the Vietnam War and his Antiballistic Missile System.

Yet there is more to getting the history straight than showing that the present is not altogether new, that it has precedents. It also enables the kind of perspective that leads to understanding. It's helpful to know where we have been in order to analyze where we may be going. Consider just the trends during the decades following World War II. To the degree that federal science was politicized during that era, it was in relationship to national security and big-technology projects. Part of what is different about science policy under the Bush administration is that its politicization has reached into key areas outside defense such as global warming and human stem-cell research. Far more can be learned about the forces at work in contemporary science policymaking by invoking a still longer and broader historical perspective, one that begins in the late nineteenth century and takes into account fundamental changes in the dynamics of American politics.

GENERAL UNDERSTANDING HAS IT THAT FEDERAL SUPPORT OF SCIENCE before World War II was insignificant and that before the 1930s little if any science of consequence was done in the United States. That view is mistaken, not least because, beginning in the post-Civil War years, the earth and certain branches of the life sciences were pursued in the United States with considerable distinction and no small degree of government patronage.[2]

The Republican Party dominated national politics during the period, and the expansion in federal patronage for science expressed the GOP's enthusiasm for using federal resources to foster national economic development. Its commitment translated munificent support for the construction of the transcontinental railroad through subsidies in the form of vast land grants given to the states and, in the territories, the railroad companies directly. Its patronage of science, part of the same devotion to nation building, was directed primarily to the disciplines relevant to exploration, settlement, and economic development, especially in the far West.

In 1878, the venerable Coast Survey, established during the administration of Thomas Jefferson, was renamed the Coast and Geodetic Survey, signifying the enlargement of its duties beyond the mapping the shoreline to determining the intensity and inclination of the earth's magnetic field throughout the continental United States. In 1870, the United States Army Signal Corps established the country's first federal weather service. In the early 1880s, a center in Washington, D.C. was gathering reports of local weather that were telegraphed from across the country, collating them into predictions, and supporting research into meteorology by a small staff of physicists.

By then, the U.S. Geological Survey, created in 1879, led all other federal scientific agencies in the scope and prominence of its work, thanks to the energy, imagination, and political skills of its director after 1881, John Wesley Powell. The survey's work in pure and applied geology rapidly achieved world-class distinction. Between 1881 and 1884, Powell's budget jumped fivefold, reaching $500,000 a year. The sum was by no means inconsiderable, since it took up a manyfold greater fraction of the federal budget than the Geological Survey commands today, and in any case, was enough to make a significant difference in the science of the time.

However, the expansion of federal science in the post-Civil War years was plagued by tensions between its practitioners and the political system, some of it familiar to our contemporary ears. Critics contended variously that its scope was too broad; that it was engaging in abstract work of no utility—for example, meteorological studies that would not lead to more reliable weather prediction or paleontological investigations that seemed to satisfy no public want. They claimed that much of federal science would better be left to private enterprise, that it needed to be cut back, and brought under closer control.

Part of the dissent came from western Republicans, unhappy with John Wesley Powell's proposals to reconfigure land and water management in the arid region west of the 100th meridian. His ideas struck directly at their economic interest in local development. But a significant source of the opposition arose from Democrats, especially in the South. There a coalition of fiscal conservatives and budding agrarian populists impelled by a degree of anti-intellectualism and an insistence that if there was to be federal science, the enterprise should be preeminently practical in its focus, with direct benefits in the short term to farmers.

In the 1880s, the dissents, coupled with the expansion of the research agencies, led to the first congressional investigation of federal science, a two-year joint venture by a House and Senate commission that was chaired by Senator William B. Allison of Iowa, one of the most powerful members of the Senate. In the hearings, federal scientists responded to the charges that they were indulging in excessive abstract research—that, as one government scientist put it, the surveys were not "fomenting science." They were doing "practical work for practical purposes." John Wesley Powell hotly declared that not even "a hundred millionaires" could support the research of the federal agencies and that the progress of American civilization should not have to wait on the philanthropic inspiration of a hundred rich men. The national government should support and publish whatever science advanced the people's welfare (Kevles, 1995: 47, 57).

Federal science, protected by Senator Allison and his Republican allies, survived this investigation virtually intact. But the political winds began to shift in 1892, on the eve of the great depression of the 1890s. Amid the mounting economic difficulties, economy-minded conservatives gained ground in the Congress and, especially in the House, so did agrarians of both parties, who, sensitive to the mounting populist revolt on the cotton fields, plains, and prairies, wondered why the government should allocate funds for research on the slimy things of the earth when human beings were earning too little to keep their farms. The agrarians and the pro-economy Democrats, each for his own reasons, formed a coalition that sharply reduced expenditures for superfluous science. In 1893, because of the depression, the order of the day in the White House and on Capitol Hill was retrenchment. The secretary of agriculture announced that he would drop all "useless scientists from the Weather Bureau," explaining: "What the people most want is knowledge beforehand of what is to happen . . . rather than a scientific diagnosis . . . after it is all over" (Kevles, 1995: 65). The great expansion in federal patronage of the earth sciences seemed not only to have ended but to have been reversed. The halcyon days of federal science appeared to be over.

When prosperity returned to the country in 1897, however, appropriations for the surveys swung upward once again, more than doubling by 1914. Yet the transition to renewed prosperity did not yield just more of the same. The forces of political economy that had produced the cutbacks in federal science during the 1890s masked a fundamental change in the national agenda. The frontier was closed, the nation swiftly urbanizing and, after the Spanish-American War, the country also began to flex its muscles as a world power. The new agenda was concerned much less with the acquisition of new land and resources and much more with the conservation of the land and resources already in the nation's possession and with the exploitation of nature to produce new goods for domestic and foreign markets.

After the turn of the century, the new overall agenda included a reconfiguring of the purposes of federal science. Federal emphases in the earth and life sciences turned partly to conservation, responding to the environmental movement of the day. And new stress was placed on federally supported agricultural research—agricultural experiment stations at land-grant colleges and universities, where research was encouraged in the new field of genetics—in the belief that it would boost productivity on the farm and make American agriculture more competitive on the world markets. Yet perhaps the most salient feature of the new agenda was its attentiveness to assisting what is known as the "second industrial revolution"—the revolution that depended on the exploitation of the laboratory sciences of physics and chemistry to produce new products. In response, in 1901 Congress created a National Bureau of Standards, enabling the agency not only to establish and maintain standards of measure but also to engage in whatever research might be necessary to do so. During congressional hearings on the matter, Secretary of the Treasury Lyman Gage had declared, expressing a salient feature of the new national agenda in applied science and trade: "in all the great things of life," the United States was in competition with the older and more thoroughly established nations of the world (Kevles, 1995: 67).

By the end of World War I, the great things had come to include military competition, too. The army and navy established new agencies devoted to research in particular areas of the physical sciences and their applications, notably the Chemical Warfare Service, the Naval Research Laboratory, and the National Advisory Committee for Aeronautics, which pioneered the practice of granting funds for research to universities. At the time, proposals were advanced to establish federal program of support for scientific research and development in the nation's colleges and universities to bolster its economic and military strength. They came to naught, partly because of the country's retreat into isolationism and partly because of disputes within the academic community, and partly because the Republican Party, a steadfast friend of federal science for almost a half century, was now in thrall to the tight-fisted conservatism that swept Warren Harding into the White House in 1920 and maintained the GOP's control of both ends of Pennsylvania Avenue through the 1920s.

WELL INTO THE 1920S, THE NATION'S SCIENTIFIC LEADERSHIP, MOST of which was Republican, did not count Democrats among the friends of federal science. In 1918, George Ellery Hale, a prominent astrophysicist and leading entrepreneur and politico in American science, expressed the reasons, drawing on a conversation with the lawyer and former Secretary of State Elihu Root:

It is almost never possible to obtain any Congressional assistance for scientific projects outside of the Government Departments, and then only under a Republican administration. . . . [According to Root, in one case a few years ago] the Democratic Senators spoke eloquently against all such organizations [as the American Academy in Rome] for research and advanced study and . . . demanded that attention be concentrated on the needs of the "the Little Red School House on the hill," standing for light and leading to the lowly of the land!. . . Although it contains some notable exceptions, the Democratic party as a whole represents the most depressing elements in American life. The National Academy [of Sciences] would never dream of going to a Democratic Congress for funds, as it would be sure to lose rather than gain by doing so (Kevles, 1995: 152 n1).

With the onset of the Great Depression of the 1930s, however, President Franklin Roosevelt refashioned the Democratic Party into a coalition of southern conservatives, northern liberals, labor unions, and ethnic, religious, and racial minorities that gave birth to the New Deal and the welfare state. The vast enlargement of the federal government's role in advancing the general welfare included an expansion of its patronage of scientific research and training, notably in agriculture, conservation, and health. Particularly noteworthy, in 1937 Congress established the National Cancer Institute, the first of many health-related research institutes to come, which operated its own laboratories in Washington and provided grants and contracts to university research.

These developments helped pave the way for the mobilization of science in World War II. Producing such militarily decisive innovations as microwave radar, solid fuel rockets, penicillin, and the atomic bomb, wartime science demonstrated the indispensability to national security of scientific knowledge and expertise. Amid the emerging cold war, the needs of national security and the general welfare translated into the establishment of a sprawling system of federal patronage for science and technology. Between 1945 and 1950, the military proliferated with research agencies, including the wide-ranging Office of Naval Research. Congress created the Atomic Energy Commission, the National Science Foundation, and some half-dozen new National Institutes of Health. The expansion of federal science continued in response to events—with, for example, the creation, stimulated by Sputnik, of the National Aeronautics and Space Administration, in 1958, and of the Environmental Protection Agency, in 1970, which was prompted by the new environmental movement.

The expansion was accompanied by widespread reliance on scientific advisers in virtually every technically related area of government policymaking. The authority of the advisory system appeared to be undercut when the physicist J. Robert Oppenheimer, a key figure in the design and development of the atomic bomb during the war and an influential policy adviser afterward, was denied a security clearance in a star-chamber-like security hearing in 1954. As one observer put it, the ruling expressed "not merely the personal defeat of a leading scientist, but the removal of scientists as a group from their high place in the political order" (Kevles, 1995: 382). But the Oppenheimer ruling was not an attack against scientists in policymaking as such. The Eisenhower administration kept appointing scientists to advisory panels, boards, and committees without significant political test, and in 1958, Eisenhower established the President's Science Advisory Committee (PSAC) to assist him directly. Scientists did a great deal to shape policymaking in the national security area, notably with the Test Ban Treaty. And although President Nixon abolished the PSAC, President Gerald Ford signed into law, in 1976, a bill reestablishing a White House science advisory apparatus.

The long expansion in federal science, including its advisory component, was undergirded by a bipartisan political consensus. While the consensus suffered setbacks from time to time, notably during the Vietnam War and the high-inflation 1970s, it continued through both Democratic and Republican administrations at least to the end of the cold war. The principal elements of the consensus included the over-lapping moderate and fiscally conservative wings of the Republican Party, whose attitudes toward federal investment in the type of capital goods represented by science echoed those popular in the days of William B. Allison. It enjoyed the support of a broad range of welfare-state Democrats. While southern Democrats lost their enthusiasm for elements of welfare-state policy and bitterly resisted the liberal embrace of the civil rights movement, they remained supporters of federal patronage of science related to defense, health, and economic development, especially if the patronage translated into big projects that benefited their region—for example, the nuclear reactor on the Savannah River and the NASA installations at Cape Kennedy, Huntsville, Alabama, and Houston, Texas.

The consensus remained in place for so long not least because the federal investment in science and technology paid such handsome dividends. The payoff premise may have been oversold in specific parts—the promises, for example, of invulnerable defenses or miracle cures for disease tomorrow—but the investment yielded a stunning arsenal of effective, high-tech intelligence systems and weapons from pin-point surveillance satellites to laser-guided bombs. It also generated a cornucopia of products to suit multiple business needs and consumer tastes—notably, mainframe computers and personal computers, jet aircraft, microwave ovens, and cable TV, antibiotics, CAT scans, and MRI machines, computer games, CDs, DVDs, and IPods.

Yet despite the flood of new technologies, a sea change has come over American politics that has impacted the consensus for science. The shift began in the 1970s. It was heralded by, among other developments, the call for deregulation of the economy, the claims that government was the problem rather than the solution, and the renewed emphasis on privatization and entrepreneurship that was signified by the emergence of the biotechnology industry. Its advent was also signaled by the backlash against the civil rights, the reaction against the libertinism of the 1960s, women's liberation, and *Roe v. Wade,* and by the emergence of the religious right.

When the civil rights acts were passed in the mid-1960s, President Lyndon Johnson rightly remarked to an aide that the legislation spelled the death of the Democratic Party in the South. A major element in the sea change was the increasing absorption of southern Democrats into the Republican Party. Many were social conservatives, convinced that scientific research must conform to the tenets of their literalist Christian beliefs, especially where human embryos were concerned. Others were fiscal conservatives, reminiscent of the southerners who plagued John Wesley Powell with their insistence that the federal government had no business in supporting abstract science. Both found a comfortable home in the Republican Party of the late twentieth century. The party formed a big tent, welcoming in every region social conservatives, expectant entrepreneurs, and leaders of corporate business. The occupants of the tent coexisted uneasily. The entrepreneurs and industrialists tended to be social liberals, eager to keep the government out of the bedroom, while the evangelical Christian right wanted nothing of social libertarianism either in the bedroom or the public square. The lure of power nevertheless has kept the occupants in the tent, making for a Republican Party beholden to sharply divided constituencies on key issues in science policy—and making for a recognizably new politics of science.

The new politics was inevitably affected by the degree to which science and technology had become pervasive in American national life. The nuclear arms race, of course, had provoked anxieties about Armageddon, but questions of science and national security tended to be remote from everyday experience. In contrast, science and technology now raise questions that strike at people directly, often in their personal and familial lives. They concern the air we breathe, the water we drink, and the temperature of the climate. They ramify into what television brings into our living rooms and into whether we can count on private communications remaining private. They figure in how we are conceived and born and how we die. All these matters affect us in visceral, immediate ways, and it is no wonder that they are on the radar screen of both political parties, though especially of the Republican

Party, given the engagement of its major constituencies with, variously, hi-tech industry, sexuality, and the fate of the human embryo.

The new politics of science emerged in force after the end of the cold war, which ushered in a struggle over the federal science policy. The absence of cold war competition combined with the recession of the early 1990s had diluted support for federal science on Capitol Hill. In 1993, Congress killed the project to build the Superconducting Super Collider, a gargantuan machine whose estimated cost had reached $11 billion. Senator Dave Durenberger, a Minnesota Republican, explained: "If we were engaged in a scientific competition with a global super-power like the former Soviet Union, and if this project would lead to an enhancement of our national security, then I would be will-ing to continue funding the project. But . . . we face no such threat" (*Congressional Record* , 1992: S11165) In constant dollars, federal expen-ditures for R&D turned downward in 1989, were driven lower by the recession, and in the budget passed in 1994 were only some 80 percent of what they had been in 1987.[3] By then, the federal share of R&D spend-ing in the United States had fallen from slightly less than half the total to only a little more than a third of it (Raymond, 1995: 2).

By then, the privatization of public science was in full swing. Exploiting the Bayh-Dole Act of 1980, universities were patenting the products of their laboratories, licensing them to start-up and estab-lished firms, and increasingly interleaving their activities with those of industrial capitalism. Limited government was the order of the day, especially in the economic arena, and so was a devotion to the entrepre-neurial free market.

Privatization was pushed to an extreme when the Republican-dominated 104th Congress rolled into Washington in January 1995, ferociously committed to the enactment of its balanced-budget Contract with America. Here was dramatic evidence of how the change in the configuration of the Republican Party could affect federal science. In June, the Republican majority drove through a budget resolution that would maintain military research at roughly its current level but that was estimated to slash nondefense R&D, not including biomedical research, by some 30 percent by the year 2002. Biomedical research was slated to fall slightly, then level off, which meant that at even moderate inflation rates, its buying-power budget would be reduced by 25 percent. The proposed cuts threatened an earthquake in federal science, including extensive reductions in the programs of space, energy, and atmospheric research, a sharp contraction in the number of grants that the National Science Foundation could afford, and the outright abolition of the United States Geological Survey (U.S. Council of Economic Advisers, 1995: 13; Broad, 1995: 12; "Crippling American Science," 1995: 16; Gibbons, 1995: 28). The survey, already feeling the squeeze, soon announced that it would fire 500 of the employees in its geological division, and the Bureau of Mines was in fact abolished (Reich, 1995, 3; *Science and Government Report*, 1995: 1).

The *New York Times* called the proposed cuts "shocking," and one of the friends of science on Capitol Hill was prompted to snap, "We're dominated by fools" "Crippling American Science," 1995, 16; Broad, 1995: 1). Know-nothingism appeared in vogue on Capitol Hill. Congressman Dick Chrysler, a Republican from Michigan who spear-headed a drive to abolish the Department of Commerce, was asked about eliminating the Commerce-housed Weather Service. Not every-one thought he was joking when he replied, "We don't need the government; I get my weather from the Weather Channel." Leaders of the federal Center for Disease Control, in Atlanta, Georgia, predicted that the proposed reductions would severely hamper its ability to identify and track epidemic diseases. Susan Tanaka, vice president of the Committee for a Responsible Federal Budget, a bipartisan group devoted to eliminating the federal deficit, suggested that the center's leaders were indulging in unjustifiable special pleading, explaining, "Diseases grow and wane. Some have gone away and we don't have to worry about them anymore" (*What's New*, 1995; Cimons, 1995: 4)

Experience, and President Bill Clinton's resistance to the contract agenda, forced the Republicans to recognize that the country did need government and did need science, but once the GOP gained control of both ends of Pennsylvania Avenue, in the elections of 2002, their responsiveness to scientific expertise appeared to diminish. The Bush administration has resisted sound scientific advice on global warming. And it has largely ignored consensus science in the reproductive area as well as human stem-cell research.

Scrutinized more closely, however, Republicans have not so much rejected scientific advice as such as found scientific advisers resonant with their own ideological predilections. Liberal reformers had long relied on technical expertise to advance the agenda of, say, environmental preservation or occupational health and safety. In the 1960s, conservatives took a leaf from the liberal book and began establishing their own expert think tanks, many of them in Washington, D.C., such as the Heritage Foundation and the American Enterprise Institute. Responding to the increasing dependence of regulatory policy on technical knowledge, they went on to establish various science-specific think tanks, including the Annapolis Center for Science-Based Public Policy, which is heavily funded by industry, and the George C. Marshall Institute, a center of doubters of global warming whose principal funders include Exxon. The main institutional engine of the crusade for intelligent design—the religious right's alternative to Darwin's theory of evolution by natural selection—is the Discovery Institute, based in Seattle, Washington.[4]

"Manufacturing uncertainty" is how a tobacco company document once described the industry's use of research to contest the regulation of its product (Mooney, 2005: 67). Drawing on the think tanks among other sources, conservatives, many of them allied with the Republican Party, have similarly employed marginal science in the interest of their causes. The theory that human activity is causing global warming commands a consensus of the overwhelming majority of the world's climate scientists. Never mind. Conservatives combat the claim, with all its implications of the imperative need for greater restrictions on the burning of fossil fuels, by stressing the views of a small dissenting minority. Senator James Inhofe, a hard-core conservative Republican from Oklahoma, proclaimed in a Senate speech in 2003, "With all of the hysteria, all of the fear, all of the phony science, could it be that manmade global warming is the greatest hoax ever perpetrated on the American people? It sure sounds like it" (Mooney, 2005: 84).

In the vein of many anti-global warming activists, the religious right uses science to cloud rather than to clarify, emphasizing claims that fall well outside mainstream science. It insists, for example, that condoms are ineffective in preventing HIV and other sexually transmitted diseases and that abortion elevates the risk of breast cancer or mental illness in women. In a recent, informative book on these trends, the journalist Chris Mooney has noted, "Where religious conservatives may once have advanced their pro-life and socially traditionalist views through moral arguments, they now increasingly adopt the veneer of scientific and technical expertise" (Mooney, 2005: 208).

Democrats have also indulged in politicizing science, but in recent years Republicans appear to have outdone them. The Bush administration has been heavy-handed in its policymaking for human stem-cell research. The administration's fealty to the religious right has blocked it from allowing the expenditure of federal funds to create or use any embryonic stem-cell lines beyond those authorized by the president in August 2001. Overt political interference has also appeared in the management of several environmental agencies—for example, the Fish and Wildlife Service, where according to a survey by the Union of Concerned Scientists, almost half of respondents working on endangered species said that they had been "directed, for nonscientific reasons, to refrain from making [findings] that are protective of species." Last year, the Food and Drug Administration refused to approve a so-called morning-after pill despite a 23-4 recommendation from its scientific advisers (Mooney, 2005: 159, 218). (Its decision widely denounced, the FDA recanted in August 2006, announcing that the pill would be available over-the-counter to women 18 and older; see the *New York Times,* August 26, 2001.)

But recall that the Bush administration is compelled to deal with the divisions in the Republican Party. If it has to respond to the demands of the religious right, it also has to attend to the preferences of its socially moderate to liberal hi-tech industrial base. The latter includes many parts of the biotechnology industry, many patient groups, and enthusiasts of global competitiveness who want to see human stem-cell research proceed. For that reason, the president did not reject such research outright but crafted a policy allowing it in a way that sought exquisitely to satisfy these principal interest groups as well as the religious right.

The new initiative for science that Bush announced in his State of the Union address is clearly a response to his party's hi-tech industrial constituency. The goad is the rising global competition from India and China and its threat to the United States in the international marketplace. The initiative emphasizes the production of more scientists and engineers and renewed investment in the advancement of practically related knowledge in areas such as nanotechnology. Whether the initiative will be significantly funded, however, remains an open question, given the administration's absorption with tax cuts and its commitment to the costly war in Iraq.

What, then is the new politics of science? Partly it is the old politics of enlisting the federal government in the cause of scientific research and training with the long-standing aims of fostering national security, economic growth, and better health. The newness of it arises from the diffusion of science into so many other arenas of American life, particularly those that touch us directly. And a key feature of the new politics is the multiple interest groups that issues such as the environment, human reproduction, and sexually transmitted diseases have reinforced in their purposes or called into being. Seen in this light, the new politics of science is not rooted in hostility to science as such. Rather, it is energized by the readiness of these diverse interest groups to deploy types of science—or what they call science—that suit them. The social and economic right in the United States has learned how to mobilize expertise on behalf of the issues it cares about. It acknowledges that the republic has need of savants. It simply prefers to use the savants it likes and, since 9/11, with a propensity for secrecy and misrepresentation.

NOTES

1. As of April 2006, some 8,000 people, including several dozen Nobel laureates, had signed on to the UCS statement. Kurt Gottfried, e-mail to the author, April 12, 2006.
2. The historical discussion that follows draws on a number of works, including Kevles (1995); Dupree (1975); Greenberg (2001); and Maier et al. (2006).
3. See appendix, table, and figure 1 in McIlwain (1995): 3.
4. For the developments discussed here, see Mooney, 2005.

REFERENCES

American Association for the Advancement of Science (AASS). "Congress Caps Another Disappointing Year for R&D Funding in 2006" (January 4, 2006) <http://www.aaas.org/spp/rd/upd1205.htm>.

Branscomb, Lewis. "Science, Politics, and U.S. Democracy." *Issues in Science and Technology* (Fall 2004): 53-59.

Broad, William J. "G.O.P. Budget Cuts Would Fall Hard on Civilian Science." *New York Times*, May 22, 1995.

Cimons, Marlene. "CDC Lab Sees Budget Cuts as Deadly Threat." *Los Angeles Times*, May 19, 1995.

Congressional Record. 102nd Cong., August 3, 1992.

"Crippling American Science." Editorial, *New York Times*, May 23, 1995.

Dupree, A. Hunter. *Science in the Federal Government: A History of Policies and Activities to 1940.* Cambridge: Harvard University Press, 1975.

Gibbons, John H. "Choices Amidst Change: S&T Resource Priorities for U.S. Global Leadership." *Science, Technology, and the 104th Congress: Perspectives on New Choices, Remarks made at the Science Policy Association of the New York Academy of Sciences.* Ed. Susan Raymond. New York: New York Academy of Science, 1995.

Greenberg, Daniel S. *Science, Money, and Politics: Political Triumph and Ethical Erosion.* Chicago: University of Chicago Press, 2001.

Hershberg, James G. *James B. Conant: From Harvard to Hiroshima.* New York: Knopf, 1993.

Kevles, Daniel J. *The Physicists: The History of a Scientific Community in Modern America*. Cambridge: Harvard University Press, 1995.

Maier, Pauline, et al. *Inventing America: A History of the United States*. 2nd ed. New York: Norton, 2006.

McIlwain, Colin. "Cost-Cutting and Downsizing Take Their Toll on U.S. R&D." *Nature* 378 (November 2, 1995).

Mooney, Chris. *The Republican War on Science*. New York: Basic Books, 2005.

Park, Bob. *What's New*, September 22, 1995 <http://bobpark.physics.umd.edu/WN95/>.

Raymond, Susan U., ed. *Science, Technology, and the 104th Congress: Perspectives on New Choices, Remarks made at the Science Policy Association of the New York Academy of Sciences*. New York: New York Academy of Science, 1995.

Reich, Kenneth. "Geological Survey to Fire 500 Workers." *Los Angeles Times*, August 15, 1995.

Science and Government Report (Washington, D.C.), December 15, 1995.

"Transcript of State of the Union Speech." *Washington Post*, Jan. 31, 2006 <http://www.washingtonpost.com/wpdyn/content/article/2006/01/31/AR2006013101468.html>.

U.S. Council of Economic Advisers. "Supporting Research and Development to Promote Economic Growth: The Federal Government's Role." October 1995.

Vasquez, Emily, and Kate Hammer. "New York Women See 2 Sides of Prescription-Free Morning-After Pill." *New York Times*, August 26, 2006.

Wang, Jessica. *American Science in an Age of Anxiety: Scientists, Anticommunism, and the Cold War*. Chapel Hill and London: University of North Carolina Press, 1999.

II. Health

Katayoun Chamany
Introduction

HEALTH POLICY HAS ALWAYS BEEN INFORMED BY BOTH SCIENTIFIC research and political will. Though the National Academies of Science was established in 1863 with the role of informing government on scientific matters, President Dight D. Eisenhower was the first president to appoint a science adviser. James Killian, a former MIT president, recognized the importance of his newly appointed advisory role, and created the first President's Science Advisory Committee (PSAC), which was followed some years later by the Office of Technology and Assessment (OTA). The creation of the presidential science adviser position, the PSAC, and the OTA were in response to an increasing need to better understand our nation's capabilities and shortcomings as they related to space research and national security. However, over the years, this position, and its related offices and committees, have been dismantled and resurrected to be more in line with each incoming administration's goals.

We currently lack an OTA, our bioethics council is appointed by the president, and the presidential scientific adviser position has been demoted to a staff position with very little technology expertise in the supporting office. Though we continue to look to science for matters of defense and energy, we have arrived at a critical juncture in health policy. We have a populace that suffers from age- and lifestyle-related disorders and a growing HIV/AIDS epidemic. Without specific agencies in place with balanced representation among members, it is not clear how we will incorporate science and its ethical implications into reproductive health policies that relate to education, family planning, and stem cell research.

Policy governing scientific research has shifted over the years and is often tightly tied to economic and business interests. Early on, government played a domineering role that gradually gave way to a more inclusive approach that involved members of the general public and the scientific community. As scientists developed new technologies, the scientists themselves took the lead in preparing guidelines for research conduct, but quite coincidentally, scientific research increasingly began to take place in the private sector, releasing scientists from the ethical oversight that accompanied federally funded projects.

As we move into the twenty-first century, government's role in the formation of health policy has begun to return to past practices that exclude community involvement, involve manipulation of scientific data, and lack ethical consistency. Many scientists and public health scholars believe that scientific discovery and sound health practices are being squelched by policies that reflect ideology and represent a flight from reason. Some have decided to relocate to other countries, while others have moved into the private sector, be it in companies or academia. Still others have become more vocal, insisting that scientists do a better job of communicating their work to a democracy that can vote on these policies in an informed manner. In some cases, states have joined the movement and enacted laws that are at odds with federal funding restrictions.

The essays in this section represent some of the fallout of such policies. Elders and Santelli, both leaders in adolescent health, walked away from government positions and continue to pursue their research goals in academia. Hurlbut and Cohen have moved in the other direction, becoming increasingly more involved in policymaking as it applies to stem cell research and in vitro fertilization techniques.

Cohen's essay eloquently quotes Max Weber and reminds us that science needs help. Surely this is true, considering the moral implications involved in stem cell research and other scientific endeavors; however, he extends his analysis more broadly as he points out that a balanced deliberation has been in question for some time. While the Bush administration has continued to push a pro-life agenda, Cohen reminds us that the Clinton Bioethics Council did not have a single member who opposed embryonic research. He argues that the need for balance goes beyond council membership and should be reflected in policies that allow for scientific progress while maintaining dignity for human life.

This point is taken up by the essays authored by Santelli and Elders that demonstrate how the Bush administration has taken the opposite approach when it comes to sex and adolescent health education; the government has employed policies that do not value human life but rather jeopardize it. Both authors use data from multiple research studies to demonstrate that the president's abstinence-only education initiative has resulted in more teenage youth engaging in unsafe sex practices during the course of their sexual lives and the result is an increase in STD rates and unplanned pregnancies.

These essays represent how information is communicated in different sectors of society, as each author describes his or her personal journey navigating the science and politics of health policy. As you read the essays, take note of the presentation of data and the use of language. The Hurlbut and Cohen essays provide a bioethics perspective and use language for which there are no universal definitions (dignity, life, etc.). In Santelli's essay, he remarks on the use of language to set the tone for political discussion long before one word is exchanged (sexual predators, chaste, partial birth abortions). Hurlbut introduces two sophisticated scientific methods for deriving embryonic stem cells that might satisfy those who oppose the destruction of a "living" embryo and makes a plea for respectful dialogue. Cohen also challenges the way language and data are presented to suggest that American stem cell research progress is falling behind (rate versus absolute numbers). Both Santelli and Elders provide concrete scientific data that are difficult to refute, and ask readers to question why the data have not entered mainstream conversations. Elders takes this one step further, suggesting that despite great advances in science and medicine, current health policy continues to marginalize those who are most vulnerable: women, children, and the poor

Before this issue went to press, President George W. Bush held a press conference announcing his veto of the Stem Cell Research

Enhancement Act, his approval of the Fetal Farming Prohibition Act, and his disappointment in the failure to pass the Alternative Pluripotent Cell Therapies Act. Collectively, the bills restrict stem cell research to embryonic stem cell lines established before August 9, 2001, by misrepresenting scientific research practice as it relates to the number and source of embryonic stem cells, and by exploiting the notion of uncertainty as it relates to the therapeutic potential of adult stem cells.Just after the veto, a Gallup Poll reported that 58 percent of those polled disapproved of the president's veto of the Stem Cell Research Enhancement Act and of those, 61 percent believed the president made his decision based on personal moral beliefs rather than to gain political advantage.

Sex education policy has also been shaped by both scientific research findings and moral beliefs. Former House Representative Tom Coburn (R., Ok.) coupled human papillomavirus (HPV) education to the abstinence-only education campaign in proposing the HPV Education and Prevention Act, which was approved by Congress in 2000 and 1) requires educational materials to include information about lack of condom effectiveness, 2) requires the Food and Drug Administration to reexamine condom labels, and 3) requires the Centers for Disease Control to determine the prevalence of HPV in the United States. It is important to note that this policy was exported to the international health community through the US Leadership Against HIV/AIDS, Tuberculosis, and Malaria Act, which was passed in 2003.

As we look to the future, it will become increasingly more important for citizens to become knowledgeable about the philosophical underpinnings of public health and to become familiar with the nature of scientific research and its applications. Perhaps with increased public engagement, we can move forward despite having lost formalized political agencies like the Office of Technology Assessment. Honest presentation of scientific data, increased understanding of science and ethics, and critical questioning of the proposed policies by groups with diverse membership will be key components in the success of such a public movement. The essays in this section provide a glimpse of the varied approaches to health policy and the outcome of such practices, and serve as stepping stones for continued conversation, activism, and research.

Eric Cohen
The Permanent Limits of Modern Science— From Birth to Death

ONE OF THE GREATEST EFFORTS TO THINK ABOUT THE MEANING OF modern science is Max Weber's essay on "science as a vocation." Weber's meditation was originally given as a lecture in 1918, with the bloodbath of World War I in the immediate background, and with some of the Enlightenment optimism of the previous decades shattered by the dark specter of high-tech warfare and the haunting images of dead young bodies. Weber came to defend the dignity of science, but also to describe the permanent limits of science on questions of value, which is to say, the great human questions that matter most. He came to rebuke those who seek false comfort in old gods that no longer exist, or in churches that provide shelter from the real dilemmas of modernity. But he came also, first and foremost, to remind scientists that they serve gods, too—or ideals and interests that the modern science of nature can aid but cannot vindicate. As Weber put it, citing the novelist Tolstoy: "'Science is meaningless because it gives no answer to our question, the only question important for us: 'What shall we do and how shall we live?' That science does not give an answer to this is indisputable. The only question that remains is the sense in which science gives 'no' answer, and whether or not science might yet be of some use to the one who puts the question correctly" (Gerth and Mills, 1946: 143).

Over the past few years—and past few centuries—there has been intense debate about the role of science in society. There has also been considerable discontent among scientists about what they see as the "unscientific" or "antiscientific" character of contemporary politics. But this discontent—over stem cells, global warming, intelligent design, sex education—has rarely helped to "put the question correctly." What we need to ask is: What moral principles should govern the conduct of science, and what moral priorities should govern the actions we take on the basis of current scientific knowledge, especially when fundamental human goods seem to be in conflict? This is a question about science but not a scientific question. The modern scientific method equips us with wonderful new powers and new knowledge, both to improve human life and to destroy it. But science itself does not tell us how to live or what to value in a world made new by scientific knowledge. The principles of biology cannot tell us whether to develop bioweapons or destroy human embryos for research. The principles of physics cannot tell us whether to build nuclear power plants or atomic weapons. Science needs to be governed by philosophical ethics and democratic politics.

This essay aims to explore the complex relationship between the scientific study of nature and democratic deliberation about the civic and human good. It begins by trying to reframe our general approach to science, ethics, and politics; then it looks at two specific controversies in health policy—at the end of life and the beginning of life—in which science offers no intrinsic limits or guidance to govern the unintended consequences of its achievements or the insatiable character of its ambitions. Finally, the essay tries to show, by specific example, that even those who disagree bitterly about some areas of science policy can nevertheless work together to set some limits on science, especially when unfettered experimentation threatens those aspects of our humanity that elevate us above the very nature we seek laboriously to study and master.

PERHAPS THE ONLY VALUE INTRINSIC TO SCIENCE IS THAT KNOWLEDGE is good and more is better. The good scientist makes discoveries, and his discoveries make him good in both senses of the term—skillful as a knowledge-seeker and virtuous for seeking knowledge. But, of course, some knowledge is not good—if put in the wrong hands, or put to the wrong uses, or acquired in the wrong way, or deforming of human life by its very possession. This means that we have reason from the beginning to be skeptical of science as a guide to ethical action, precisely because acquiring knowledge sometimes seems to require conducting unsavory experiments or working for unsavory patrons. If knowledge of nature is the highest end of human life, then we always risk making some human beings mere means to the pursuit of other men's knowledge. And if scientific freedom to experiment is the highest good, then other types of freedom risk being devalued or transgressed.

Indeed, it is at least ironic, in the context of the stem cell debate, that some scientists and policymakers from Western democracies have praised China as a bastion of scientific freedom. For we all know that China is hardly a bastion of intellectual freedom in general. And historically, we know that both the Nazi regime and the Soviet regime—no friends of liberty—were home to many scientific and technological achievements. To despots, scientists are tools, means to their political ends. Yet we must at least contemplate whether the reverse is also potentially true: to scientists, even despots are potential tools, means to their end of seeking knowledge without moral limits and thus with the freedom to experiment in ways that democratic societies may find abhorrent. For there is nothing in nature, at least nothing discoverable by modern scientific methods, that refutes the morality of despotism. Liberty and scientific liberty, it turns out, are not exactly the same. What is good for science, devoted first and foremost to the pursuit of knowledge, is not necessarily good for human beings, precisely because scientific knowledge of nature is not the highest good in human life.

Most of the time science is man's great benefactor, and most scientists have only the best motives: improving the quality of life, healing the sick, educating the young. And, of course, most of the time, free societies like America are far better for science than regimes like China, which restrict the free flow of information even if they might permit the freedom to experiment without significant moral constraints. But even and perhaps especially in democratic societies, science cannot be its own guide. Because human beings are limited, we need to decide which types of knowledge are most worth supporting with public funds, public prestige, and public education. In ages past, kings and queens made such decisions, and scientists were either the beneficiaries of their generosity or the targets of their animus. Today, citizens rightly set limits and priorities democratically, with scientists playing a special dual role in this democratic process: they are experts who can tell us what is possible, and they are fellow citizens helping to discern what is worthy. As experts, scientists know more than the rest of us; as citizens, they are just like the rest of us—sometimes wiser than most, and sometimes more foolish, especially when they falsely believe that their knowledge of scientific facts qualifies them to act as the lone moral arbiters of scientific research.

Good ethics surely requires knowledge of the facts. But knowledge of the facts hardly guarantees good ethics or good judgment. Knowing the remarkable promise of embryonic stem cell research hardly makes one the best judge of the morality of destroying human embryos. Knowing the genetic character of Down's syndrome hardly makes one the best judge for deciding whether to abort a fetus with Down's syndrome. Knowing the neurological pathology of Alzheimer's hardly makes one the best judge of whether life with dementia still has value.

Even on an issue like global warming, knowing the facts, which themselves are often in dispute, does not settle the best course of action. How much short-term economic pain are we willing to endure to prevent the potential long-term dangers of global warming? To what extent are we willing to limit personal freedom and expand the regulatory power of government to reduce greenhouse gases? How do environmental concerns relate to other urgent problems, whether the looming crisis of old-age entitlements or the threat of a nuclear Iran? Many scientists, experts in their own subdisciplines, come to think that the "crisis" they know best is the only crisis that matters, and they demand that all "enlightened" politicians govern accordingly. But in reality, democracy, informed by science but not ruled by it, is often more enlightened than scientists alone, striking a balance among many urgent problems and priorities. This fact is often forgotten amid all the endless chatter about "politicizing science."

Indeed, it is usually not a compliment to be accused of politicizing science. But this phrase actually has at least two meanings—one negative and one positive. The first meaning involves distorting scientific evidence to promote one's own ideology or agenda. The temptation to engage in such a disgraceful practice exists (and sometimes prevails) on all sides of the political spectrum: environmental activists tempted to exaggerate the threat of global warming; industry advocates tempted to downplay the ecological effects of oil exploration; pro-life activists tempted to overhype the promise of adult stem cells; embryo research advocates tempted to promise cures for dreaded diseases based only on preliminary animal experiments. It is true that many of the most ideologically intense debates about science involve areas where the scientific facts themselves are open to question, where nature's realities and possibilities are still obscure to the human mind. But even then, everyone should resist the temptation to assume that the best hypothesis is the one most convenient for one's own chosen cause, or to highlight only those facts that advance one's chosen agenda. Such "politicization" is rightly condemned by responsible people on all sides.

The second meaning of "politicizing science," however, is not a problem but a virtue. Politics, rightly understood, is the activity of ordering our life together, and insofar as science both affects and depends on civic life, it is rightly a political issue. Indeed, all democratic societies need to debate the relative importance of different scientific projects—such as curing AIDS or exploring new planets. We need to debate the relative risks and benefits of certain areas of scientific research—such as creating artificial viruses or developing nuclear power. We need to consider the ethical dilemmas of proceeding or not proceeding with certain types of experiments—such as embryo research or experimentation on children. Science alone cannot answer the types of questions that science sets before us, and a self-governing people must govern the direction of science, especially (but not only) when citizens are paying the bills.

Which brings us back to the fundamental question: What values or ideals ought to govern scientific ambition? The most obvious ideal is the technological ideal, the drive for material progress, the effort to make life better for oneself or one's fellow citizens. That science has succeeded in this technological venture is obvious, and we should all be grateful, resisting the temptation to glorify premodern life and its supposed simplicity. But the elevation of man through science always needs to be grounded in the ideals that elevate man above the rest of nature—namely, his special dignity as a rational and moral being, and his unique capacity to treat seemingly unequal fellow human beings as morally equal. That man evolved from lower animal forms seems clear; that he is different from every other animal seems obvious. These ideals—the human difference from the rest of nature and human equality despite natural differences—rightly shape the governance of science, especially biological science, and especially at the edges of human life: conception and death.

LET US BEGIN WITH THE END OF LIFE BEFORE RETURNING TO (AND focusing largely on) the beginning. In the years ahead, as America and Europe become mass geriatric societies, one of the greatest health policy challenges will be caring well for the elderly, especially the elderly with dementia. In this case, we can hardly be anything but grateful for the new world that modern biomedical science has made possible—a world where long life is the norm, long enough for most of us to see grandchildren married and the cycle of the generations continued. But we also cannot sever medicine's sweetest fruits from its sourest consequences: science prevents earlier, acute causes of death but leaves us more vulnerable to extended decline, bereft of all mental and bodily powers, left in the hands of adult children in an age when familial bonds are being severely tested by divorce, geographical separation, and the ethic of autonomy.

The advance of biomedical science helped create this new world of longevity. But what can science tell us about how to live well in it, about what it means to honor our father and mother during that long decade of decline, about how to balance the good of the young and the old both within families and within society? And the answer, alas, is very little. Modern medical research can tell us what Alzheimer's does to the brain. It can explore risk factors, strategies of prevention, and possible cures. But everything else—what to do and how to live an aging society—is a matter of interpretation. Some may enlist science as the justification of their values. But the values they choose are not themselves scientific.

The neuroscientist, for example, might defend the compassionate killing of our elders before their dementia gets worse. After all, if human beings are nothing more than our minds, as some neuroscientists believe, then life with dementia is subhuman. Euthanasia is an act of generosity. Noble suicide before dementia robs us of our faculties; it is a last act of human greatness, a revolt against our natural origins as merely survival-seeking beasts or matter-in-motion.

The geriatrician, by contrast, might defend caring for our demented elders until the very end. Nature may drive us to devalue those whose will is gone and whose reproductive years are long past. But our capacity to love even those whose lives seem so diminished reveals our special humanity; our capacity to treat the severely disabled as equal members of the human family shows that we are more than Darwinian beasts. The utilitarian economist might retort that devoting endless resources to such futile lives seems immoral, while the techno-optimist might say that keeping the demented alive is our moral duty, in the hope that science will eventually reverse the death sentence of nature and restore those powers taken away by disease.

The point is that both nature and the scientific mastery of nature offer little guidance about how to live as natural beings with more than natural moral aspirations. Max Weber, interestingly enough, saw this very dilemma many decades ago:

> Consider modern medicine, a practical technology that is highly developed scientifically. The general "presupposition" of the medical enterprise is stated trivially in the

assertion that medical science has the task of maintaining life as such and of diminishing suffering as such to the greatest possible degree. Yet this is problematical. By his means the medical man preserves the life of the mortally ill man, even if the patient implores us to relieve him of life, even if his relatives, to whom his life is worthless and to whom the costs of maintaining his worthless life grow unbearable, grant his redemption from suffering. Perhaps a poor lunatic is involved, whose relatives, whether they admit it or not, wish and must wish for his death. Yet the presuppositions of medicine, and the penal code, prevent the physician from relinquishing his therapeutic efforts. Whether life is worthwhile living and when—this question is not asked by medicine. Natural science gives us an answer to the question of what we must do if we wish to master life technically. It leaves quite aside, or assumes for its purposes, whether we should and do wish to master life technically and whether it ultimately makes sense to do so (Gerth and Mills, 1946: 144).

Whatever course one follows, whatever values one allows to govern the care (or noncare) of the demented, it is possible to enlist science as a justification, even though science cannot actually tell us what values to serve—equality, nobility, utility, longevity. As Hans Jonas put it: "The scientist himself is by his science no more qualified than others to discern, nor even is he more disposed to care for, the good of mankind. Benevolence must be called in from the outside to supplement the knowledge acquired through theory: it does not flow from theory itself" (Jonas, 2001: 195).

This is true in every area of public life where science and morality intersect: on stem cells, scientists can tell us the potential benefits of destroying human embryos, but not whether the progress of medicine justifies the willful destruction of nascent human life. On drilling in Alaska: scientists can estimate the potential oil reserves and the potential harm to the biosphere, but not whether we have a moral responsibility to expand the domestic oil supply or a moral responsibility to preserve the unsullied wonders of animal nature even at economic harm to ourselves. On the human exploration of space: scientists can estimate the economic and human costs of putting a human on Mars and the potential benefits of such a mission to the advance of human knowledge, but they cannot say whether human greatness in space is more worthy of public funds than ongoing research into curing AIDS. Science is power without wisdom about the uses of power. Science is, as Weber told us, silent about the very values it serves.

WHICH RETURNS US TO THE FUNDAMENTAL QUESTION: WHAT VALUES DO scientists wish to serve? What ideals do scientists hold dear? What makes modern scientists—and especially modern biologists—believe that they are true benefactors of mankind? For some, the pursuit of knowledge is its own justification. Their fellow citizens exist to serve the cause of knowing, rather than the activity of knowing existing to serve their fellow citizens. For the most part, this means providing public funds for scientific research; sometimes it means enlisting (or even using) human beings as tools for experimentation. But most scientists are driven, too, by compassion for the sick and suffering, afflicted with the inequities of disease—like infertility, or childhood leukemia, or Parkinson's. Scientists are emotional creatures, it turns out, or at least appeal to emotion in their public defense of science—as we saw so vividly in the 2004 campaign in California for stem cell research, with advertisement after advertisement evoking the pathos of disease as the justification for destroying embryos. Faced with the absurdity of sickness—why does a child get sick, after all?—scientists seek rational means to correct the irrational imperfections of nature.

But here we discover that the cause of science has a problem—one revealed clearly in debates about reproduction and embryo research. True compassion is grounded in the ideal of human equality—a belief that others, weak or strong, old or young, rich or poor, are worthy of compassion. But it is precisely the principle of human equality that is violated by the very practices of embryo research and pre-implantation genetic diagnosis. To the untutored eye, the human embryo looks like an ordinary cell, no smaller than the period at the end of this sentence. But to those who understand modern embryology, the embryo is a life in process—weak and vulnerable, barely visible, but unquestionably a member of the human species. As science knows, our eyes can deceive us. And as we learned (or should have learned) from the civil rights movement, appearance is not the true criteria for human dignity. Stem cell scientists may tell us that the embryo is just a clump of cells. But they seem to want that clump of cells quite desperately, and it seems dishonest to separate the special powers that an embryo possesses from the special entity an embryo is. Those who oppose embryo research may be religious, but their argument rests on the twin pillars of democratic equality and modern science: every life is equal; a human embryo is a life unfolding before our eyes; to use one vulnerable life to help another is unjust. Of course, the embryological facts do not tell us what to believe; rather, they tell us what is required of us if we believe in the protection of intrinsic human equality.

Likewise when it comes to pre-implantation genetic diagnosis—a new way of screening embryos to decide which are worthy and which are not, which to keep and which to discard. Such a process of reproduction by exclusion is rooted in the rejection of equality—the belief that some lives are not worth welcoming and protecting. In the name of compassion, it engages in ruthless genetic discrimination.

In all likelihood, the bitter debates about embryo research and new technologies of reproduction will continue interminably. It would be much better for everyone if they proceeded more honestly and more civilly: without scientists promising cures long in advance of the evidence; without politicians claiming that President George W. Bush's stem cell policy "bans" embryo research, when in reality such research is entirely legal in nearly every state of the union; without research advocates dishonestly claiming that research cloning is just "nuclear transplantation to produce stem cells," hiding the fact that getting those stem cells requires producing and destroying a cloned human embryo; and without all the loose talk about the inquisition of Galileo.

One hesitates even to dignify such charges, and yet they come from deans of leading medical schools (for example, Stanford dean Philip A. Pizzo) and members of Congress (Senator Arlen Specter, Representatives Christopher Shays and Jim McDermott). So let us answer them once and for all: many opponents of embryo research, as said earlier, are religious believers, but the argument against embryo research rests on a moral interpretation of the biological facts, not an appeal to parochial religious authority. To believe human embryos are human beings worthy of protection is a very rational position—and arguably the only rational position compatible with our democratic ideal of equality. Moreover, those scientists who claim the mantle of Galileo fail to understand or acknowledge the crucial distinction between the free pursuit of knowledge and the experimental deeds required to acquire that knowledge. Studying the planets from afar and destroying nascent human life up close are very different acts. Restrictions on federal funding and the Inquisition of ages past are very different matters. The comparison—and the attitude behind it—is absurd.

IN THE POLICY ARENA, THE GREATEST CONFUSION—AND IN SOME CASES, disingenuousness—has surrounded the character and consequences of President Bush's decision to limit federal funding of human embryonic stem cell research to a specific number of eligible lines. Most egregious is when critics of the policy willfully misrepresent scientific data, in prestigious scientific publications, to make their public case. It offers a classic example of believing that any public policy that does not necessarily promote the maximum amount of scientific research is necessarily unscientific, and then allowing one's pro-science views to justify making an unscientific (or scientifically distorted) defense of scientific progress.

In its April 2006 issue, the journal *Nature Biotechnology* published a short paper entitled "An International Gap in Human ES [Embryonic Stem] Cell Research" (Owen-Smith and McCormick, 2006: 391-392). The authors, Jason Owen-Smith of the University of Michigan and Jennifer

McCormick of Stanford, carefully reviewed all scientific publications involving the use or derivation of human embryonic stem cells, starting with the first paper in 1998.

Their aim, very clear in the tone and tenor of the text, was to show that American stem cell scientists were falling behind their counterparts abroad, and that the Bush administration's funding policy was to blame. "Expanding the purview of federal [human embryonic stem] cell funding can still prevent the United States from slipping off the leading edge of developments in this vital field," the authors write (391). A press release accompanying the article proclaims that "the fear that United States researchers might lose ground to their international counterparts in human embryonic stem cell research now appears to have become a fact" ("U.S. Falling Behind," 2006).

Coverage of the study took much the same tone. "The United States is falling behind other countries in human embryonic-stem-cell research," UPI reported ("Study: U.S. Lagging," 2006). The *Washington Post* began its brief report on the study by telling its readers that "American scientists are falling behind researchers elsewhere in stem cell discoveries because of U.S. limits on the use of federal funding, a study has found" ("Findings," 2006).

The study itself, however, tells a different story. Owen-Smith and McCormick reviewed the 132 human embryonic stem cell articles published in 55 scientific journals since 1998. Far from showing the United States lagging behind in the field, they found that American scientists had by far the most publications—46 percent of the total, while the other 54 percent was divided among scientists from 17 other countries. They also found that the number of papers in the field published by Americans has increased each year, with a particularly notable growth spurt beginning in 2002.

How, then, to support the image of Americans "falling behind"? The best the authors could do was to note that, as their accompanying press release claims, "human embryonic stem cell research has been accelerating at a faster pace internationally" ("U.S. Falling Behind," 2006). They point out that while in 2002 a third of the papers published in the world came from the United States, in 2004 only a quarter did. Their data also show, however, that in 2002 there were only 10 papers published on human embryonic stem cells (of which 3 were American), while in 2004 there were 77 papers, of which 20 were American. So the number of American publications in the field was nearly seven times greater in 2004 than it was in 2002—a trend that hardly supports the image of research stifled or held back by government policy.

To advance the perception of American science in crisis, Owen-Smith and McCormick compare the output of American scientists to that of their counterparts in the rest of the world combined, hoping to obscure the inconvenient fact that no single country comes close to challenging America's dominance of embryonic stem cell research. Another recent study, highlighted by *The Scientist* magazine in March 2006, found the same to be the case in the larger field of stem cell research (Stafford, 2006). Between 2000 and 2004, 42 percent of all scientific publications in stem cell research were by Americans. America's nearest competitor was Germany, far behind with only 10 percent of the total.

But the most extraordinary aspect of the Owen-Smith and McCormick study—which the authors conveniently and deliberately fail to highlight—was what it said about the use of those embryonic stem cell lines approved for federal funding under President Bush's 2001 policy. Besides claiming that America is falling behind, critics of the Bush policy have argued relentlessly that the presidentially approved lines are inadequate or even useless. But this claim is also severely undermined by the study.

Grudgingly, and almost in passing, Owen-Smith and McCormick note that "Only 14.4% (19) of publications described the use or derivation of lines not approved by the NIH" (2006: 391). In other words, more than 85 percent of all the published embryonic stem cell research in the world has used the lines approved for funding under the Bush policy. Since this is almost twice the number of papers published by Americans, it is clear that a great deal of the work done abroad has also involved these lines, even though most of it could not have been funded by the NIH. The lines are used, in other words, because they are useful, not only because they are eligible for federal support.

Many critics of the Bush policy claim that the Bush lines are useless because they are contaminated with mouse-feeder cells. This claim also seems largely specious. Two recent studies have shown methods of culturing the NIH-funded lines that leave them free of all trace of animal materials. Discussing his company's use of the Bush-approved lines, Geron CEO Tom Okarma recently told *Wired News*, "the stuff you hear published that all of those lines are irrevocably contaminated with mouse materials and could never be used in people—hogwash. If you know how to grow them, they're fine" (Edwards, 2006).

In April 2006, the *Wall Street Journal* reported similar sentiments from other researchers in the field. While scientists would always welcome more funding for their work (who wouldn't?), those reached by the *Journal* seem not to see Bush's policy as the intolerable impediment his political opponents suggest it is. "There is a lot going on in the U.S.," said Renee Reijo-Pera, codirector of the Human Embryonic Stem Cell Center at the University of California, San Francisco. "The official story [of stem-cell advocates] is how we are falling behind in tragedy and dismay. And I don't think that is the case" (Regalado, 2006).

Of course, the argument for the Bush administration's funding policy does not finally rest on scientific utility but on moral and democratic principle. As the president has put it: "We should not use public money to support the further destruction of human life." (Bush, 2005) This means that some types of research, even if beneficial, should never be conducted with federal dollars. The current limit would not move—and the moral principle it upholds would not change—even if it were true that it "crippled" American stem cell science. And supporters of the Bush policy should be up-front about the fact that some useful research may not advance as quickly or at all, at least in America, because of such limits. Surely more could be done, and more quickly, if more public dollars were spent on more lines—that is, if the profound ethical dilemmas involved were simply ignored.

That said, it is dishonest to obscure the useful research that the Bush policy has indeed facilitated, and disingenuous to claim that America is "lagging behind" when it remains, by far, the world's leader in stem cell science. Rather than make the narrow case for funding embryo-destructive research, many opponents of the Bush policy zealously claim that the Bush policy paralyzes stem cell research in general. In doing so, they often ignore the moral issue entirely, treating stem cell policy as if it were entirely a scientific question to be settled by scientific data.

The point of the Bush policy, after all, is to show that science can proceed without violating human dignity or destroying nascent human life, even if it cannot proceed as quickly and by as many simultaneous routes. The choice it offers is not between science and ethics, but between a devotion to science and health so total that it abandons all ethical limits, and a devotion to science and health balanced and constrained by a respect for human life largely understood.

Moreover, even the various practical arguments made against the scientific utility of the policy—the lines are contaminated, there are not enough to support basic research, they are causing American researchers to fall behind their foreign counterparts—often do not stand up to factual scrutiny. The defenders of science often make their defense by distorting the empirical facts.

One can make reasonable arguments for a more permissive funding policy; one cannot reasonably claim that the policy is wreaking havoc on American science, or that America is becoming backward because only private dollars or state funds are available for the derivation of stem cells from destroyed human embryos. To make such a claim is not science or even the rational defense of science; it is fundamentalism in the name of science, employing the most unscientific means imaginable: playing with the data to advance one's cause.

WHILE THE BITTER DIVIDE OVER EMBRYO RESEARCH CONTINUES, IT IS incumbent upon us to seek whatever common ground we can find, and to see if we might break the current bioethical impasse when it comes to biotechnologies touching the beginnings of human life. In an arena of science and health policy in which values clash, we must seek out shared values. And here, the nation has a golden opportunity: to promote medical progress that every citizen can celebrate, to set wise ethical limits that most scientists can live with, to seek the widest possible consensus in a divisive political environment, and to show that even those with different first principles can work together on science policy.

In his 2006 State of the Union address, President Bush laid out a new bioethics agenda, calling on Congress to prohibit the creation of man-animal hybrids, the harvesting of fetuses as a source of biological spare parts, and the buying, selling, or patenting of human embryos. (Bush, 2006) These policy proposals offer a partial way forward in the bioethics debate, and even those who vigorously support embryo research should support the great bulk of this new agenda. This is, in other words, an example of science policy at its best.

Of course, combining human and animal cells is already standard practice in many biological laboratories, and no one is proposing that such experimentation should stop. But creating chimeras by combining human eggs and animal sperm (or vice versa) crosses a new and important ethical line by blurring the boundaries between human and nonhuman species. One need not believe that human embryos are fully human to defend the dignity of humanity as a whole by preventing the creation of embryonic hybrids.

Likewise, even the most vocal supporters of embryo research and research cloning have pledged their support for establishing some upper limit on embryonic development in the research setting. They wish to preserve the right to use early embryos in research, but abhor the prospect of harvesting embryos to later fetal stages as a source of "spare parts." On this point, all sides seem to agree, and it is to the credit of both President Bush and Congress that America banned this practice in summer 2006 by prohibiting the harvesting of fetuses in human and animal wombs solely for research purposes.

Finally, the most thoughtful defenders of embryo research recognize the moral gravity of what they seek to advance and defend. They recognize that the human embryo deserves at least "special respect," and should be used only for the most important scientific experiments. Such respect demands that embryos not be treated as mere articles of commerce, bought and sold on the open market.

But setting such moral and legal limits is not enough. We all hear the cries of the sick and suffering afflicted with dreaded diseases like Parkinson's. And we all admire the compassionate motives of those scientists who seek to come to their aid with novel stem cell cures. The disagreement has always been about the scientific means, not the medical end. For as we all know, the pursuit of health is one good that all modern individuals agree on, even when they disagree on much else.

For the past few years, scientists and advocates have claimed that the only way to make stem cell research really pay off is by using cloned embryos, which would allow us to produce pluripotent stem cells with genomes we control. Such genetic control is important for two reasons: it allows scientists to build stem cell models of diseases, and in the future it may allow us to produce rejection-proof stem cell therapies. Ordinary embryos—such as those left over in fertility clinics—lack these crucial biological qualities.

Until recently, it seemed as if research cloning was well under way, and that it was the most promising method to achieve these vaunted scientific goals. But in late 2005 and early 2006, the world discovered that research cloning was not as far along as we thought, because the world's first and only research cloners, a team of South Koreans led by Hwang Woo Suk, were engaged in a gargantuan scientific fraud. In the meantime, a series of papers published in *Science* and *Nature* suggested that there might be alternative ways to produce genetically tailored pluripotent stem cells without creating or destroying human embryos at all.

One of these alternative methods, variously called "altered nuclear transfer" or "oocyte assisted reprogramming," involves modifying the technique of cloning to produce a pluripotent stem cell directly, without ever producing an embryo. An even more technically advanced and morally responsible method—because it does not require using eggs, and because it has already been done in humans—is called "cell fusion." It involves combining an existing embryonic stem cell line—like one of the "Bush lines" already eligible for federal funding—with an ordinary human cell from an ailing human donor. The result, if it works, is a new embryonic stem cell line with the genetic make-up of the cell donor, giving us all the benefits of research cloning (stem cell models, rejection-proof therapies) without the moral hazards or political divisions.

One can forgive those citizens who find the bioethics debate bewildering: the science is changing fast and the ethical stakes are monumental. But one cannot forgive policymakers for missing the opportunity to find common ground in this arena of science policy even amid deep disagreement. On the moral standing of the embryo, public argument will surely continue, and it should continue more civilly. But over the past year, the room for agreement has also widened. We can come together to prevent the most egregious practices—such as producing man-animal hybrids or engaging in embryo commerce. And we can come together to promote promising science that everyone can support—such as creating pluripotent stem cells without destroying human embryos. With a dose of goodwill and prudent moderation on all sides, we can get beyond some of the old arguments, or at least govern alongside them. That would surely be the politicization of science at its best, and a great improvement over the bitterness of the past few years. It might also have a spillover effect in other areas of science policy, in which acrimony and contention now seem to reign.

STEPPING BACK FROM THE SPECIFIC MORAL AND POLICY DILEMMAS confronting us at the beginning and end of human life, we need to reexamine more generally how we understand the encounter of science and values in a democracy. We need, as Weber once hoped, to put the question correctly, but we cannot rely upon science alone, or science predominantly, to help us do so. What we need, in fact, is a reinvigoration of philosophy, beginning with a serious philosophy of nature. As animals, we are part of nature—yet we are also the only animals with a science of nature, a technological mastery of nature, and an explanation of our origins within nature. We are the only animals that understand the meaning of nature's imperfections, and the fact that our natural bodies will one day fail us for reasons we can explain mechanistically but not metaphysically. We are also more than natural beings, seeking to correct nature's brutal laws of survival with moral concern for those who cannot survive on their own, and seeking to transcend the limits nature imposes upon us, with a thirst for immortality that drives both modern biology and ancient religion. Only by grappling with who we are—as natural beings, curious about nature, confronted by nature's limits, with more than natural aspirations—will we begin to understand the meaning of modern science. And only then, can we try to govern science wisely, hoping to preserve those lofty elements of our humanity that elevate us above the natural world.

REFERENCES

Bush, George. W. "President Discusses Embryo Adoption and Ethical Stem Cell Research." May 24, 2005 <http://www.whitehouse.gov/news/releases/2005/05/20050524-12.html>.

Bush, George W. "State of the Union 2006." January 31, 2006 <http://www.whitehouse.gov/stateoftheunion/2006/>.

Edwards, Steven. "Scrutinizing a Stem Cell Trial." *Wired News* (March 29, 2006) <http://www.wired.com/news/technology/medtech/0,70521-0.html>.

"Findings: U.S. Lags in Stem Cell Research." *The Washington Post,* April 7, 2006 <http://www.washingtonpost.com/wpdyn/content/article/2006/04/06/AR2006040601763.html>.

Gerth, H. H., and C. Wright Mills, trans. and eds. *From Max Weber: Essays in Sociology*. New York: Oxford University Press, 1946.

Jonas, Hans. *The Phenomenon of Life: Toward a Philosophical Biology*. Evanston, IL: Northwestern University Press, 2001 (1966).

Owen-Smith, Jason, and Jennifer McCormick. "An International Gap in Human ES Cell Research." *Nature Biotechnology* 24:4 (April 2006): 391-392.

Regalado, Antonio. "Embryonic Stem-Cell Research Spreads Despite Curbs." *Wall Street Journal,* April 4, 2006 <http://www.stemcellnews. com/articles/stem-cells-research-grows.htm>.

Stafford, Ned. "Stem Cell Density Highest in Israel." *The Scientist* (March 21, 2006) <http://www.the-scientist.com/news/display/23240/>.

"Study: U.S. Lagging in Stem-Cell Research." UPI, April 7, 2006 <http:// www.upi.com/HealthBusiness/view.php?StoryID=20060407-023128-6458r>.

"U.S. Falling Behind in Embryonic Stem Cell Research, Study Says." University of Michigan News Service, April 6, 2006 <http://www. umich.edu/news/?Releases/2006/Apr06/r040606b>.

M. Joycelyn Elders
The Politics of Health Care

DESPITE ALL OF OUR SCIENTIFIC PROGRESS IN THE AREAS OF HEALTH and biological sciences, we still have a huge unfinished agenda and multiple problems that must be addressed. We confront problems with health care access for all of our citizens. Ours is a health-illiterate society, yet we refuse to provide comprehensive health education for all children. Scientists have unraveled the secret of the cell, explored and mapped the human genome; they have developed methodology for controlling human reproduction, created lasers that can read license plates in Japan, designed scanning images for every part of the body, carried out stem cell research that can cure diseases. Yet, we have health policies that limit optimal benefit for our population.

We deny comprehensive health education and support abstinence-only education when we know that more than 50 percent of our children are not abstinent. We have one of the highest teenage pregnancy rates in the industrialized world; 50 percent of all of the 1.9 million sexually transmitted diseases (STDs), including human immunodeficiency virus (HIV), occur annually in young people less then 24 years of age. We downplay the value of condoms when scientific data support their use in the prevention of unplanned pregnancy and certain sexually transmitted diseases, including HIV and human papilloma virus (HPV). The illogical nature of these circumstances often is the result of short-term political gain by some who capitalize on the sensationalism of the word "sex" brought up in any context.

The human population continues to increase exponentially; it doubled from 2.5 billion to 5 billion between 1950 and 1989, reaching 6 billion in 1996 and, if trends continue, could reach 12 billion by 2050.

Almost nothing is being done in most nations to promote effective family planning programs. Instead, there is widespread ideological, political, and religious resistance to contraception. This is aggravated in many developing countries by female illiteracy and restrictions on the rights of women. The United States has been complicit in this gender inequity by cutting family planning budgets, both foreign and domestic, while supporting abstinence-only education.

There is major political debate about a recently developed vaccine against the HPV. Now Supreme Court judges are appointed based on their stand on abortions and pharmacists are allowed to deny women emergency contraceptives pills, which have been ordered by their physician, based on their moral stands (Gee, 2006). Politics and health care are strangely entangled with little regard for the healthy outcome of the populace.

We have many crises to overcome in trying to create a healthy society for the twenty-first century. The first is a crisis of vision. While we have the best doctors, nurses, hospitals, support staff, and cutting-edge research, we do not have the visionaries to design the system to serve all of our people. Our present system costs too much, delivers too little, is not comprehensive, coherent, or cost effective, does not allow choice, is not equitable, and is not universal.

Our second crisis is a crisis of anticipation. We are not looking to the future, not using all available resources, not realizing that prevention is far better than intervention or that if a school nurse prevents one girl from getting pregnant or one boy from using drugs, that she has saved her state more than she is paid.

The third is a crisis of creativity. We in medicine must learn to think out of the box and develop a health care system that is available, affordable, assessable, high quality, and culturally competent.

There are many social and behavioral problems that affect the health of our people: smoking, poor dietary habits, lack of exercise, alcohol abuse, the use of illicit drugs, abuse of prescription drugs, and violence. These determine up to 50 percent of our health status, but receive only 4 percent of our national health expenditures. At the same time, access to care influences only 10 percent of our health status and receives 88 percent of our national health expenditure of $1.9 trillion.

Nutritional disorders such as obesity, diabetes mellitus, hyperlipidemia, and hypertension can all be influenced by dietary regulations. With 60 percent of our society overweight, we took physical education out of schools.

We have accomplished much in public health. However, we have not met the goals of *Healthy People 2000* or *Healthy People 2010*. We will need to use multiple strategies to achieve the nation's goals of *Healthy People 2010*, which are to:

▸ increase the quality and years of healthy life,
▸ eliminate health disparities, and
▸ provide access to primary preventive care for all citizens.

We need educational strategies, access strategies, prevention strategies, intervention strategies, leadership strategies, political strategies as well as strategies of compassion.

Quality health care, a universal concern, is dependent upon a few key interrelated factors, number one of which is a sound scientific basis with continuing scientific discovery. It is dependent upon having a heath care system that is coherent, comprehensive, cost effective, offers choice of providers, is accessible and equitable. It involves the education of providers, patients, and the community. Providers must be trained to be culturally sensitive and culturally competent.

In January 2006, poll results revealed that 89 percent of Americans agree that "our health care system is broken and 86 percent support reforming it to provide affordable health coverage for all" (Americans for Health Care, 2005). Health care is a powerful issue to most Americans that is not adequately addressed by political leaders. Likely, it is because our health care system is truly broken, not merely out of adjustment. Therefore, it needs a difficult overall rebirth rather than a superficial makeover. We are constantly looking for quick fixes to make points in an election, make more money for our corporation/business, or to promote our agenda rather than working hard for a long-term solution to the difficult problem of providing universal access to health care for all Americans.

Our health care system is not a health care system; rather, it is a very expensive sick care system. Consider the statistics:

- More than 46 million people have no health insurance, including over 18 percent of our non-elderly population.
- Forty-two percent of the uninsured population consists of minorities.
- Eighty percent of the 46 million uninsured people work every day or live in families in which at least one member works every day.
- Fifty-six percent of the uninsured earn less than 200 percent of the federal poverty guidelines for a family of four and many more are underserved by our health care system.

Our population is growing older, living longer (women, 80 years; men, 76 years), and have more chronic disease and disabilities.

We are the richest country in the world and the only industrialized country that does not provide health care for its entire people. Health care, which now consumes one-seventh of GDP, or $1.9 trillion in 2005, continues to grow in its appetite for our economic resources while the United States continues to fall in overall health care for its citizens in comparison with the remainder of the industrialized world (Blumenthal, 2006: 85). We own 25 percent of the wealth of the world, while constituting only 5 percent of the people of the world and still do not offer health care to all Americans. In its 2000 world health report, the World Health Organization (WHO) carried out the first-ever analysis of the world's health systems. Using five performance indicators—overall level of population health or disability-adjusted life expectancy (DALE), health disparities within a population, a health system's responsiveness to the needs of the population, the distribution of responsiveness (rich vs. poor; goodness vs. fairness, and distribution of financial burden (who pays?)—it was found that the United States stood:

- first in spending 14 percent of its gross domestic product on health care;
- thirty-seventh out of 151 countries according to its health care performance

▸ seventy-second in its performance on health level (DALE);

▸ fifty-fourth in its fairness ("Health Systems," 2000).

If the rest of the industrialized world can manage to serve all its citizens on less, why can we not?

Where is the money going? Earlier, Congress agreed that through legislation, managed health care was the answer to fix the broken health care system. However, it has not managed to provide health care for everyone, nor has it reduced the rapid increase in health care expenditure. Americans often think that government is wasteful and makes a poor provider for health care dollars. However, the opposite is true. Government health care programs often use fewer dollars to administer health programs than health insurance corporations do.

Increasing numbers of Americans have difficulty receiving adequate health care (Citizens' Health Care Working Group, n.d.). Insurance premiums have increased 73 percent since 2000 (15 percent in 2004 alone) while wages have increased only 4 percent. Seventy-four percent of those without insurance come from working families. Almost 1 million of those who lost their health insurance in 2004 had a full-time job. Health care costs were $6,300 per person in 2004 and are projected to increase to $12,300 per person in 2015 (Americans for Health Care, n.d.). It is no wonder that people lament the cost of health care, and that doctors and hospitals grieve over litigation costs.

Those individuals earning more than $75,000 who lost their insurance increased 28 percent in 2004. A college education is no guarantee of insurance, since the percentage of those without in that group increased by 29 percent in 2004. This creates a slippery slope for increasing numbers of working Americans. People are making life decisions based on access to health care.

Access to affordable health care is diminishing in the United States. Many people benefit from advances in medical science. However, the delivery of medical care is not only not coherent, comprehensive, cost effective, equitable, universal; it also does not provide choice. On average, adults receive only 55 percent of the recommended care for many common conditions (McGlynn et al., 2003). Moreover, "a person's race, ethnicity, and socioeconomic status continue to be associated with differences in the quality of care provided, the person's access to care, and the person's overall health" (Defend Science! 2006).

Our health care system is at a crossroads: it is the biggest item in the budget, outpacing expenditures for housing. Of the 300 million people in America, 18 percent do not have health insurance. We have 739,000 doctors, with 16,813 new students entering medical school each year. Prescription drug costs increased from $3 billion in 1960 to $12 billion in the year 2000 and they are projected to be $243 billion in 2008. We have fewer solo practitioners, more managed care HMOs, PPOs, and IPAs. We have more lawsuits and threats of suits and inadequate preventive health care. We have wide disparities in health care (race, language, gender, socioeconomic). We have the world's best doctors, nurses, hospitals and academic health centers, along with cutting-edge research. Our population is growing older, more diverse. And the burden of disease is shifting from acute illnesses to chronic diseases, mental illnesses and lifestyle behavior problems. We have healthier children than ever before but many are at risk.

Yet, in light of this, a seeming unending lack of decision on health care is maintained by the uncompromising positioning of groups favoring their own self-interest.

Politicians ask, "What would be the political fallout?" Politicians want to please their constituents enough to have them support their campaigns financially and to gain votes in political contests.

Religious leaders ask, "Does this reflect what I believe?" Religious leaders want to promote their own ideologies or their specific beliefs and organization. The line between government and religion is blurring, possibly because some religious groups can deliver large voting blocs to politicians.

Scientists ask, "Is it scientifically accurate or correct? Science seems increasingly less respected except as a moneymaker in today's political climate. The scientific community wants to understand all the facts and to develop and improve drugs for healing of disease. Scientists have:

▸ decoded the human genome system,

- developed better anesthesia,
- developed better microtechnology,
- developed better nanotechnology,
- improved communication, and
- helped women better control their reproduction.

Through its interest in discovery, science develops new ideas. While science makes astonishing new discoveries, its role does not include a delivery system. Therefore, scientific inroads in practical application depend upon other disciplines for practical application. Basic research in discovery is invaluable; likewise, practical application that includes a delivery system to people is invaluable. Not all of our citizens are recipients of our progress.

Corporations ask, "How does it affect our bottom line?" Corporations have gained strength with the government through sheer control of wealth. In some ways they have become more like supercitizens, with rights that are greater than that of individuals. Most corporations want to spend as little as possible to offer the health care required by the government or demanded by workers. The vested interest of corporations is in building the corporation itself to provide investors with financial returns rather than spending dollars on health care. All this notwithstanding, "sixty-two percent of the non-elderly population had health care coverage through employer-sponsored insurance in 2004" (Fronstin, 2005). It is clear that the US practice of substantial reliance on employer-sponsored health insurance is unique among countries. It was an unplanned concept that evolved without the benefit of intentional design.

Medical doctors and other health care professionals ask, "Will it create more healthy people in a healthy community?" They know that health is about more than the absence of disease. Health is about the flourishing of persons rather than a bare subsistence survival. Therefore, health is about nutrition, education, safe drinking water, safe affordable housing, equitable lifestyle, safety, security, secure employment, and adequate income.

Health is present when children are nurtured, loved and care for by the society in which they develop. Health is productive, creative, constructive, and practical; the absence of health is decay of not only the individual but of society.

Philosophers, ethicists and bioethicists ask, "Is it ethical?" The insufficiency of our health care system affects every American, because our society as a whole is adversely affected. Author Kurt Vonnegut writes, "We are healthy only to the extent that our ideas are humane." Can we say individually or collectively that we are humane when health care is a major concern for so many? We have tinkered with health care so much but yielding so little that it is time to keep our eye on the goal and work as long and as hard as it takes to accomplish the humane task of meeting the health needs of Americans in the twenty-first century.

Educators ask, "Why should it be our job and not the job of health care professionals to train the population about health care?" People cannot be educated if they are not healthy and they cannot maintain health without the benefit of education. Education must do more than teach the 3 R's of reading, 'riting, and 'rithmetic; it must teach our young people to be physically, mentally, and emotionally fit. Young people can be taught to: eat a healthy diet, exercise, keep clean, maintain sexual health, avoid engaging in high-risk behaviors, and be responsible for their own health. Public policy that denies young people important information about their health or provides misinformation on how to protect themselves is irresponsible and negligent. Age-appropriate, medically accurate and science-based sexuality education delays the onset of sexual intercourse, decreases the frequency of intercourse, decreases the number of sexual partners, and increases condom and contraceptive use, thus decreasing pregnancy, abortion, and disease.

We cannot let what we cannot do stand in the way of what we can do. We can improve education by making certain that every child enters school ready to learn. Early childhood education is an investment not an expense. We can teach children to be healthy by having comprehensive health education in schools from kindergarten through the twelfth grade. We should teach our children not to smoke, drink, and take drugs. We should teach them about sexuality, including sexually transmitted infections (STIs), AIDS, and teenage pregnancies. We should also teach them about conflict resolution and to exercise, along with good nutrition and eating appropriately.

We can provide primary preventable health care for all children in inner cities, *colonias*, and rural area schools where there is a high percentage of underserved children. We can make a difference by providing primary preventive health care to communities in need and clinicians who care.

If we are able to combine the forces of scientists, politicians, philosophers, religious leaders, and corporations to search for common goals, we may have a beginning to improve the health care of our people. Representation at the table necessarily would include all age groups, working groups, and ethnic groups.

None of these forces is likely to come to any table without the loud authoritative voice of the people demanding that universal health care be delivered to Americans. Even if polls find that Americans do want universal health care, they might not actually vote to change health care, education, or for other social improvements. Therefore, if we actually expect to change, people must make it clear that they support change.

Americans might appreciate remembering that the 1948 Universal Declaration of Human Rights states in Article 25 that "Everyone has the right to a standard of living adequate for the health and well-being of himself and of his family, including food, clothing, housing and medical care and necessary social services, and the right to security in the event of unemployment, sickness, disability, widowhood, old age or other lack of livelihood in circumstances beyond his control."

Individuals, government, and businesses are experiencing difficulty meeting the medical needs of Americans. Since 56 other industrialized nations provide better health care to their citizens than the United States, we could begin by studying their health care systems.

There are barriers that many patients face when attempting to access health care. Barriers include financial access, provider access, cultural access, and transportation access. We have increased our physician pool from 339,000 in 1960 to 739,000 in 1996. However, we have not had an impact on access to health care in rural and inner city urban areas. We have too many specialists and not enough generalists, and too few minority health professionals. Minorities constitute 27 percent of the population with only 12 percent minority health professionals. Many people have financial barriers to health care, lacking either money or insurance.

Transportation access is a major barrier, especially for many of our elderly and rural populations. It is cheaper to train bus drivers than it is to train doctors.

In addition to the professional, financial, and transportation barriers, people often face cultural access barriers once they finally arrive at the health center a great distance from their homes. Cultural barriers include language barriers, cultural differences, and lack of respect. For instance, appearing undressed even for health care professionals is difficult in some cultures.

The relationship between poor health and economic status is well documented. People with less education live in least desirable neighborhoods, work at the least prestigious jobs, and are more likely to die earlier than people at the other end of the economic scale. Therefore, we cannot just blame the individual. We must create a health care system that meets the needs of the poorly served, the underserved, and the never served members of our society. Minorities are over-represented in inner city urban populations and under-represented in health care and decision-making positions. We have powerless people in need of powerful friends.

The disparity in health for the underserved begins at conception. A disproportionate number of black infants is born to children before they become adults, 92 percent of whom are unplanned. A disproportionate number of these babies have low birth weights, and the infant mortality for black infants is more than twice as high as that for white infants (14.6 vs. 6.9). Many are born into poverty to mothers who are too young, use illicit drugs, drink alcohol excessively, and do not receive prenatal care. Then they grow up to be members of the "Five-H Club": hungry, healthless, homeless, hugless, and hopeless.

Epidemiological data painstakingly gathered over a number of years clearly show a wide disparity between the health of minority Americans and the nation's population as a whole. Despite the availability of data, which is collected so that it can be analyzed, evaluated, and used to improve the status, the gap between minority Americans and the nation as a whole has widened, suggesting we did not use the data collected, did not interpret it properly; that the strategies used were not tailored to the population to be served or our investment was insufficient to get he job done.

The prevalence for risk factors for certain diseases—teenage pregnancy, HIV/AIDS, diabetes, obesity, poverty, increased exposure to a noxious environment, accidents on the job, severe stress, underutilization and lack of accessibility of quality health care, lack of minority providers—all contribute to the disparity (Institute of Medicine, 2002).

An adequate health care system that would guarantee affordable health care for every American includes:

1. Financial access
‣ supporting academic health centers and biomedical research
‣ guaranteeing health insurance coverage to all Americans (medical, including health maintenance, dental, mental and long-term)
‣ eliminating unfair insurance practices
‣ providing subsidies for the unemployed and impoverished, and
‣ preserving and strengthening Medicare.

2. Provider access
‣ providing services where people live, work, and go to school
‣ training more primary care doctors and doctors who are culturally sensitive
‣ increasing incentives for doctors to practice in underserved areas, and

3. Cultural access
‣ training more minority doctors and nurses
‣ providing culturally sensitive health care information and services—"informed access"
‣ providing outreach (translation and transportation services)

4. Transportation access

How can health care professionals better use the enormous and accumulating volume of new scientific discoveries to improve public policy, address the needs of the 300 million people in the US, 46 million of whom have no health insurance and many more who have limited benefits? We must become leaders and advocates for our patients. It is a part of our mission as physicians. It is not enough just to provide good clinical services—we must support high-quality research and become leaders and advocate for our patients in clinics and in the media as well as the halls of Congress. Health care professionals often say they do not want to be politically involved but we cannot continually sit on the sidelines and let non-health care professionals decide all health policy. As leaders we must listen to our patients, learn what needs to be done and provide the leadership to get it done. We must educate ourselves about health policy; educate our patients on how to take care of themselves, nutritionally, physically, emotionally, sexually, and mentally. They must be empowered with the knowledge to make appropriate choices for their own health so that they understand political decisions. Health care providers must not only be aware of the problems, but they must become advocates for health care and develop an action plan for accomplishing the implementation of a new health care system. We must realize with determination that it is our responsibility to develop a health care system that is coherent, comprehensive, offers choice, and is cost effective, equitable, and universal.

What are some of the strategies we must take if we are to be as proud of our health care system as we are of our Department of Defense? What is our vision for health in America? In its overview of the American health care system, the Institute for the Future in its report, *Health and Health Care 2010*, provided guidelines for the future. Can we accomplish the goal? Can we make our health status among nations fit our health care expenditure?

1. We must aim for a society of healthy individuals and healthy communities.
2. We need to design and develop a health care system that is consumer responsive, prevention focused, and affordable for all of our citizens.
3. We need a health care system that empowers individuals, fosters

individual responsibility, human dignity, improved health status, and enhanced quality of life.
4. We must care. Care enough to share and have the courage to do what needs to be done. We must be aware of the problems, become advocates for the problem, and develop an action plan to get it done. We must reach out and be responsible, use all of our resources and yes, take some risks.
5. Finally, we must educate and empower our people to be healthy (Institute for the Future, 2000).

Health care costs have increased from $27 billion annually in 1960 to $1.9 trillion in 2004, or from 5 cents of every dollar to 15 cents of every dollar (Blumenthal, 2006: 85). Costs are projected to increase even more in the years ahead.

Despite spending the most money, we do not necessarily spend wisely. For instance, we provide 25 percent of our health care costs in the last year of our patients' lives. Most patients want to die at home and only 15 percent do that. Ninety-three percent would like to die pain free; only 30 to 50 percent achieve this goal. We have limited coverage for prescriptions drugs, mental health, and long-term care. We are well aware that our health care is not equitable, that race, ethnicity, and socioeconomic status are associated with differences in quality of care provided, access to services, and a person's overall health.

Health care professionals cannot reasonably abdicate their responsibility to politicians and seriously expect medical justice to be done. Congressional seats are overwhelmingly filled with attorneys who understand law and law making rather than health care and public health policy. A real substantive change in our health care system will remain an elusive goal until health professionals demand specific changes that only they fully recognize on behalf of our patients.

REFERENCES

Americans for Health Care. "Health Care in America: The Crisis at a Glance" <www.americansforhealthcare.org/facts/groups/glance.cfm>.

Americans for Health Care and Center for American Progress National Survey. Frequency Questionnaire. Questionnaire conducted November 15-22, 2005 <http://americansforhealthcare.org/docUploads/HEALTHCARE%5FTOPLINES%2Epdf>.

Blumenthal, D. "Employer-Sponsored Health Insurance in the United State: Origins and Implications." *The New England Journal of Medicine* 355:1 (2006:):82-88.

Citizens' Health Care Working Group. *The Health Report to the American People* <http://www.citizenshealthcare.gov/healthreport/healthreport.php>.

"Defend Science!: An Urgent Call by Scientists" <http://www.defend-science.org>.

Fronstin P. "Sources of Health Insurance and Characteristics of the Uninsured: Analysis of the March 2005 Current Population Survey." Issue brief no. 287. Washington, D.C.: Employee Benefits Research Institute, 2005 <http:www.ebri.org/pdf/briefspdf/EBRI_IB_11-20051.pdf>.

Gee, R.E. "Plan B, Reproductive Rights, and Physician Activism." *New England Journal of Medicine* 355:1 (2006): 4-5.

"Health Systems: Improving Performance." *Health Report 2000*. Geneva: World Health Organization, 2000.

Institute for the Future. *Health and Health Care 2010: The Forecast, the Challenge*. Princeton: Jossey-Bass Publishers, January 2000.

Institute of Medicine. *Unequal Treatment: Confronting Racial and Ethnic Disparities in Health Care*. Washington, D.C.: National Academies Press, 2002.

McGlynn, E. A., et al. "The Quality of Health Care Delivered to Adults in the United States." *New England Journal of Medicine* 348:26 (2003): 2635-2645.

William B. Hurlbut
Science, Religion, and the Politics of Stem Cells

IN JULY 2005, AMERICA'S ONGOING DEBATE OVER EMBRYONIC STEM cell research reached a dramatic moment during a Senate subcommittee hearing.* In a conference room crowded with television camera crews, newspaper journalists, fellow legislators, and a panel of expert witnesses ranging from scientists to bioethicists, Senator Tom Harkin (D., Iowa), in a long and impassioned statement, asserted there are no moral issues here, just personal religious views parading as political principle ("Transcript Hearing," 2005).

In making this comment, Senator Harkin was joining a wider chorus of critics labeling President George W. Bush's policy on stem cells a conflict between the objectivity of secular science and the cultural variability of traditional religion—with religion here relegated to the category of partisan ideology.

The policy under attack is the president's August 9, 2001, executive order limiting federal funding to already existing stem cell lines. At that time President Bush declared that during his administration, no further embryo-destructive research would be supported by the American taxpayers. Now, however, as Congress threatens a legislative override of this policy—which the president, in turn, promises to veto—there is an ever more vocal outcry that this is not mere politics, but the imposition of religious beliefs, a deeper matter violating the established order of separation of church and state.

A May 26, 2005, editorial in the *New York Times* declared: "His actions are based on strong religious beliefs on the part of some conservative Christians, and presumably the president himself. Such convictions deserve respect, but it is wrong to impose them on this pluralistic nation" ("Stem Cell Theology," 2005).

From a broad social perspective, this difficult dispute over federal funding of embryonic stem cell research (ESCR) might be seen simply as democracy in action, the social process essential for progress into any new and unfamiliar technological terrain. Yet when one pauses to ponder exactly what is at issue and the nature of the controversy, it is clear that this conflict is driven by more fundamental forces—forces that challenge us at the most basic level as a cooperative society.

At the immediate political level, the issue is the federal funding of research that involves the destruction of early but incipient human life. That alone qualifies as a matter of profound social and ethical significance. But beneath this issue, the dispute involves the most basic assumptions concerning the foundation of the moral principles on which our civilization is built: What is the source of our moral principles and how do we govern amid a plurality of perspectives? Indeed, recognizing the immensity of the issues and the depth of the division, we must acknowledge we are at a crisis of science, religion, and politics.

The recognition of this foundational conflict has become increasingly clear in American culture. Most analysts agree that the results of the last presidential election reflect a widening divide within American society over matters of faith. It is also clear that with advances in our understanding and control of biology, our social division increasingly involves different basic assumptions concerning the source and significance of the natural world—most specifically, the meaning of human nature as grounded in natural human embodiment, and the possibility of its degradation or destruction through technological manipulation. This conflict over the use of biotechnology to intervene in human life has reached its deepest point of disagreement over the issue of cloning to create human embryos for scientific experimentation.

The historical background of this conflict reflects changes in both our basic religious values and scientific knowledge, and, most important, the way these relate to each other. The situation in the

United States is, in turn, just a subset of a growing global dispute based on differing worldviews, as is evident in the recent UN declaration on human cloning. Nearly three-fourths of national delegations (including some of the most technologically advanced nations of the world) voted for a nonbinding mandate condemning human cloning for any purpose—reproduction or research.

Most commentators from the scientific community interpreted this UN mandate as a sign of the over-extension of religious values, an inappropriate interference in the realm of science. And, indeed, authorities from the major religious traditions have weighed in on these important issues. Christian, Confucian, Buddhist, and some Hindu and Jewish scholars have spoken up strongly against any destruction of human embryos for research.

But even here, the situation is not simple; there are differences in understanding of human life between religious traditions and this points to the complex relationship between religion and the ongoing advance in scientific knowledge. Clearly, the religious traditions of the world are seeking to uphold a comprehensive moral frame for understanding and respecting human life. But each is based on some evidence and interpretation that might be rightfully labeled "scientific knowledge," albeit scientific knowledge from a particular social and historical perspective now culturally encoded within a tradition of transcendent authority.

However, if we return to the criticisms of President Bush's policy, largely from those sympathetic to the scientific goals of embryonic stem cell research, the situation is even more disturbing. Claiming to rise above all religious ethnocentricities, those who advocate a purely objective scientific approach merely smuggle in their own arbitrary markers of moral meaning—and, in some cases, manage to override or obscure honest science in the process.

Consider the confident assertions of the now discredited South Korean scientist Woo Suk Hwang: "'What we are doing is not creating embryos. An embryo basically presupposes a birth of a life. But we have no intentions or goals whatsoever to create life.' So, it's not an embryo if you don't intend to make a baby out of it" (Kim, 2005).

The *New York Times* seems to agree: "The president's policy is based on the belief that all embryos, even the days-old microscopic form used to derive stem cells in a laboratory dish should be treated as emerging human life and protected from harm" ("Stem Cell Theology," 2005). But here the president is scientifically correct: human embryos are a form of emerging human life. My medical dictionary, written before the need for more politically convenient definitions, defines embryo as "the human organism from fertilization to the end of the eighth week" (Stedman's, 1966).

Likewise, former New York Governor Mario Cuomo, speaking of the "religious morass created by President Bush's position on embryonic stem cells,' states: "No doubt the president's view that human life begins with fertilization is shared by millions of Americans, including many Christians and evangelicals. But it remains a minority view" (Cuomo, 2005). As a remedy to the president's "sincere religiosity," he prescribes an objective panel to consider testimony from bioscience experts describing when consciousness and viability outside the womb occur.

Current proposals for federal support of embryonic stem cell research draw a sharp limit declaring no research on human embryos beyond 14 days. But by Governor Cuomo's criteria, this could morally be extended to the onset of consciousness or viability, both currently considered to be at about six months of gestational age.

Fourteen days, forty days, consciousness, viability at six months—where is the moral boundary? All of this adds up to a troubling prospect. There are no clear global standards among the religious traditions in defense of human life—at least until well into development. And, likewise, science by the very limitations of its methodology and domain of knowledge is unable to draw its own moral boundaries. Neither religion nor science seems independently adequate to answer these new and unfamiliar challenges.

RESPECTFUL DIALOGUE

There are compelling social, scientific, and medical arguments for the importance of a respectful and constructive dialogue between science and religion in an effort to open the positive prospects of stem cell biology.

We are at a crucial moment in the process of scientific discovery. The dramatic advances in molecular biology throughout the twentieth century have culminated in the sequencing of the human genome and increasing knowledge of cell physiology and cytology. These studies were accomplished by breaking down organic systems into their component parts. Now, however, as we move on from genomics and proteomics to discoveries in developmental biology, we have returned to the study of living beings. When applied to human biology, this inquiry reopens the most fundamental questions concerning the relationship between the material form and the moral meaning of developing life. The current conflict over embryonic stem cell research is just the first in a series of difficult controversies that will require us to define with clarity and precision the moral boundaries we seek to defend. Chimeras, parthenotes, projects involving the reaggregation of embryonic-stem-cell-derived products into functional human parts (organs and organ systems), and a wide range of other emerging technologies will continue to challenge our definitions of human life. These are not questions for science alone, but for the full breadth of human wisdom and experience.

The scientific arguments for going forward with this research are compelling; and the best way to do this would be with federal funding through the National Institutes of Health (NIH). The convergence of these advancing technologies is delivering unprecedented powers for research into the most basic questions in early human development. Beyond the obvious benefit of understanding the biological factors behind the estimated 150,000 births with serious congenital defects per year, it is becoming increasingly evident that certain pathologies that are only manifest later in life are influenced or have their origins in early development. Furthermore, fundamental developmental processes (including the formation and functioning of stem cells), and their disordered dynamics, seem to be at work in a range of adult pathologies including some forms of cancer. Research in these realms is so broadly foundational to the whole of biomedical science that only the NIH can provide the wise governance, ethical oversight, and measure of funding essential for cooperative collaboration on a national level.

Yet from the moral and social perspective there are serious concerns. It is important to acknowledge the many scientific projects for which human embryos could be used. Beyond their destruction for the procurement of embryonic stem cells, some fear the industrial scale production of living human embryos for a wide range of research in natural development (cell differentiation, imprinting, and morphogenesis), toxicology, and drug testing. Beyond that, there is concern about the commodification and commercialization of eggs and embryos and worry about the implications of ongoing research to create an artificial endometrium that would allow the extracorporeal gestation of cloned embryos to later stages for the production of more advanced cells, tissues, and organs.

Furthermore, from a social perspective, do we really want to have "red state medicine/blue state medicine"? The emerging patchwork of policies on the state level threatens to create a situation in which a large percentage of patients will enter the hospital with moral qualms about the research practices on which their treatments have been developed. What was traditionally the sanctuary of compassionate care at the most vulnerable and sensitive moments of human life is becoming an arena of controversy and conflict.

Clearly, both sides of this difficult debate are defending important human goods—and both of these goods are important for all of us. The issues under discussion are not simply matters of empirical evidence. Whatever objectivity there may be on the level of the physical sciences, this mode of knowledge does not extend to the depths of the moral. Concepts such as dignity and decency are grounded in values and an understanding of the world that is beyond the reach of the empirical process of science.

But, more fundamentally, science itself rests upon an interpretive frame—unproven *a priories*—an account of the world not so different in character than the foundations of religious understandings.

Science, too, is its own form of grand narrative—one that developed out of and expresses a distinct moral order comprising particular, historical perspectives, traditions, and worldviews. As the sociologist Christian Smith has pointed out, human beings are intrinsically and irreducibly moral believing animals: "Science as we know it can only ever proceed by first placing faith in a set of unprovable cosmological, metaphysical, and epistemological assumptions and commitments " (Smith, 2003: 25.)

Furthermore, religions, far from being simply calcified traditions, are the distillations of accumulated human experience, an integration of observation and comprehensive understanding. They give stability to the central core of human values while sustaining personal identity and social cohesion through periods of transition, cultural innovation, and periods of renewal such as our own.

The current conflict in the political arena is damaging to both science and religion and is, I believe, completely contrary to the positive pluralism that is the strength of our democracy. What is needed is to draw back from the polarized positions of political rhetoric and to respectfully reflect on the meaning of the moment we are in. Advances in biomedical technology pose a profound challenge to our civilization, and, indeed, to our species. As we enter the coming era of advance in developmental biology, we must pause to ponder deeply the significance of our emerging powers and their practical implications—our very humanity may depend on it.

In the spirit of such a dialogue I offer the perspective that follows.

THE MORAL MEANING OF EMERGING LIFE

Assessing the moral status of the embryo begins with affirming the moral status of human life in general. The principle that human life constitutes the fundamental good serves as the cornerstone of law for our civilization. In no circumstance is the intentional destruction of the life of an innocent individual deemed morally acceptable. This valuing of human life is indeed the moral starting point for both advocates and opponents of cloning for biological research, and it flows from the reciprocal respect that we naturally grant as we recognize in the other a being of moral equivalence to ourselves. It leads to the principle of inviolability of human life and the prohibition against using human life instrumentally.

From the perspective of those who object to research involving the destruction of embryos, any evaluation of the moral significance of human life must take into account the full procession of continuity and change that is essential for its development. With the act of conception, the life of a new human being is initiated with a distinct genetic endowment that organizes and guides the growth of a unique and unrepeatable individual person. The gametes (the sperm and egg), although alive as cells, are not living beings: they are instrumental organic agents of the parents. The joining of the gametes brings into existence an entirely different kind of entity: a living human organism. With regard to fundamental biological meaning (and, by this perspective, moral significance), the act of fertilization is a leap from zero to everything.

In both structure and function, the zygote and subsequent embryonic stages differ from all other cells or tissues of the body; they contain within themselves the organizing principle for the full development of a human being. This is not an abstract or hypothetical potential in the sense of mere possibility, but rather a potency, an engaged and effective potential-in-process, an activated dynamic of development in the direction of human fullness of being.

Unlike an assembly of parts in which a manufactured product is in no sense "present" until there is a completed construction, a living being has a continuous unfolding existence that is inseparable from its emerging form. The form is itself a dynamic process rather than a static structure. In biology, the whole (as the unified organismal principle of growth) precedes and produces the parts.

It is this implicit whole, with its inherent potency, that endows the embryo with its human character and continuity of identity from the moment of conception and therefore, from this perspective, inviolable moral status. To interfere in its development is to transgress upon a life in process. The principle of this analysis applies to any entity that has the same potency as a human embryo produced by natural fertilization, regardless of whether it is the product of in vitro fertilization (IVF), cloning, or other processes.

ACCRUED MORAL STATUS

The major alternative to the view that an embryo has an inherent moral status is the assertion that moral status is an accrued or accumulated quality related to some physical dimension of form or function.

The three arguments currently given in support of a 14-day limit on embryo research—lack of differentiation, lack of individuation, and pre-implantation status—are based on a kind of "received tradition" that dates back to the 1996 Warnock Commission in the United Kingdom (United Kingdom Report, 1984). But this commission explicitly acknowledged the continuous nature of embryonic development, stating: "There is no particular part of the developmental process that is more important than any other" (Saletan, 2005). In a recent memoir, Mary Warnock discussed the utilitarian grounding of her commission's analysis, acknowledging that her committee's task was "to recommend a policy which might allow the sort of medical and scientific progress which was in the public interest" (Saletan, 2005). Indeed, recent advances in embryology do not support this commission's conclusions, and any designation of 14 days (being ungrounded in either scientific evidence or sound moral reasoning) will be vulnerable to extension based on projections of further medical promise.

However much one may or may not agree with the moral analysis given above, it is important to acknowledge it is grounded in a reasoned interpretation of the scientific evidence, not in purely mystical assumptions drawn from abstract religious beliefs. It is not religious, any more than any other interpretation of these biological realities; empirical science is simply unable to extend its realm to confident statements concerning matters of value within the moral sphere.

Moreover, this view is consistent with 2,500 years of medical science—as recently as 1948, the Physicians Oath in the Declaration of Geneva, echoing the enduring traditions of Hippocratic medicine, proclaimed: "I will maintain the utmost respect for human life from the time of conception."

ALTERED NUCLEAR TRANSFER

In light of the arguments that human moral worth is based on a continuity of embodied form from fertilization to natural death, it would seem that we are at an irresolvable impasse. If embryonic stem cells can be obtained only by the destruction of human embryos this may, in fact, be the case. But a white paper released in May 2005 by the President's Council on Bioethics suggests otherwise ("Alternative Sources," 2005). This report describes four proposals put forward as possible means of obtaining embryonic stem cells without the creation and destruction of human embryos. As the author of one of these proposals, Altered Nuclear Transfer, I will discuss this approach as an example of the scientific advances and moral reasoning that may lead us to a technological solution to our conflict over embryonic stem cell research ("Alternative Sources," 2005b).

As described earlier, natural conception signals the activation of the organizing principle for the self-development and self-maintenance of the full human organism. In the language of stem cell biology, this capability is termed "totipotency": the capacity to form the complete organism. In contrast, the term "pluripotency" designates the capacity to produce all the cell types of the human body but not the coherent and integrated unity of a living being. This is a difference between the material parts and the living whole.

Altered Nuclear Transfer (ANT) would draw on the basic technique of SCNT (popularly known as "therapeutic cloning") but with an alteration such that pluripotent stem cells are produced without the creation and destruction of totipotent human embryos.

In standard nuclear transfer the cell nucleus is removed from an adult body cell and transferred into an egg cell that first has its own nucleus removed. The egg then has a full set of DNA and, after it is electrically stimulated, starts to divide like a naturally fertilized egg. This is how Dolly the sheep was produced.

Altered Nuclear Transfer uses the technology of nuclear transfer but with a preemptive alteration that assures that no embryo is created. The adult body cell nucleus or the enucleated egg's contents (or both) are first altered before the adult body cell nucleus is transferred into the egg. The laboratory construct that is produced by ANT has only partial developmental potential. It lacks the integrated unity that characterizes a human embryo so the above ethical analysis would permit harvesting its embryonic stem cells.

Altered Nuclear Transfer is a broad concept with a range of possible approaches; there may be many ways this technique can be used to accomplish the same end.

One variation involves the preemptive silencing of a gene necessary for the integrated development that characterizes an embryonic organism. As described in an January 2006 paper in *Nature* magazine, stem cell biologist Rudolf Jaenisch has established the scientific feasibility of this approach in a series of dramatic mouse model experiments in which he procured fully functional embryonic stem cells from a construct that is radically different in developmental potential than a human embryo (Meissner and Jaenisch, 2006?).

Unfortunately, the news reports have emphasized the inability of the ANT entity Jaenish produced to form the placenta. The alteration he employed, however, results in a failure of formation that is earlier and far more fundamental than simply an inability to implant in the womb. Due to the alteration, the first division into different cell lineages does not occur, the body axes (top/bottom, front/back) cannot form, and the basic human body plan is never established.

At this stage a critical "deficiency" is more rightly considered an "insufficiency,' not a defect *in* a being, but an inadequacy at such a fundamental level that it precludes the coordinated coherence and developmental potential that are the defining characteristics of an embryonic organism. Jaenisch concurs with this conclusion. In testimony to a Senate subcommittee, he stated: "Because the ANT product lacks essential properties of the fertilized embryo, it is not justified to call it an 'embryo'" (Jaenisch, 2005).

Another variation of ANT called Oocyte Assisted Reprogramming (ANT-OAR) has been put forward by Markus Grompe, director of the Stem Cell Center at the Oregon Health Sciences University. This approach involves a kind of "jump-starting" of cell differentiation to bypass entirely the totipotent cells of the cleavage stages of natural embryogenesis. In this variation of ANT, alterations of the nucleus of the adult body cell and the enucleated egg's contents before nuclear transfer would force early expression of genes characteristic of a later and more specialized cell type that is capable of producing pluripotent stem cells. Such a creation, from its very beginning, would never have the actual configuration or potential for development that character-izes a human embryo and would therefore not have the moral standing of a human being. As documented in a joint statement posted at the Ethics and Public Policy Center website, this proposal has drawn wide endorsement from leading scientists, moral philosophers and religious authorities. (Joint Statement, 2005).

Each of these variations on ANT draws on our increasing scien-tific knowledge and deepening moral reflection on the meaning of developing life. We are beginning to recognize the complexity of inter-related parts that are essential for generating the coordinated coher-ence of growth that characterizes the living being to which we rightly assign moral worth.

The very word *organism* implies organization, an overarching principle of unity, a cooperative interaction of interdependent parts subordinated to the good of the whole. As a living being, an organ-ism is an integrated, self-developing and self-maintaining unity under the governance of an immanent plan. The philosopher Robert Joyce (1978) explains: "Living beings come into existence all at once and then gradually unfold to themselves and to the world what they already but only incipiently are" (Joyce, 1978). To be a human organism is to be a whole living member of the species *Homo sapiens,* to have a human present and a human future evident in the intrinsic potential for the manifestation of the species typical form. Joyce continues: "No living being can become anything other than what it already essentially is."

For an embryonic organism, this implies an inherent potency, a drive in the direction of the mature form. By its very nature, an embryo is a developing being, its wholeness is defined by both its manifest expression and its latent potential; it is the phase of human life in which the organismal whole produces its organic parts.

It is this living whole that is the object of our moral concern and the foundation for expression of the psycho-physical unity of spirit and matter that we designate with the concept of the human person.

THE ADVANTAGES OF ALTERED NUCLEAR TRANSFER

ANT, in its many variations, could provide a uniquely flexible investigative tool and has many positive advantages that would help advance embryonic stem cell research. Unlike the use of embryos from IVF clinics, ANT would produce an unlimited range of genetic types for the study of disease, drug testing, and possibly generation of therapeutically useful cells. By allowing controlled and reproducible experiments, ANT would provide a uniquely flexible research tool for a wide range of useful studies of gene expression, imprinting, and intercellular communication. Furthermore, the basic research essential to establishing the technique would advance our understanding of developmental biology and might serve as a bridge to other technologies, such as direct reprogramming of adult cells. Moreover, as a laboratory technique, ANT would unburden embryonic stem cell research from the additional ethical concerns of the "leftover" IVF embryos, including the attendant clinical and legal complexities in this realm of great personal and social sensitivity.

CONCLUSION

The present conflict over the moral status of the human embryo reflects deep differences in our basic convictions and is unlikely to be resolved through deliberation or debate. Yet a purely political solution will leave our country bitterly divided, eroding the social support and sense of noble purpose that is essential for the public funding of biomedical science.[1] In offering a "third option," Altered Nuclear Transfer defines with clarity and precision the boundaries that our moral principles are seeking to preserve while opening fully the promising possibilities of embryonic stem cell research.

As described in the president's council white paper, Altered Nuclear Transfer is just one of several hopeful proposals. Since publication of the council report, major scientific advances in several of these proposals have been reported in leading peer-reviewed publications. The momentum of scientific discovery that has delivered our current ethical impasse, may now provide a solution to our conflict over embryonic stem cell research.

As we enter the coming era of rapid advance in biotechnology, we will confront a range of moral dilemmas that challenge our most basic assumptions concerning the source and significance of the natural world. The approach set out in the council report would set a positive precedent for maintaining constructive ethical dialogue and encouraging creative use of our scientific knowledge. In recognizing the important values being defended by both sides of our difficult national debate over embryonic stem cell research, this approach could open positive prospects for scientific advance while honoring the diversity of opinion concerning our most fundamental moral principles. Such a solution is in keeping with the American spirit and would be a triumph for our nation as a whole.

NOTES

* Portions of this article were originally presented at the fourth Yoko Civilization International Conference, Awaji, Japan, September 2005. Proceedings in press. Portions of this essay were also drawn from Hurlbut (2006) and are used with permission.

1. The depth of this division was evident in the July 2006 congressional debates and subsequent legislative actions. By a vote of 63 to 37, the Senate approved a bill to allow federal funding of research on embryonic stem cell lines obtained from embryos to be discarded by *in vitro* fertilization clinics. This bill, which was passed by the House more

than a year before, was then vetoed by President George W. Bush. On the same day, the Senate also approved, by a vote of 100 to 0, a bill to encourage federal support for projects such as Altered Nuclear Transfer and the other proposals set out in the council's white paper. report. A few hours later, however, this "alternative sources" bill was rejected in the House, apparently with the motive of depriving the president of a positive counterbalance to the bill he would veto. The president reproached the members of the House for failing to open an avenue of hopeful scientific inquiry, and announced his intention to issue a directive to the NIH to fund these projects.

REFERENCES

Cuomo, Mario. "Not On Faith Alone." *The New York Times*, June 20, 2005.

Ethics and Public Policy Center. *Production of Pluripotent Stem Cells by Oocyte Assisted Reprogramming*. June 20, 2005 <http://www.eppc.org/publications/pubID.2374/pub_detail.asp>.

Hurlbut, William B. "Framing the Future: Embryonic Stem Cells, Ethics, and the Emerging Era of Developmental Biology." *Pediatrics Research* 59:4, pt. 2 (2006).

Jaenisch, Rudolf. Testimony of Rudolf Jaenisch, M.D., Hearing on "An Alternative Method for Obtaining Embryonic Stem Cells." Committee on Appropriations, Subcommittee of Labor, Health and Human Services, Education." United States Senate. Oct. 19, 2005.

Joyce, Robert E. "Personhood and the Conception Event." *New Scholasticism* 52 (1978): 97-109.

Kim, Ji-Soo. "Cloning Pioneer Envisions Stem Cell Bank." AP Online. June 1, 2005.

Meissner, A., and R. Jaenisch. "Generation of Nuclear-Transfer Derived Pluripotent ES Cells From Cloned *Cdx2*-Deficient Blastomeres." *Nature* 439 (2006): 212-221.

President's Council on Bioethics. *White Paper: Alternate Sources of Pluripotent Stem Cells*. Washington, D.C.: President's Council on Bioethics, 2005b <www.bioethics.gov>.

"The President's Stem Cell Theology." *The New York Times*, May 26, 2005.

Saletan, William. "The Organ Factory." July 25, 2005 <http://slate.msn.com/id/2123269/entry/2123270/>.

Smith, Christian. *Moral, Believing Animal*. Oxford: Oxford University Press, 2003.

Stedman's Medical Dictionary. 21st ed. Baltimore: Williams and Wilkins, 1966.

"Transcript Hearing. Senate Committee on Appropriations, Subcommittee of Labor, Health and Human Services, Education July 12, 2005." *Congressional Quarterly* (2005).

United Kingdom Committee Report on the Social, Ethical, and Moral Implications of Advances in Assisted Reproduction. 1984.

John S. Santelli
Abstinence-Only Education: Politics, Science, and Ethics

INTRODUCTION

UNTIL AUGUST 2004, I WORKED AT THE US CENTERS FOR DISEASE CONTROL and Prevention (CDC) as a researcher on adolescent health issues, an Institutional Review Board chairman, and a supervisor of other public health scientists.* This opportunity to do important public health research in a supportive, collaborative environment was a tremendous personal experience. CDC prided itself on excellence in epidemiologic and social science research and on science as the primary basis for its public health policy. I joined the CDC in 1991 because doing research with the centers meant that a scientist could influence critical public health issues—he or she could make a difference.

Sadly, toward the end of my 13-year stay at CDC, it was becoming increasingly difficult to conduct research on certain sensitive social issues. Although I was never overtly censored, scientific review became more labored and colleagues began to talk, somewhat ironically, about "self censorship," that is, avoiding research that might not be received favorably in Washington. A paper I had written on teen pregnancy declines, which examined the contributions of fewer teens having sex and more teens using contraception, made reviewers nervous because it could be used to support a conclusion that would have been contrary to the administration's emphasis on abstinence-only education for teenagers. Although scientific review in my own division and center seemed fair, I began to hear stories from other centers about papers and projects that had been stopped by scientific reviewers. Then, one day in 2003, under the Department of Health and Human Services (DHHS) Secretary Tommy Thompson's "one voice" initiative, the entire communications group at CDC, the group that helped us to clarify and hone our scientific messages for the public, was transferred from CDC headquarters in Atlanta to DHHS headquarters in D.C. It seemed that controlling the message in terms of its policy impact suddenly had become more important than getting the scientific content right. I became increasingly beleaguered and began to feel that creativity, an essential element of research, was not longer valued, particularly if it challenged orthodoxy. Also, after September 11th, the surgeon general had begun to discuss the idea of retraining CDC and National Institutes of Health (NIH) scientists, regardless of their specialty, as disaster preparedness experts. Feeling that my skill set was no longer as valued inside the government sector, and having an outside opportunity present itself, I joined the exodus of senior researchers from the agency. Suddenly, my shoulders felt lighter, and the air seemed clearer.

In January 2006, colleagues and I published two papers in the *Journal of Adolescent Health*. One (Santelli, 2006) was a scientific review and analysis of federal funding for "abstinence-only" education (AOE), or abstinence until marriage programs; the other was a position paper from the Society for Adolescent Medicine (SAM) on the same subject (SAM, 2006). The review paper, at considerable length, pointed out numerous scientific problems with US government support for AOE. Building upon writing from the 1990s on reproductive rights as human rights, we also pointed to what we saw as the inherently coercive aspects of a government policy that suppresses information or provides only half-truths. In February, I spoke on the issue of AOE at the New School's Politics and Science conference. And in May, I experienced an example of the current administration's interference with science.

I had submitted an abstract, which was then accepted through the peer review process, to the National STD Prevention Conference, co-sponsored by the CDC Division of STD Prevention and three professional groups. Others, including a state STD director, a graduate student, and an advocate for comprehensive sexuality education, also submitted abstracts that were each accepted through the same process. Two weeks before the meeting date in May, we began to receive e-mail messages from the CDC meeting sponsors indicating that a congressman was concerned about CDC sponsoring a meeting in which a one-sided attack on US government policy would be presented. We were informed that Rep. Mark Souder (R., Ind.) had contacted DHHS officials and questioned the panel's balance. Two panel members were subsequently uninvited (that is, removed) from the panel. In a May 9, 2006, letter, Rep. Henry Waxman (D., Calif.) asked DHHS Secretary Michael Leavitt about the change in panel membership. Waxman wrote, "In effect, it appears that presentations at a public health conference were censored because they criticized abstinence-only education. This attempt at thought control should have no place in our government" (http://www.henrywaxman. house.gov/issues/health/issues_health_HIV_current.htm). The response from Representative Souder's office, as published in the *Philadelphia Inquirer*, May 11, 2006, by Dawn Fallik, was unrepentant:

> "They're upset because we rained on their little party," said Marc Wheat, chief counsel for the drug policy subcommittee that oversees the CDC, of which Souder is chair. "They don't like to have their orthodoxy questioned." Those who organized the panel had an anti-abstinence agenda and it was the CDC's responsibility to reach out to those with other views, Wheat said.

The conference session was held, but with a panel composed of two abstinence proponents, the original state STD director, and myself. The title of my talk was changed, and my abstract was deleted from the conference website, but I was allowed to give my talk as planned, without any changes to its content. Reports in online journals (for example, www. slate.com) and national newspapers (such as the *Philadelphia Inquirer*) in the days preceding the conference ensured that session attendees were well aware of the change in panel membership. The session was packed and the debate was vigorous. The controversy insured that participants received two lessons that day: one on the issue of abstinence-only education, and the other on political intrusion into the scientific process.

This paper uses the controversy surrounding abstinence-only education to depict the current struggle between US politics and science. Herein, I attempt to illustrate how science has been misused in support of the federal government's abstinence-only education policies. I also attempt to illustrate the way in which this fight over science has become a communications battle and how the Internet has become the vehicle through which ideology is able to masquerade as science.

FRAMING SCIENTIFIC DEBATE

Thomas Kuhn, in his seminal book on the development of scientific theory, described how changing theoretical paradigms was an essential part of scientific transformations (Kuhn, 1996). Scientific revolutions involve some new data, but of greater importance are critical changes in the way we organize new and old data to understand the physical world. So, while many had seen apples fall from trees, Newton provided new insights into the operations of nature that led to a new scientific paradigm for physics. Such paradigms guide research and provide benchmarks against which to evaluate new data. They are an important aspect of the scientific consensus that guides peer review and scientific publication.

In the world of communication science, George Lakoff has described how the way we use language to frame political debates greatly influences the way we set policies and priorities (Lakoff, 2004). The framing of the debate sets an underlying paradigm for how one initially marshals the data. Thus, in a debate about "partial birth abortion," "welfare reform," or "sexual predators," much of the debate is already defined before one even gets to the data. Returning to the issue of AOE, proponents have repeatedly used the term "junk science" to criticize scientists who publish information that does not coincide with their beliefs. For example, the critique by Robert Rector of the Heritage

Foundation of a study by Peter Bearman of Columbia University uses this term (http://new.heritage.org/research/welfare/wm762.cfm). Try Googling "abstinence" and "junk science" to see how frequently the latter term has been used.

The works of both Kuhn and Lakoff are pertinent to the debate over abstinence-only education. In part, this is a debate between moral beliefs and scientific efficacy. But this is also a scientific debate over the nature of adolescence and emerging sexuality. Underlying ideological assumptions, which are often at odds with current scientific and medical consensus, are an important feature of the "science" supporting current abstinence-only policies. In fact, frequently the arguments used to support abstinence-only programs are an artful mix of science and pseudoscience.

HISTORY OF FEDERAL SUPPORT FOR ABSTINENCE EDUCATION AND THE SOCIETY FOR ADOLESCENT MEDICINE POSITION PAPER

While the federal government began supporting abstinence promotion programs in 1981 through the Adolescent Family Life Act (AFLA), there have been since 1996 major expansions in federal support for abstinence programming and a shift to funding programs that teach abstinence exclusively and restrict information about condoms and other methods of contraception (Dailard, 2002). These expansions include Section 510 of the Social Security Act in 1996, which was part of welfare reform, and Community-Based Abstinence Education (CBAE) projects in 2000. The CBAE program bypasses state governments' approval processes and makes grants directly to community-based organizations, including faith-based organizations. Both Section 510 and CBAE programs prohibit disseminating information on contraceptive services, sexual orientation, gender identity, and other aspects of human sexuality (Dailard, 2002). Section 510 provides an eight-point definition of abstinence-only education (see table 1), and specifies that programs must have as their "exclusive purpose" the promotion of abstinence outside of marriage and may not in any way advocate contraceptive use or discuss contraceptive methods except to emphasize their failure rates (Dailard, 2002).

The congressional intent of the CBAE program in 2000 was to create "pure" abstinence-only programs, in response to concerns that states were using funds for "soft" activities such as media campaigns instead of direct classroom instruction and were targeting younger adolescents (Dailard, 2002). Programs funded under CBAE must teach all eight components of the federal definition; they must target 12 to 18 year olds, and, except in limited circumstances, they cannot provide young people they serve with information about contraception or safer-sex practices—not even with their own non-federal funds (Dailard, 2002). Federal funding for abstinence-only programs has increased from $60 million in fiscal year (FY) 1998 to $168 million in FY2005. Virtually all the growth in funding since FY2001 has been in the CBAE program. The administration has promised to increase total funding for abstinence-only education from $204 million in FY2007 to $270 million in FY2009 (Dailard, 2006).

In late January 2006, just after the SAM position paper was released, the federal Administration for Children and Families issued new rules for the CBAE program that more clearly define abstinence but also more clearly prohibit dissemination of any positive information about contraception or condoms (http://www.acf.hhs.gov/grants/pdf/HHS-2006-ACF-ACYF-AE-0099.pdf). For example, grantees "must not promote contraception and/or condom use," must not "promote or encourage the use of any type of contraceptives outside of marriage or refer to abstinence as a form of contraception," and must teach that "contraception may fail to prevent teen pregnancy and that sexually active teens using contraception may become pregnant" (Dailard, 2006). While more specific, such language reveals an overt bias against contraception.

In the position paper from the Society for Adolescent Medicine, to which I was a major contributor, abstinence from sexual intercourse is endorsed as a "healthy choice for adolescents" and an important behavioral strategy for preventing human immunodeficiency virus (HIV), other

Table 1

Under Section 510, abstinence education is defined as an educational or motivational program that:

(A) has as its exclusive purpose, teaching the social, psychological, and health gains to be realized by abstaining from sexual activity;

(B) teaches abstinence from sexual activity outside marriage as the expected standard for all schoolage children;

(C) teaches that abstinence from sexual activity is the only certain way to avoid out-of-wedlock pregnancy, sexually transmitted diseases, and other associated health problems;

(D) teaches that a mutually faithful monogamous relationship in the context of marriage is the expected standard of human sexual activity;

(E) teaches that sexual activity outside of the context of marriage is likely to have harmful psychological and physical effects;

(F) teaches that bearing children out-of-wedlock is likely to have harmful consequences for the child, the child's parents, and society;

(G) teaches young people how to reject sexual advances and how alcohol and drug use increases vulnerability to sexual advances; and

(H) teaches the importance of attaining self-sufficiency before engaging in sexual activity.

---

sexually transmitted infections (STIs), and pregnancy among adolescents (SAM, 2006). However, SAM roundly castigated the federal programs that promote only abstinence and denigrate already proven risk reduction strategies to demonstrate the superiority of abstinence-only approaches. We built our case on demographic data, careful analysis of current program requirements, evaluation and observational data about abstinence-only curricula, and human rights principles. For example, we noted that many adolescents, including most younger adolescents, have not initiated sexual intercourse and many sexually experienced adolescents and young adults are abstinent for varying periods of time. We noted broad public and parental support for abstinence as a part of sexuality education. We also noted that according to demographic data, few

Americans remain abstinent until marriage and most Americans initiate sexual intercourse and other sexual behaviors during adolescence. In addition, marriage is occurring increasingly later in life: the median age for first marriage is 25 for women and 27 for men. Examining a central assertion by abstinence proponents that abstinence is 100 percent effective, we reviewed longitudinal data that indicates that abstinence as practiced by American teenagers often fails to protect against pregnancy and STIs. SAM noted that a recent emphasis on abstinence-only programs and policies appears to be undermining more comprehensive sexuality education and other government-sponsored programs. Finally, SAM concluded that abstinence-only education programs, as defined by federal funding requirements, are ethically problematic, because these programs withhold information and promote inaccurate information and questionable opinions.

The SAM position paper noted that abstinence, in specific curricula and in government policies, is frequently defined in moral terms, using language such as "chaste" or "virgin," and is frequently framed as an attitude or a commitment. For example, one study of abstinence-only program directors, instructors, and youth found that all groups defined abstinence in moral terms, such as "making a commitment" and "being responsible," as well as in specific behavioral terms, such as not engaging in coitus (Goodson, 2003). Federal regulations for domestic AOE funding adopt a moral definition of abstinence in the language above, requiring funded programs to teach that "a mutually faithful monogamous relationship in the context of marriage is the expected standard of human sexual activity." In understanding the framing of the debate about abstinence education, it should be noted that while health professionals generally view abstinence as a behavioral or health issue, many AOE advocates view abstinence as an issue of character or morality, based on their own personal religious or moral beliefs.

SCIENCE, IDEOLOGY, AND ABSTINENCE EDUCATION

It is useful to examine specific examples of clashes between ideology and science over abstinence education. These begin with particular misuses and misrepresentations of scientific data within the curricula of abstinence programs. Next, I examine the program evaluation data on abstinence-only programs and how proponents have misrepresented this data and/or used the Internet to "publish" data and conclusions at odds with peer-reviewed summaries. Attacks on research and researchers who have examined the virginity pledge movement and AOE are presented, including a poorly considered re-analysis from the Heritage Foundation of the data on virginity pledges, and attacks on my own credibility. Finally, we review the damage caused by this injection of ideology into public health, and the ethical issues raised by providing adolescents with partial information or misinformation regarding protection of their sexual health.

Abstinence-only curricula make extensive use of "science," or what appears to be science, in describing the dangers of sex. These curricula commonly use data from the CDC, NIH, and other research groups regarding the STD risk among teenagers, the incidence of STDs, the frequency of unintended pregnancy, and the consequences of such events. As such, they often provide risk information similar to other sexuality education curricula, but they present different prevention messages. However, some curricula may also exaggerate risk and/or diminish other prevention approaches such as condom use.

Abstinence-only education may also exaggerate or misrepresent the mental health consequences of sex during adolescence or sex before marriage. For example, federal AOE funding language requires teaching that sexual activity outside the context of marriage is likely to have harmful psychological effects. The SAM review found no scientific data suggesting that consensual sex between adolescents is harmful. We noted that most Americans initiate intercourse during adolescence and virtually all do so before marriage. Also, research shows that early sexual activity and pregnancy are associated with adverse childhood experiences, including unwanted sexual intercourse, sexual abuse, unsupportive social environments, and individual mental health problems such as conduct disorder and substance abuse (SAM, 2006). Thus, certain mental health problems are associated with early sexual activity, but these peer-reviewed studies suggest that sexual activity is a consequence of pre-existing mental health problems. We found no reports showing that initiation of adolescent sexual intercourse itself has an adverse impact on mental health. We also noted the paucity of data on whether purposively remaining abstinent until marriage promotes either personal resiliency, or sexual dysfunction in adulthood.

As unwanted or coercive sexual experiences are associated with mental health consequences, one must control for such experiences when examining the psychological consequences of sexual initiation. AOE advocates have recently pointed to a 2005 longitudinal analysis (Hallfors, 2005) using National Longitudinal Study of Adolescent Health (also known as "Add Health") data that found substance use, sexual experimentation, and having multiple sexual partners among females was predictive of depression one year later. However, that study did not control for sexual coercion. Moreover, the authors themselves noted that they had found few previous studies where sexual behavior and depression were temporally linked. Another recent study found that forced sex was related to poorer psychological health (Else-Quest, 2005); however, premarital sex absent these coercive experiences was not related to psychological problems. Advocates of AOE appear more interested in justifying their beliefs about abstinence than dealing with the complicated realities of adverse childhood experiences, conduct disorder, and substance abuse.

In a related area, opponents of abortion (which include many of the groups promoting AOE) have created a pseudo-scientific psychological diagnosis: "postabortion syndrome." This "diagnosis" is not recognized by either the American Psychological Association, or the American Psychiatric Association. In fact, studies of psychological reactions following abortion have consistently shown that the risk of psychological harm is low, and postabortion reports of distress and dysfunction are lower than preabortion rates (Adler, 1992). Long-term rates of psychological distress among women after having an abortion are generally the same or lower compared to that of the general population (Adler, 2003). Longitudinal studies with adolescents show similar findings of improved psychological functioning postabortion, and low rates of distress with one- to two-year follow up.

A content review of commonly used, abstinence-only curricula conducted by the minority staff of the Committee on Government Reform of the House of Representatives (led by Representative Henry Waxman) found that 11 of the 13 curricula contained false, misleading, or distorted information about reproductive health, including inaccurate information about condom and other contraceptive effectiveness, the risks of abortion, and other scientific errors. These curricula promoted gender stereotypes as scientific fact and blurred religious and scientific viewpoints (http://www.democrats.reform.house.gov/Documents/20041201102153-50247.pdf). The committee staff found multiple examples of such errors.

Likewise, Representative Waxman in a July 2005 letter to DHHS Secretary Michael Leavitt criticized an abstinence-inspired DHHS website (www.4parents.gov) as inaccurate and ineffective, promoting misleading and inaccurate information on STIs and condoms, and providing a narrow focus on abstinence (http://www.democrats. reform.house.gov/story.asp?ID=888). The website used content from the National Physicians Center for Family Resources, a supporter of AOE, instead of the expertise of scientists from NIH or CDC, or physicians from mainstream leading professional organizations such as the American Academy of Pediatrics or Society for Adolescent Medicine.

Although opponents of AOE have consistently attacked these programs for a lack of efficacy in reducing adolescent risk behaviors, based on the SAM review it is probably fair to say that there is a paucity of well-designed studies on which this assertion can be made. Three recent systematic reviews examined the evidence supporting abstinence-only programs and comprehensive sexuality education programs designed to promote abstinence from sexual intercourse (Kirby, 2001; Kirby, 2006; Manlove, 2004). These reviews were published as monographs; each underwent peer review, and each examined primarily curricular evaluations published in peer-reviewed journals. These reviews employed similar scientific criteria in selecting studies for evaluation and were based on criteria that are commonly used to evaluate comprehensive sexuality education programs, including use of experimental or quasi-experimental research design, and measurement of behaviors and not just behavioral intentions. Each review concluded that comprehensive sexuality education effectively promoted abstinence as well as other protective behaviors. In contrast, these reviews found no scientific evidence that abstinence-only programs demonstrate efficacy in delaying initiation of sexual intercourse. Manlove and Kirby identified the lack of rigorously evaluated programs as a major problem in evaluating the effectiveness of abstinence-only education. The most recent review by Kirby (2006) finds a few additional well-designed evaluations of abstinence-only educational programs, but no deviation from the conclusion that these evaluations have not demonstrated an impact on delay in initiation.

Doug Kirby's 2001 review of AOE program evaluations was challenged by Robert Rector of the Heritage Foundation in a paper published on the Foundation's website (http://www.heritage.org/Research/Family/BG1533.cfm). Rector identified evaluations of AOE programs that he believed demonstrated behavior change as a result of program participation. Rector reports, "There are currently 10 scientific evaluations that demonstrate the effectiveness of abstinence programs in altering sexual behavior. Each of the programs evaluated is a real abstinence (or what is conventionally termed an 'abstinence only') program; that is, the program does not provide contraceptives or encourage their use." Kirby, responding on the website of the National Campaign to Prevent Teen Pregnancy, noted that few of these evaluations identified by Rector met the minimum scientific criteria used by Kirby in his review, and all contained flaws in methodology or interpretation of the data that could lead to significantly biased results (Kirby, 2002).

Proponents of AOE assert that a variety of AOE programs have been shown to be effective, including those studied by Lerner, Cabezon,

Devaney, Maynard, and Borawski, but there are problems with these assertions. The evaluation by Lerner (2005) of the Best Friends program suffers from serious problems in research design, including the comparison of data from self-selected program participants to community-wide data from the Youth Risk Behavior Survey. The Lerner analysis was specifically rejected by Kirby in his reviews of abstinence programs because of these methodological limitations. The evaluation of the Teen Star program in Chile by Cabezon (2005) is adequately designed but the program is not an abstinence-only program; it specifically provided students with information on contraception and fertility awareness. The study by Devaney and Maynard under contract to the DHHS Office of the Assistant Secretary for Planning and Evaluation is very well designed and is referenced in the SAM review. The first two reports (Devaney, 2002; Maynard, 2005) from their evaluation document some increase in abstinence intentions and small (but positive) effects on teen norms and perceived risk; other intermediate variables did not change. It is important to note that the second report (Maynard, 2005), which presented the one-year impact of the program, failed to provide any behavioral data, although the baseline report suggested such data would be included in the second report. Finally, the Borawski (2005) evaluation is well designed but failed to demonstrate an impact on delay in initiation of sexual intercourse. It did demonstrate behavioral impact, increasing secondary abstinence and reducing multiple partners. The Borawski evaluation also found a worrisome reduction in intentions to use condoms along with an increase in abstinence intentions.

A critical study in the debate about AOE involves the work of Peter Bearman, former chairman of Sociology at Columbia University. Using longitudinal data from Add Health, Bearman and colleagues examined the virginity pledge movement, estimating that over 2.5 million American adolescents have taken public "virginity pledges." Bearman initially found that pledgers were more likely to delay initiation of intercourse by 18 months on average for adolescents 12 to 18 years (Bearman, 2001). This initial study was warmly received by AOE advocates. However, a second study involving a longer follow-up period (six-year follow-up) found that the prevalence of STIs (chlamydia, gonorrhea, trichomoniasis, and HPV) was similar among those taking the abstinence pledge and nonpledgers (Bruckner, 2005). Moreover, many teens who intended to be abstinent failed to do so, and when abstainers did initiate intercourse, many failed to protect themselves by using contraception. While pledgers had fewer sexual partners compared to nonpledgers, they were less likely to report seeing a doctor for an STI concern and were less likely to receive STI testing. Although pledgers tended to marry earlier than nonpledgers, if married, most pledgers initiated vaginal intercourse before marriage (88 percent). Virtually all married nonpledgers also initiated sex before marriage (99 percent).

AOE advocates were angered by the second report. Robert Rector of the Heritage Foundation has re-analyzed the Add Health data and severely criticized the Bruckner study at a DHHS conference and in a paper published on the Heritage Foundation website (http://www.heritage.org/Research/Welfare/whitepaper06142005-1.cfm). The Rector analysis has been severely criticized for manipulating statistical norms for significance in an online critique by a Princeton statistician (http://slate.msn.com/id/2122093/). A serious flaw in Rector's analysis stems from his selection of a less valid dependent variable. He used self-reported STIs, instead of laboratory-reported infections as used in the Bruckner analysis. This is problematic given that many STIs are asymptomatic and that Bruckner demonstrated that pledgers were less likely to have received STI testing.

Abstinence proponents have also vociferously attacked both the SAM position paper and the review paper on abstinence-only education. Immediately after the two papers were released in January 2006, the Abstinence Clearinghouse in a press release suggested that the "Society for Adolescent Medicine needs a health education of its own" (http://abstinence.net/library/index.php?entryid=2463). The Medical Institute on Sexual Health (MISH) in May 2006 also issued a 24-page

Internet critique (Hendricks, 2006) of the papers, admonishing the lead author (myself), the peer reviewers for the journal, and the journal editor. This critique found

> a significant number of serious omissions, misrepresentations, deviations from accepted practices, and opinions presented as facts. Logic, if employed, was often faulty. However, the authors should not be given full credit for these shortcomings, as even a handful of such errors in an article submitted for publication to most peer-reviewed journals would have caught the attention of at least one reviewer or editor. . . . The scholarship in this review article is generally lacking in rigor. The authors employ nonstandard research methods. Key points are substantiated by non-peer-reviewed sources.

This critique is itself full of striking misrepresentations and twisted logic. For example, the authors criticized the use of web references but then "published" their critique on a website. The MISH authors asserted that we "paint educational policies having moral components as patently unscientific." We had pointed out the moral basis for many AOE curricula and the scientific mistakes in commonly used AOE curricula. We never asserted that morality is incompatible with science. The MISH critique claims that we were erroneous in saying that the American Academy of Pediatrics (AAP) and the American Public Health Association (APHA) vigorously supported "comprehensive sexuality education." In an amazing feat of logic, they document this "error" by quoting the AAP policy as supporting "accurate and comprehensive education about sexuality." They then quote the APHA statement as encouraging government leaders to ensure that "sexuality education programs include comprehensive, medically-accurate information." These two verbal quibbles appear to be examples of distinctions without differences.

DAMAGE TO PUBLIC HEALTH PROGRAMS

Our review suggested that the politics around AOE programs is caus-ing systematic harm to a variety of domestic public health programs and international HIV-prevention programs. Abstinence-only education appears to be replacing more comprehensive forms of sexuality educa-tion in many communities. For example, in 2004 the Texas Board of Education decided to remove most information about contraception from new health education textbooks. Recent reports in the popular media describe teachers and students being censured for responding to questions or discussing sexuality topics that are not approved by the school administrators (Joint statement from the National Coalition against Censorship, 2002), as well as restricted access to HIV/AIDS experts from the classroom, and censorship of what experts and teach-ers can say in the classroom.

The abrupt cancellation by DHHS of Programs that Work from the Division of Adolescent and School Health at the Centers for Disease Control and Prevention is another example of politi-cal interference with public health. One day in 2002, the program and website disappeared. Programs that Work used a rigorous peer-reviewed process to identify programs that were effective in chang-ing adolescent sexual risk behaviors; the cancellation is believed to have been the result of CDC's failure to identify any abstinence-only programs as effective (http://www.thememoryhole.org/health/healthsites-scrub.htm).

Surveys on health educational practice in the United States provide further evidence of an erosion of comprehensive sexuality education, coincident with the rising emphasis on abstinence educa-tion. Data from the School Health Policies and Programs Study in 2000 found that 92 percent of middle and junior high schools and 96 percent of high schools taught abstinence as the best way to avoid pregnancy, HIV, and other STDs (CDC, 2002). Only 21 percent of junior high and 55 percent of high school teachers taught the correct use of condoms. Between 1988 and 1999, sharp declines occurred in the percentage of teachers who supported teaching about birth control, abortion, and sexual orientation and in the percentages who actually taught these subjects. For example in 1999, 23 percent of secondary school sexuality education teachers taught abstinence as the only way to prevent pregnancy and STDs, compared with only 2 percent who had done so in 1988 (Darroch, 2000). In 1999, one-quarter of sex education teachers said they were prohibited from teaching about contraception.

An emphasis on abstinence has influenced important public health programs. For example, federal and state governments provide support for family planning programs, which are available to adolescents through Title X of the Public Health Service Act. Starting in the FY2004 service delivery grant announcements, the Office of Population Affairs announced that program priorities for Title X grantees would include a focus on extramarital abstinence education and counseling, increasing parental involvement in the decisions of minors to seek family planning services, reporting of statutory rape, and working with faith-based organizations. Thus, Title X grantees are now expected to focus on these new priorities, while continuing to provide condoms and other contraceptive services, STI- and HIV-prevention education, cancer screening, and other reproductive health services. Many who work in the Title X program are concerned that these changes may weaken efforts to provide effective reproductive health services for adolescents and unmarried individuals who are sexually active (Dailard, 2003).

Likewise, language stressing abstinence has also appeared in CDC's Interim HIV Content Guidelines for AIDS-Related Materials. These guidelines require that "All programs of education and information receiving funds under this title shall include information about the harmful effects of promiscuous sexual activity and intravenous substance abuse, and the benefits of abstaining from such activities" (Office of the Federal Register, 2004).

Abstinence-only policies by the US government have also influenced global HIV-prevention efforts. Human rights groups have reported that government policy has become a source for misinformation and censorship in other countries (Human Rights Watch, 2004). US emphasis on abstinence may also have reduced condom availability and access to accurate information on HIV/AIDS in some countries (Human Rights Watch, 2004). The President's Emergency Plan for AIDS Relief (PEPFAR), focusing on 15 countries in sub-Saharan Africa, the Caribbean, and Asia that have been severely affected by AIDS, requires grantees to devote at least 33 percent of prevention spending to abstinence-until-marriage programs. Since the publication of the SAM position paper, the Government Accountability Office (GAO), which is the investigative arm of Congress, has issued a critique of US foreign policy support for abstinence-only education. PEPFAR in-country prevention teams reported that spending requirements "present challenges to their ability to respond to local prevention needs" and "can limit their efforts to design prevention programs that are integrated and responsive to local prevention needs" (http://www.gao.gov/new.items/d06395.pdf). The GAO report underscores our contention that abstinence-only policies undermine public health and health education efforts. At the urging of Representative Waxman, the GAO is currently conducting a review of the federal government's domestic abstinence-only education programs.

SCIENCE, ETHICS, AND HUMAN RIGHTS

Scientific ethics has often focused on the protection of human subjects in research, the responsible conduct of research by scientists, and distributional justice in access to the benefits of medical advances. The SAM position paper and our review paper both raised ethical concerns about AOE based on the principle of informed consent, suggesting that abstinence-only curricula withhold information from teenagers and thus are inconsistent with commonly accepted notions of medical ethics. Access to complete and accurate HIV/AIDS and sexual health information has been recognized as a basic human right and essential to realizing the human right to the highest attainable standard of health (Freedman, 1995). As such, governments have an obligation to provide accurate information to their citizens and avoid the provision of misinformation; such obligations extend to government-funded health education and health care services (Freedman, 1995).

International treaties provide that all people have the right to "seek, receive and impart information and ideas of all kinds," including information about their health. The UN Committee on the Rights of the Child, the UN body responsible for monitoring implementation of the Convention on the Rights of the Child, and which provides authoritative guidance on its provisions, has emphasized that children's right to access adequate HIV/AIDS and sexual health information is essential to securing their rights to health and information. The United Nations Guidelines on HIV/AIDS and Human Rights provide guidance in interpreting international legal norms as they relate to HIV and AIDS. These guidelines similarly call on states to "ensure the access of children and adolescents to adequate health information and education, including information related to HIV/AIDS prevention and care, inside and outside school, which is tailored appropriately to age level and capacity and enables them to deal positively and responsibly with their sexuality." Access to accurate health information is a basic human right that has also been described in international statements on reproductive rights such as the Programme of Action of the International Conference on Population and Development, Cairo, 1994.

Similarly, we asserted in our papers that patients and students have rights to accurate and complete information from health teachers and health care professionals, and that health professionals have ethical obligations to provide accurate health information. Health care providers may not withhold information from a patient in order to influence their health care choices, nor should health teachers. Such ethical obligations are based on the principle of respect for persons and are operationalized through the process of providing informed consent. Informed consent requires provision of all pertinent information to the patient. Similar ethical obligations should apply to health educators.

CONCLUSIONS AND RECOMMENDATIONS

Given the clash between ideology and science, how will scientists and medical providers be able to influence the policy debate over abstinence education? It is unlikely that simply providing more data or better evaluations will resolve these debates rooted in cultural and religious beliefs. Part of the resolution may be for scientists to become better communicators to the public about scientific principles and findings. However, in a clash between belief and science, improved communication is likely to fail. Nathanson (2006) has described the contingent power of experts in deciding public health issues, particularly the example of the United States, where no single group seems to have scientific supremacy, and considerable mistrust of scientific authority is evident. If scientists (and citizens) are interested in improving sexuality education, we need to rely on science but may find it more advantageous to reframe our arguments around themes that perhaps have greater cultural salience. "Medical accuracy" and "medical ethics" are two potential themes. While appeals to human rights may be an important adjunct strategy (with greater global resonance), medical ethics is likely to provide a broader appeal to US voters and parents.

Recognizing and appealing directly to the concerns of parents may also be effective in public policy debates. Parents overwhelmingly support education about abstinence *and* about condoms and risk reduction. Home-spun language such as "parents want their kids to be protected" and "kids need all the facts to protect themselves" may appeal to parents. Finally, while becoming more effective communicators, scientists must remain true to the data and the methods of scientific inquiry. Let us not fall into the rhetorical trap that has snared the proponents of abstinence-only education.

NOTES

* This commentary draws upon a review paper, "Abstinence and Abstinence-Only Education: A Review of U.S. Policies and Programs," by Santelli et al. (2006) and a similar position paper from the Society for Adolescent Medicine, both published in the *Journal of Adolescent*

Health in January 2006. I would like to thank my coauthors for their insights and encouragement in understanding and analyzing the science and politics around abstinence. This paper builds upon our previous efforts. I took this opportunity to update the data and my own understanding of the issues. Also, I would like to thank Lila J. Lande for her writing assistance.

REFERENCES

Adler, N. E., E. J. Ozer, and J. Tschann. "Abortion among Adolescents." *American Psychologist* 58:3 (March 2003): 211-217.

Bearman, P. S., and H. Bruckner. "Promising the Future: Virginity Pledges and First Intercourse." *American Journal of Sociology* 106 (2001): 859-912.

Borawski, E., E. S. Trapl, L. D. Lovegreen, N. Colabianchi, and T. Block. "Effectiveness of Abstinence-only Interventions in Middle School Teens." *American Journal of Health Behaviors* 29:5 (Sept.-Oct. 2005): 423-434.

Bruckner, H., and P. S. Bearman. "After the Promise: The STD Consequences of Adolescent Virginity Pledges." *Journal of Adolescent Health* 36:4 (April 2005): 271-278.

Cabezon, C., P. Vigil, I. Rojas, M. E. Leiva, R. Riquelme, W. Aranda, and C. Garcia. "Adolescent Pregnancy Prevention: An Abstinence-Centered Randomized Controlled Intervention in a Chilean Public High School." *Journal of Adolescent Health* 36:1 (January 2005): 64-69.

Dailard, C. "Abstinence Promotion and Teen Family Planning: The Misguided Drive for Equal Funding." *The Guttmacher Report on Public Policy* 5:1 (February 2002): 1-3.

———. "Title X Program Announcement Articulates New Priorities for Nation's Family Planning Program." *The Guttmacher Report on Public Policy* 6:5 (December 2003): 13.

———. "The Other Shoe Drops: Federal Abstinence Education Program Becomes More Restrictive." *Guttmacher Policy Review* 9:1 (Winter 2006): 19-20.

Darroch, J. E., D. J. Landry, and S. Singh. "Changing Emphases in Sexuality Education in U.S. Public Secondary Schools, 1988-1999." *Family Planning Perspectives* 32:5 (Sept.-Oct. 2000): 204-211.

Devaney, B., A. Johnson, R. Maynard, and C. Trenholm. "The Evaluation of Abstinence Education Programs Funded under Title V Section 510: Interim Report to Congress on a Multi-site Evaluation." Princeton: Mathematica Policy Research, Inc., 2002.

Else-Quest, N. M., J. S. Hyde, and J. D. DeLamater. "Context Counts: Long-term Sequelae of Premarital Intercourse or Abstinence." *Journal of Sex Research* 42:2 (May 2005): 102-112.

Freedman, Lynn P. "Censorship and Manipulation of Reproductive Health Information." *The Right to Know: Human Rights and Access to Reproductive Health Information.* Ed. Sandra Coliver. Philadelphia: University of Pennsylvania Press, 1995.

Goodson, P., S. Suther, B. E. Pruitt, and K. Wilson. "Defining Abstinence: Views of Directors, Instructors, and Participants in Abstinence-Only-Until-Marriage Programs in Texas." *Journal of School Health* 73:3 (March 2003): 91-96.

Hallfors, D. D., M. W. Waller, D. Bauer, C. A. Ford, and C. T. Halpern. "Which Comes First in Adolescence: Sex and Drugs or Depression?" *American Journal of Preventive Medicine* 29:3 (October 2005): 163-170.

Hendricks, K., P. Thickstun, A. Khurshid, S. Malhotra, and H. Thiele. "The Attack on Abstinence Education: Fact or Fallacy?" Technical paper. MISH/SR/TP - 20060505. Austin, Tex.: Medical Institute for Sexual Health; May 5, 2006 <http://www.medinstitute.org/includes/downloads/sr_tp20060505.pdf>.

Human Rights Watch. "The Philippines. Unprotected: Sex, Condoms, and the Human Right to Health." New York: Human Rights Watch, May 2004.

Kirby, D. "Emerging Answers: Research Findings on Programs to Reduce Teen Pregnancy." Washington, D.C.: National Campaign to Prevent Teen Pregnancy, 2001 <http://www.teenpregnancy.org/resources/research/reports.asp>.

——. "Do Abstinence-Only Programs Delay the Initiation of Sex among

Young People and Reduce Unintended Pregnancy?" Washington, D.C.: National Campaign to Prevent Teen Pregnancy; 2002 <http://www.teenpregnancy.org/resources/data/pdf/abstinence_eval.pdf>.

Kirby. D., B. A. Laris, and L. Rolleri. "The Impact of Sex and HIV Education Programs in Schools and Communities on Sexual Behaviors among Young Adults." Research Triangle Park, N.C.: Family Health International, 2006 <http://www.fhi.org/NR/rdonlyres/e2saa3gkcwbr422uoeyiitlrre6pd62cyh63x7rmw7xaibtztb2zvox-px4sb7oxmq7hugymp722f5n/KirbyFinallongreportv251.pdf>.

Kuhn, Thomas S. *The Structure of Scientific Revolutions.* Chicago: The University of Chicago Press, 1996.

Lakoff, George. *Don't Think of an Elephant: Know Values and Frame the Debate-The Essential Guide for Progressives.* White River Junction, Vt.: Chelsea Green Publishing Company, 2004.

Lerner, R. "Can Abstinence Work? An Analysis of the Best Friends Program." *Adolescent and Family Health* 3:4 (April 2005): 85-192.

Manlove, J., A. Romano-Papillo, and E. Ikramullah. "Not Yet: Programs to Delay First Sex among Teens." Washington, D.C.: National Campaign to Prevent Teen Pregnancy, 2004.

Maynard, R. A., C. Trenholm, B. Devaney, A. Johnson, M. A. Clark, J. Homrighausen, and E. Kalay. "First Year Impacts of Four Title V, Section 510 Abstinence Education Programs." Princeton: Mathematica Policy Research, Inc., 2005.

Nathanson, C.A. "The Contingent Power of Experts in the Marketplace of Knowledge." In press, 2006.

The National Coalition Against Censorship. "Abstinence Only Education? A Joint Statement." New York: The National Coalition Against Censorship, 2002.

[Office of the] Federal Register. *2004 Federal Register.* Washington, D.C.: National Archives and Records Administration; June 16, 2004; 69 (115).

Santelli, J. S., M. A. Ott, M. Lyon, J. Rogers, D. Summers, and R. Schleifer. "Abstinence and Abstinence-Only Education: A Review of US Policies and Programs." *Journal of Adolescent Health* 38 (2006): 72-81.

Society for Adolescent Medicine. "Abstinence-only Education Policies and Programs: A Position Paper." Prepared by J. S. Santelli, M. A. Ott, M. Lyon, J. Rogers, and D. Summers. *Journal of Adolescent Health* 38 (2006): 83-87.

III. Keynote Address

Neal Lane
Politics and Science: A Series of Lessons

OF COURSE, POLITICS IS IN THE NEWS ALL THE TIME AND SOME FOLKS
have been a bit cynical about it.

I grew up in Oklahoma, which is a little south of Nebraska, the
home state of the New School president and former senator from
Nebraska, Bob Kerry. Oklahoma is the birthplace of a cowboy come-
dian, Will Rogers, who had many wise and witty sayings about politics.
I really wanted to use his quips when I was in Washington—but Will
Rogers said things like: "I'm not a member of any organized party—I'm
a Democrat!" or "A fool and his money are soon elected!" or "Be thank-
ful we are not getting all the government we are paying for!" It just
wouldn't have worked.

Although an Okie, I am not quite as cynical about American politics
as Will Rogers. With all its faults—and they are very much in evidence
these days—there doesn't seem to be a superior model out there.

I would agree that politics in this country has been particularly ugly since the mid-1990s. One turning point was the election of
1994, which brought us the Gingrich revolution and the turmoil that
followed.

But in some ways things got even worse as we experienced
"shock and awe" at the dawn of the new millennium. First, it was the
presidential election of 2000—at least it shocked Democrats. Then, on
9/11, we were stunned by the horrors of terrorist attacks on American
targets, including the destruction of the World Trade Center in New
York City, and the tragic deaths of nearly 3,000 innocent people. That

was followed by the administration's story of weapons of mass destruction in the hands of Saddam Hussein, ready to nuke us. Finally, we had the Pentagon's prediction of how a blitzkrieg on Baghdad would render Iraq's people "in shock and awe," breathless and defenseless—with Iraqi soldiers unable or unwilling to fight. Well, the blitzkrieg occurred in March 2003 and, as with many predictions, this one came up short. And US politics as well as the morning news have been in a sad state since. I'm not sure any of us have the capacity for much more "shock and awe" in US politics.

Science also gets into the news, usually not on the first page, unless there is some scandal—for example, the exposure earlier this year of fraud in the case of the much heralded South Korean breakthroughs in stem cell research. This incident shocked the world of science and medicine. Stem cell research was already controversial in this country. This scandal made it even more difficult to move forward in a very important field of medical research.

The intersections of "science and politics"—and the tensions between the two—have also been in the news, not only in connection with stem cell research but in other areas as well, such as the allegations of a pattern of misuse and misrepresentation of science by the current administration. So I greatly appreciate the effort made at the conference where this paper was presented, and in this volume, to bring serious thinking to what I believe are very important matters, especially at this uncertain time in our nation's history.

Let me make an assertion and then we can see if it stands up: "Science and politics, at least in the US system, are bound together in diverse ways—and a divorce would not be good for either."

My qualifications to speak on this topic are slim indeed.

I am a theoretical atomic physicist, not a political scientist or credentialed policy scholar. But I had almost eight years in Washington, working on the front lines of science policy and politics, which left me with some impressions—along with some scars and bruises. I'll share a couple of examples in a few minutes.

Often, I find that when scientists talk about science and politics they are worried about "politicizing science," their concern being that politicians might exert undue influence on who does science, what kind of science gets done, and how science is used (or abused). For these reasons, and because there aren't enough hours in the day, most scientists avoid politics, aside from occasionally lobbying for funding. Two notable exceptions are Congressmen Rush Holt, Democrat from New Jersey, whose remarks at the conference appear later in this volume, and Vern Ehlers, Republican from Michigan, both of whom are Ph.D. physicists.

But the relationship between science and politics is, of course, more complicated than these views would suggest. I would like to address the complications.

First, a little American history.

WE COULD GO BACK TO THE BEGINNINGS OF OUR GREAT NATION, TO Benjamin Franklin, at a time of Enlightenment (a word you don't hear so much these days). Franklin was the first American scientist and was acclaimed for his studies of electricity, which he carried out successfully even without an National Science Foundation grant. I am not aware of any political interference with Franklin's research, although some folks preferred the notion that lightning was an "act of God."

It was really in World War II, over 60 years ago, that science, mathematics, and engineering received the bipartisan attention of the federal government by proving their worth, not just with the Manhattan Project, which produced the atomic bomb, but with radar, the proximity fuse, solid fuel rockets, electronics, penicillin, sulfa drugs and medical treatments proven on the battlefields of Europe and the Pacific.

At the close of the war, MIT engineer and president of the Carnegie Institution of Washington, Vannevar Bush, who was the wartime science adviser to Presidents Franklin Roosevelt and Harry Truman, wrote an influential report entitled "Science—The Endless Frontier." In it he argued convincingly that the science that won the war could also assure America decades of peace and prosperity.

Peacetime turned out to be the terrifying cold war with the Soviet Union. As a result, research funding grew significantly through this period. And along with the money came political influence over the level of federal funding, the kind of research that received supported and the people who did it. Initially, defense agencies led the way in supporting university research. And following the Soviet Union's launch of Sputnik in 1957, NASA's Apollo moon program was created by President John Kennedy in response to Sputnik.

The National Science Foundation (NSF) and National Institutes of Health (NIH), which emerged and grew during this period, focused entirely on nondefense research projects, selected by a process of competitive peer review. Even so, these agencies also have been subjected to political influence. With the NSF, Congress has always been concerned about geographical distribution of grants. With the NIH, the issue has been whether more money should go to heart disease or cancer or Parkinson's disease and, more recently, possible conflicts of interest with NIH researchers. Both agencies draw fire when a grant title sounds silly or sexy. That said, NSF and NIH have enjoyed strong bipartisan support and have avoided pork-barrel earmarks.

With that very incomplete description of the history of federal research funding, I want to turn to more recent times. I apologize, in advance, for the anecdotal nature of these next remarks, but I felt that a couple of specific examples with "lessons learned" might help make a few points.

I worked in Washington for most of the Clinton administration, first at the NSF (from fall 1993) and then, starting in 1998, in the White House. From the day I arrived in Washington, I saw in stark terms just how closely connected research funding is to politics. Given that the NSF is the only federal agency with a mandate to assure "progress of science" and traditionally has focused on basic research, where the idea is to fund the best people with the best ideas, I had some surprises coming.

My freshman year at NSF (1993-1994)—I'll call the "Year of Senator Barbara Mikulski." When I arrived at NSF, Sen. Barbara Mikulski (D-Md.) was the powerful chair of the Senate Appropriations Subcommittee that controlled the NSF budget (as well as NASA and some other agencies). She felt that NSF should be reorganized to align itself better with the economic problems the nation was facing and the needs of industry.

Specifically, she felt NSF should focus more of its budget (actually, 60 percent) on "strategic research"—for example, research directly related to computing, networking, biotechnology, materials, manufacturing, and so forth.

It took a year to figure out how to accommodate Senator Mikulski's concerns without radically changing the NSF and its programs and to establish a solid relationship with this important senator. It would have been easier had it not been for some science reporters with a nose for controversy.

My lesson here was that you can't take things personally and you must have a good working relationship with the chairs of your appropriations subcommittees and other leaders in the Congress. Of course, the same holds for the White House. Otherwise, you might as well go home.

A second lesson was that science reporters are much like other reporters. They like a good story, and controversy is always a good story. You really have to be careful what you say.

My sophomore year at NSF (1994-1995)—I'll call it the "Year of the Gingrich Revolution." You'll recall that in the election of 1994, the Republicans took over both the House and Senate. This meant that all the committees were now controlled by Republicans. People traded offices, staffs were fired (fewer Ds) and new staff hired (more Rs)—pretty much everything changed.

Right after the election, my—by that time—good friend Senator Barbara Mikulski (who, of course, would no longer chair the subcommittee) told me: "My advice to you, Neal, is to keep your head down!" (Meaning that things will likely get pretty rough, there will be a lot of shooting back and forth, best to not get caught in the crossfire.) I did that, but even so, budgets that had been going up reversed direction. NSF did better than most agencies, but we still got cut. It would have been much worse had we not had strong supporters of science on both sides of the aisles.

My lesson here was that the science community is very fortunate to have champions of science in both parties, who will fight back when necessary. I am worried that they may be getting tired and increasingly fed up with trying to do some good in a dysfunctional environment.

A second lesson was that "when a friend in Congress tells you to duck, you'd better duck!"

My Junior year (1995-1996) was the "Year of the Government Shutdown." Just as Barbara Mikulski had warned, it was not long before the shooting started. The new Republican leadership in Congress, feeling that it was in the driver's seat, believed they could force President Clinton to accept the Republican agenda, no questions asked. The conflict resulted in a shutdown of most of the federal government in the snowy winter of 1995-1996. Most workers had to stay home, and nobody was being paid. I was nearly alone in the building answering the phone: "Hello, this is the National Science Foundation—please hold!" Ultimately, Congress gave in and we opened our doors, just before a huge snowstorm arrived and shut down the city.

Perhaps the lesson here was that you never know how the political winds (or the snow) will be blowing when you decide to take a job like this. Things can change fast—and the changes can be huge. You just have to make the best of it, keep your job skills up, and drink in moderation!

My senior year and, let us say, early postgrad year (1996-1998), included a number of tussles with Congress. One influential member of Congress decided NSF should stop supporting the social sciences, or perhaps let the chemists and physicists decide which political science grants were funded. I spent a lot of time on the Hill explaining why the research was so important. The social science communities got organized, and cards and letters began arriving in congressional offices. It also required the help of some "friends of science" in Congress to get that turned around.

A lesson here was that the research community can influence political outcomes, if it speaks with one mind and uses solid arguments.

My last year at NSF (1997-1998) was the "Year of Trying to Get the NSF Budget Back on an Upward Path" in the wake of the earlier stormy struggle between the White House and Republicans in Congress. I'm very happy to say that we got that done.

I LOVED THE NSF JOB, BUT IN THE SUMMER OF 1998, EITHER BECAUSE President Clinton liked what I was doing at NSF or he didn't, he asked me to come over to the White House as his science adviser, following the legendary Jack Gibbons. And he appointed Rita Colwell to become the next NSF director.

The White House was and is a very political place.

The morning senior staff meeting set the priorities for the day, week, month; and the president's chief of staff assigned responsibilities. What got attention were matters that were urgent, vital to national security, politically important "goings on" in Congress, and frontpage news. And everyone stayed focused on the president's priorities and agenda.

With a few exceptions, science was not urgent, politically important, or on the front-pages of the morning's papers. That had its pluses and minuses. But, as science adviser, if you wanted to get the attention of the president—and his circle of political advisers—on any matter, you had to find a way to connect science to the larger policy and political agenda—health, national and domestic security, energy and environment, education and workforce, the economy, etc. That was one of the challenges.

In my own case, there was the extra challenge of trying to sell science and technology inside the White House at a time when many Republicans in Congress were trying to kick the president out of office.

But, I must tell you that all during this unfortunate episode, the president stayed focused on his job and asked us to do the same. As a result, the American people saw that the country's important business moved forward, at least in the executive branch.

I was also amazed that, while I knew of Vice President Al Gore's considerable interest and knowledge in science and technology, I found that President Clinton had an insatiable curiosity and considerable knowledge about science as well. In his last budget request, he asked Congress to give the NSF almost double the largest dollar increase the agency had ever received. He requested increased funding for all other federal research programs as well, and launched the $500 million National Nanotechnology Initiative.

But for most people working in the White House (and the same was true of Congress), it was not obvious that most important policy issues are intimately connected with science and technology. Just in the two and one half years I was in the White House, my office dealt with: the human genome; cloning and stem cells; clean air and water; endangered species; carbon emissions and global warming (Kyoto); national security; terrorism; missile defense; HIV/AIDS and other infectious diseases; food safety; energy; the space station; the federal research budget; and many others. Fortunately, I inherited an outstanding staff, including Henry Kelly, whose introduction to a group of papers presented at the conference appears earlier in this volume.

It is also true that most of the issues that connect science and technology with larger societal needs involve controversy of one kind or another, have advocates and opponents among different special interest groups and get the attention of one or more members of Congress—usually more!

In the case of carbon emissions, global warming, and climate change, the United States had already signed the Kyoto agreement by the time I arrived in the White House, but the Senate had not ratified it. We spent much of our time responding to endless Republican congressional requests for files and e-mails with any connection to climate change. President Clinton and I were named in a lawsuit, filed by several anti-global warming groups, in an effort to prevent publication of a federal report on the possible impact of global warming and climate change on the United States. The report was published, but today you may have a hard time finding it on the government's websites.

My lesson here was that some members of Congress and lobbyists will use whatever means they can find, including the courts, to exercise their political will. And these powerful groups will not hesitate to attack scientists whose findings they don't like. Anyone who takes on these Washington jobs must have a good lawyer close at hand and always keep an eye in the rearview mirror.

I'll just give one more example: stem cells and cloning.

President Clinton's Bioethics Advisory Committee, chaired by former Princeton president Harold Shapiro, found that ethical considerations, on balance, favored the use of discarded embryos to develop embryonic stem cell lines, since the possibilities of stem cell therapy in medicine were so promising.

President Clinton agreed, up to a point, and was willing to allow the NIH to fund such research on stem cell lines derived with private money, but was not willing to use federal money to develop these lines. However, the Republican-led Congress, bowing to the religious right, wanted none of it and, through the Dickey Amendment (passed in 1996) caused such research to be delayed until President Clinton was out of office.

The lesson was that some policy actions that relate to science arouse passionate resistance by people whose religious beliefs are in conflict with such actions; and that resistance is increasingly directed against scientists and their funding.

There are other examples I could cite; many of them also were frontpage conflicts between science and politics at the moment.

So, is there anything really new with science and politics? What's special about the G. W. Bush administration? To be frank, it's hard to even know where to start.

Over 60 scientists, including myself and many Nobel laureates and members of both political parties, signed a statement two years ago with the heading "Restoring Scientific Integrity in Policymaking" that criticized the administration for its misuse of science. Since then, over 8,000 scientists have signed the statement, which is posted on the Union of Concerned Scientists (UCS) website.

I won't take time to review the events that led up to our decision to sign this statement, which was based on UCS research, since I think this material is covered in other contributors' papers. Suffice it to say that we were concerned about a "pattern of misrepresentation of science and undermining the integrity of the scientific advisory process" that we felt endangered the health of Americans and could erode the public's trust in science.

Was it a good idea for scientists to speak out?

Some have said that our statement was "politically motivated," especially coming out within a year of the presidential election. I can only speak for myself. I did not, for a minute, believe the statement would have any effect at all on the outcome of the election. In fact, in the discussions among many of the signers prior to issuing the statement, I don't recall anyone mentioning how the statement might influence the election. My hope, and I believe that of my colleagues, was simply that someone would put a stop to this bad behavior. In fact, we called for legislative action.

Some have said that by speaking out in this way, we made it much harder for those trying to reverse the recent slide in federal research funding. But, it did not appear to have upset the president, who talked about science in his State of the Union address.

My view, in any case, is that maintaining the integrity of science is exceptionally important. So, on occasion, if we feel strongly enough that science is being threatened in more fundamental ways than money, we just have to speak out.

I also want to add the comment that in all the time I worked in the Clinton administration, I was never asked to misrepresent scientific findings or appoint unqualified people to important positions, nor was I aware of anyone else doing so.

Is there a lesson here? Each of us will have our own view about that. Also, it's too early to know whether speaking out, in this particular instance, did any long-term good or not.

One immediate tangible result, as is widely known, was an amendment to the appropriations bill funding the Department of Health and Human Services, which essentially tells the administration to "cease and desist" imposing political litmus tests on nominees for scientific advisory committees and misrepresenting science in government documents and web sites. The president signed that bill into law on December 30, 2005. The amendment got its impetus from Congressman Henry Waxman (D-Calif.) and Senator Richard Durbin (D-Ill.) and was actively advocated by the Union of Concerned Scientists. The UCS will work for similar language in all relevant appropriations bills next time around.

Furthermore, the most recent outrageous attempt by the administration to silence one of the world's foremost experts on climate change, Dr. James Hansen, of NASA Goddard (as reported in the January 30, 2006, *New York Times*), seems to have backfired. The administration's bungled effort got more front-page news than did Dr. Hansen's original comments. Congressman Sherwood Boehlert, Republican from New York and chairman of the House Science Committee, blasted the agency over that one. And this morning's *New York Times* carried an editorial on the incident—appropriately titled "Censuring Truth." Dr. Hansen, of course, has since spoken out frequently, including at this conference, and his paper is included in these proceedings.

I want to finish my remarks by saying something about the future—as if I knew anything about the future. Even Einstein said "I never think of the future—it comes soon enough." Or in the words of that great sage, Yogi Berra, "The future ain't what it used to be."

On climate change, the United States cannot simply "go it alone" on such an obviously important global matter. I don't expect any international agreements to come out of this administration. (Unless I missed it, there was no mention of global warming in the State of the Union address.) But, whichever party is next in the White House, I think the United States will be at the table talking about carbon credits, emissions reductions, and so forth. The science will get better and better; and as it does, a looming disaster of unprecedented consequences will be impossible to ignore. (The Evangelical Climate Initiative is a striking example of the increasing alarm of Americans.) Even with the best efforts by all nations, the enormous energy demands in the coming decades will require revolutionary technologies and know-how to keep from destroying the planet.

On embryonic stem cell research, we will continue to see strong opposition by some religious fundamentalist groups in this country who believe that the fertilized egg is a human being. And, in his State of the Union speech, President Bush called on Congress to outlaw "all forms of human cloning," which I take to include therapeutic cloning. This ban would apply to every researcher, regardless of who supports the work; and it would be a serious blow to stem cell research in this country. But, the promise of stem cell therapy is real, and the American people care about their health. The first proof that a serious illness or physical disability has been helped by stem cell therapy will result in public pressure to fund a large stem cell research program.

There are three broader areas of policy that affect the health of scientific research in all fields. The first is finding the money to do science. Research budgets have flattened out, actually decreasing in some fields for many years; grant sizes are too small and too short in duration; too little attention is given to truly innovative ideas; and the nonbiomedical sciences are seriously underfunded. I am now very worried about NIH funding as well. This is all likely to get worse, with an $ 8 trillion debt, large deficits, expanding security budgets, an expensive Iraq war, and large tax cuts.

The second, on my list, is finding the people to do the research. For several decades, we have been unable to attract a sufficient number of our young people, particularly underrepresented minorities and women, to careers in science and engineering. Part of the problem is our troubled K-12 school system; but that has a lot to do with what we value in this country, a "get rich quick" attitude, our lack of respect for the teaching profession, and our turning away from the view that a quality education for every American is a national responsibility and vital to the welfare of all Americans.

Meanwhile, this nation has become dependent on young men and women from other parts of the world to do much of the nation's research and fill many of the technical positions in universities and industry. And we were fortunate that they came. Well, they have not been coming in such large numbers anymore, due to visa problems, our image abroad, and opportunities available elsewhere.

I might interject here that the recent preliminary report, "Rising Above the Gathering Storm," called for by Republican Senator Lamar Alexander and Democratic Senator Jeff Bingaman and drafted by a committee of the National Academies chaired by former CEO of Lockheed-Martin, Norman Augustine, makes some bold and thoughtful recommendations that address both research funding and education. It has gotten good bipartisan vibes in Congress. President Bush, in his State of the Union address, announced education and innovation initiatives, which include additional funding, although the total for science and technology is down.

The test will be in how Congress deals with the many cuts President Bush is proposing in his budget and how strongly the administration fights for these initiatives during the appropriations process. I noticed that his announcement did not generate rousing cheers from the Congress, even though many individual members have been pushing hard for budget increases in these areas! A lot has to happen before these initiatives become reality.

If ever there was a time to write/fax/e-mail/call/visit your congressman and senator about whatever you believe to be important, this is it.

The third on my list of three is improving people's understanding of science and retaining their trust. This one is the most troublesome of all, because, I think, it reflects some things about our value system in this country at a very fundamental level.

The general public does not know much about science. The good news is that 70 percent of the American people understand that the earth goes around the sun. But, if you ask how long it takes, you lose 20 percent. Only half the American people know the answer is one year. This is the same fraction that believes humans lived with dinosaurs.

Interestingly, roughly half of the American people believe all sorts of things that lack any scientific evidence at all—for example, ghosts and haunted houses, ESP, astrology, and intelligent design or creationism.

And as long as so many people don't understand science—how scientific research is done, why scientific knowledge is not simply one opinion, no better than any other opinion—there is the danger that people will lose confidence in the value and trustworthiness of science. Moreover, there are people and organizations who will use or misuse science in any way that suits their purpose. All of this threatens the integrity of science.

And, while we're at it, let's add one more matter that should be a concern to all of us: freedom—in science, in teaching, in everyday life. It is by far the most important. Because I believe that without personal freedom none of the rest of what I have talked about matters much.

Albert Einstein had something to say about freedom in 1931, at a time when Europe was facing another World War, with the United States soon to follow. In Einstein's words, "everything that is really great and inspiring is created by the individual who can labor in freedom."

But, when people are insecure, frightened and confused, as they are in our country right now, governments can take away their freedoms—our freedoms—quite easily. Once gone, those freedoms are hard to get back.

Benjamin Franklin warned us about this 250 years ago with his famous statement, "They that can give up essential liberty to obtain a little temporary safety deserve neither liberty nor safety."

I wonder what Ben would think if he were with us today.

I'll close by returning to my opening assertion that "Science and politics, at least in the US system, are bound together in diverse ways—and a divorce would not be good for either." This bonding has a lot to do with federal funding, but it also is inevitable because of the large impact science and technology have on pretty much everything Americans need, want and do in their lives. By and large it has been a good marriage.

But, at this uncertain time in our nation's history, it will challenge both sides to ensure that the marriage remains a fruitful one, with many positive offspring for our society. We all have much work to do.

I HOPE THESE CONFERENCE PROCEEDINGS WILL SPAWN MANY MORE such events, raising the profile of the issue of science and politics and engaging a widening circle of participants in the dialogue.

And, let me end on a note of optimism, in the words of my former boss, Bill Clinton. At the 2004 Democratic National Convention, he said, "Strength and wisdom are not opposing values." That is a not-so-subtle thought for our nation's leaders. And in his first inauguration address (January 20, 1993), we all heard a message of hope from that very wise man from Hope, when Clinton said, "There is nothing wrong with America that cannot be cured with what's right with America."

Whether original or not, I know firsthand that our former president believes that to be true and would challenge each of us to do whatever we can to prove him right.

IV. The Environment

NATURAL RESOURCES JOURNAL

The Natural Resources Journal takes a multi-disciplinary, multi-resource approach to the widest range of national and international issues. The Journal emphasizes good writing, and innovative scholarship. It strives for technical accuracy and easy accessibility. Some articles are intensely focused; others canvass broad areas. There are always essays and book reviews.

Subject Classifications
Environmental Policy and Law; Natural Resources; Conservation; Ecology

Natural Resources Journal
School of Law MSC11 6070
1 University of New Mexico
Albuquerque NM 87131-0001
(505) 277-8659
nrj@law.unm.edu

Please enter my subscription to Natural Resources Journal for
□ Volume 46 (Year 2006) $40.00
□ Volume 46 & 47 (Years 2006 & 2007) $75.00
       Additional cost of $5.00 per volume outside the U.S.

Name _____

Organization _____

Address _____

ZIP Code_____

Payment enclosed $ _____

       MAKE ALL CHECKS PAYABLE TO
       NATURAL RESOURCES JOURNAL

URL: http://lawschool.unm.edu/nrj/index.htm

Dawn Rittenhouse
Introduction

SINCE ENVIRONMENTAL CONCERNS FIRST SURFACED AS A NATIONAL issue in the late 1960s, there has been a running argument between one side focused on protecting the environment and the other side calling attention to the need to assure continued economic development. For years this discussion played out as an either/or dilemma: a community could have a clean environment and no jobs, or jobs but a degraded environment. Nongovernmental organizations (NGOs) that were focused on the environment continued to challenge the federal, state, and local governments to create laws and regulations that would require the reduction of emissions and clean up of already degraded areas. In the meantime, many companies struggled to first understand what their emissions were and then reduce their emissions to be in compliance with these new laws and regulations.

Companies invested significant amounts in limiting their emissions and cleaning up sites to be compliance with the regulations. For the most part, America's air and rivers are cleaner then they were 25 years ago. Additionally, a number of companies found that the actions to reduce their emissions were good for their bottom line as well. In 1992 the World Business Council for Sustainable Development started to make the case that reducing waste and emissions went hand in hand with improving productivity and therefore bottom line performance. Over the decades we proved that economic development could be done with less impacts on the environment. In hindsight, that might have been the easy part.

Today's environmental challenges are more complex and challenging. Previously we were dealing with local, point-source emissions that could generally be measured and regulated. Today's issues are broad and global in scope; their solutions will require actions from governments, the private sector, and individuals. The linkage of science to environmental policy is now critical, not only in the United States, but also internationally, as we deal with global issues like climate change and the far-reaching proposals for solutions.

Science is important in environmental policymaking. It is important in terms of how we define the problem as well as what solutions that we seek to implement and in what time frame they need to be implemented. A key challenge is the interplay between the scientist and the policymakers: How can different and diverse interests be represented in the policy discussion without hijacking the entire process? Is there a right balance of input from entities with different perspectives and if so, what can be done to create that right balance?

The comments from discussion participants exemplify some of the key issues associated with how to frame the challenge: Where does one draw the line when discussing an environmental issue? As Paul Ehrlich points out, population growth will have a massive effect on almost any environmental issue. Is that part of the framing that we need to use for the policy dialogue, or can we be successful with discussions that are more limited—specifically, about climate change or ecosystem protection?

The comments also speak to many of the challenges in seeking solutions and understanding if the proposed solutions will have the desired affect. As Steve Hayward points out, in the short term no improvement—but instead escalating problems—may be seen when proposed solutions are implemented. How do we track and understand the broader system changes that may be driving what we are measuring?

And finally, there are some suggestions on what needs to be done to change the current balance of how interests are represented. Michael Oppenheimer proposes a threefold solution to the challenge. Jim Hanson writes about how to communicate the climate story in an understandable fashion.

The roundtable discussants may not have the answer to the question of how science can play an instrumental role in environmental policy development, but their thoughts add context to the challenge of how to assure freedom—the freedom to research, and the freedom to discuss the results and challenge how testing was done in a way that moves our total understanding of the issues and the possible solutions forward.

Journal of **Environmental Systems**

Editor: Sheldon J. Reaven

Associate Editor: Jeffrey B. Gillow

Managing Editor: Carole Rose

The knowledge of environmental, energy, and waste problems is burgeoning individual disciplines. There are lively, continuing disagreements among environmental professionals as to the basic theories, concepts, methods of analysis, and values that most fruitfully explore environmental issues and systems. We continue to discover the bewildering complexities of environmental systems themselves, and find that they cannot be understood within the confines of individual fields of science and engineering. It becomes ever more evident that environmental problems can be understood only in the context of their social, economic and regulatory "environments."

READERSHIP

In more than 40 countries, *JES* is read by engineers, scientists, business executives, government officials, and others involved in areas relevant to environmental systems. Leading subscribers are from the areas of: recycling and waste management; policy analysis and risk analysis; energy/resource modeling and environmental impact assessment; environmental health and safety; architecture and urban studies; civil engineering, transportation, and public utilities (energy and water); ecology and environmental engineering; law and economics; anthropology and psychology, science and technology studies.

AIMS AND SCOPE

The *Journal* defines environmental problems as systems in which complex natural phenomena affect, and are affected by, the human world of economics, regulation and law, culture, behavior, and public perceptions The *Journal* is where environmental professionals from many disciplines exchange ideas on, and devise solutions to, problems in waste management, energy and resources, local and global water, land, and air pollution.

SUBSCRIPTION INFORMATION

ISSN: 0047-2433; Online ISSN: 1541-3802

Sold by volume only (4 issues yearly)

Institutional Rate: $300.00 + $11.00 postage & handling U.S. and Canada; $20.00 elsewhere

Complimentary sample issue available upon request

BAYWOOD PUBLISHING COMPANY, INC.

26 Austin Avenue, PO Box 337, Amityville, NY 11701

call (631) 691-1270 • fax (631) 691-1770 • toll-free orderline (800) 638-7819

e-mail: baywood@baywood.com • web site: http://baywood.com

Michael Oppenheimer
Science and Environmental Policy: The Role of Nongovernmental Organizations

THIS PAPER ADDRESSES THE ROLE OF NONGOVERNMENTAL ORGANIZATIONS, or NGOs, in the science-policy nexus. I shall draw on my 21 years of experience working for a nongovernmental organization, Environmental Defense, my earlier experience as a research scientist, and my recent experience as a professor, the latter two positions at large universities. I hope this quasi-anecdotal approach is informative, but in addition, it is a necessity because there have been relatively few academic studies of nongovernmental advocacy organizations.

I shall begin by considering a question arising from the opening section of this volume: Is the special objective role of science in the policy arena, presumed by many observers to have existed in an earlier political era, about to disappear into the dust bin of history, and if so, should we act to restore such a role?

My view is consistent with Daniel Kevles's paper: science in the current policy world has just as much to do with regulation of corporate activity and, to a lesser extent, people's lives, as it does with the means to wage war or develop consumer goods like computer games. This development dates to the revolution in environmental regulation in the 1970s, as well as the expansion of regulatory attention to foods, drugs, and health care. If science formerly was viewed as a servant of people's wants and needs, science-based decision making now also functions as something of a master over people and companies by dictating restrictions. So it was inevitable in a free society, organized in part along the lines of special interests, some empowered by large financial resources, that a melee should ensue. And that is what we have today on many issues, particularly global warming, aided and abetted by a related phenomenon: government that is often disingenuous.

I argue that there is no point trying to put the genie back in the bottle, no point trying to regain an imagined status of science operating in splendid objectivity and isolation, rendering untainted judgments. It probably never was so, and I doubt it ever will be. Furthermore, it should become apparent from this paper that proposals to create a neat division between regulation and science, resembling Alvin Weinberg's earlier notion of a science court (Jasanoff, 1990), are tinged with elitism while satisfying neither side, and if they were proposed (and I have heard such rumblings) many scientists, including me, would be strongly opposed.

The relation of science to government has indeed worsened, and needs to be fixed, but whether or not the good old days ever existed, we should not aspire to return to them. To deal with current problems of the environment, science needs to be inclusive rather than exclusionary, as usually has been its tendency. We need to recognize that values and viewpoints are an inevitable part of scientific judgment in the zone where science interacts with government over many environmental problems, where systems are complex, uncertainty is endemic, and learning is slow. What questions are asked and how they are framed are a critical part of science research and science advice in this arena. A necessary part of improving the science-government interface is to avoid pretending that science advice in such an arena can be built from pure natural science. Rather, as Henry Kelly has noted, "Sound policy depends on a rough marketplace of ideas." We must all get used to this new situation.

Of course, this rough marketplace has some big downsides. The problem isn't all the voices heard. Rather, it is that some participants do not play by the usual rules, and at the same time, have disproportionate resources to amplify their message in public (Mooney, 2005) and often have differential access to the decision process (Jasanoff, 1990).

The solution I propose is threefold:

▸ First, broaden the scope of participation in the scientific process; we must welcome the barbarians at the gate, as long as they behave once inside.
▸ Second, trust the culture of science, which honors transparency and openness to new approaches, but holds claims of truth to a rigorous standard.
▸ Third, find a way to deal with the pernicious imbalance of resources—that is, money deployed in the debate over science in the public and government arena. The latter is a little like the campaign finance question and not easily solved.

These points bring me back to my main topic: the role of nongovernmental organizations.

I do not intend to go into detail about what an NGO actually is, but take for granted the understanding that I am referring to the class of environmental advocacy, and sometimes research and advocacy organizations, at the national, state, and local level that have as their mission, contributing to the protection of the environment. I include here both groups that favor expansion of environmental regulation, as well as those that oppose it. To summarize my conclusion: a strengthened NGO sector would improve policy outcomes. Let me start with an anecdote.

After the invasion of Iraq, when it became clear that there was no firm evidence at hand that Iraq possessed weapons of mass destruction, I observed a conversation between two high-ranking academic scholars—one relatively young, the other of late middle age. The younger professor was outraged that our government did not tell the truth. The older one, whose political sensibility was formed during Vietnam and Watergate, responded automatically, and with a shrug: "That's what governments do; they lie".

Although governments may not all lie all the time, they all too often withhold, distort, spin, and ignore scientific facts and that, in a nutshell, summarizes why we need a strong NGO sector.

An explosion of NGOs occurred following Vietnam and Watergate, in the wake of the participatory atmosphere that had been generated by the civil rights movement. A partial remedy for the current attack on science should be sought in strengthening the ability of such organizations to participate intelligently, rather than attempting to narrow access to the policy arena, which would in any case be impossible. NGOs perform three vital functions:

▸ NGOs' culture, like most of the culture of science, insists on transparency (at least for others; sometimes these organizations are not themselves sufficiently transparent).
▸ NGOs provide balance in the transformation of scientific information into policy; that is, the framing of scientific questions and findings as policy issues.
▸ NGOs help initiate policy examination of new problems, and even sometimes initially identify questions as proper scientific and policy concerns. They have shown an ability to convert a scientific question into a policy issue with great effectiveness. Of course, not everyone agrees that they have always been right in what they focused public attention toward, but my view of course is that scientifically literate NGOs have usually shown good judgment.

NGOs have shown their worth in this regard across a spectrum of environmental issues:

▸ Scientists employed at NGOs played a critical role in developing the basis for the Endangered Species Act, and subsequently (in cooperation with academic scientists) defending the act from radical revision.
▸ Scientists at NGOs, in cooperation with academic scientists, had a key role in developing the regimes for regulation of hazardous

chemicals during the 1970s and for increasing stringency on lead during the 1980s.

▸ In 1983, a National Academy of Sciences panel (NAS, 1983) made a serious misjudgment by recommending a 10-year delay to allow more learning before governments even considered action on climate change. Despite the prevalence of this view, NGOs, working closely with academic and government scientists who had a different perspective, played (and still play) a critical role in transforming the climate change issue from an arcane scientific question into a global regulatory regime, leading to the United Nations Framework Convention on Climate Change by 1992 (Oppenheimer and Petsonk, 2005), and ultimately the Kyoto Protocol.

▸ NGOs, particularly the American Lung Association, pressed for action against airborne fine particles when estimates of annual deaths ranged from 50,000 to zero. During the 1980s, the US government, particularly the Reagan administration, focused on the uncertainty while NGOs focused on the potentially large risk. The acid rain section of the Clean Air Act of 1990 significantly enhanced control of the sulfur dioxide emissions that generate the particles, but for a different reason (acid deposition). It was not until the late 1990s that science improved enough to support the higher estimates, but to me, NGOs were right in calling for a policy that reduced the high-end risk in advance of fuller knowledge. This is exactly the kind of decision we face again and again in environmental science.

▸ Before I hear claims that environmental NGOs can be counted on to jump on any risk, no matter how uncertain or trivial, and therefore should be discounted, let me point out several cases where NGOs acted with considerable caution: By and large they did *not* press the power-line microwave radiation exposure question, they did not press for mercury control until the science was clear, and most NGOs have been appropriately cautious on the human health aspects of the endocrine inhibitor question.

As for transparency in the policy arena, ideally it would be guaranteed by individual scientists or groups of scientists operating through a shared culture that demands it. I think our mental model here is too influenced by the old debates over disarmament and nuclear weapons, which saw some scientists willingly participate in the public arena and play extraordinary roles. In practice, society cannot now, and never could, count on scientists automatically entering the fray. Sometimes research scientists do become engaged, for example as whistle blowers, but it is not their main job and in fact, the personal incentives, particularly for young scientists, are all in the other direction.

So the heroic scientist model as the guardian of truth has severe limits, as much as we welcome and need scientists like Jim Hansen. It is truly unfortunate that while Jim and Rick Pilz and a few others have tried to keep the Bush administration from clamping down on the flow of information, many others, perhaps severalfold that number of scientists in NASA, NOAA, and other agencies, may be too frightened to speak. And who can blame them? As a result, the public discourse on climate has already been stifled. In a government dominated by one political party, there is no obvious solution to this problem within government itself. But developing a vital and scientifically educated NGO sector (as demonstrated by the recent efforts of the Union of Concerned Scientists; UCS, 2004), along with an aggressive media, would be important first steps.

This special volume also argues that science in the regulatory arena is best understood as a battle of competing interests. I will not deal here with the issue of the role of science as an interest itself that raises issues outside the current discussion. In any event, viewed as an interest group, science these days (as relevant to the environment) is in a highly weakened condition; witness the diminished role of earth observation at NASA.

Each interest in the policy arena is in a position to "purchase" the skills and knowledge of scientists. NGOs are by far the weakest in this respect, and that means the system is severely imbalanced, especially when you consider that government often acts as a representative of special interests rather than a fair broker.

Since a stronger and scientifically knowledgeable environmental NGO sector would be a critical element in assuring a properly functioning policy process (for the reasons stated earlier), the development of scientific skills at NGOs provides a welcome, if limited counterweight to the dominance of the corporate and government voices of science that usually dominate the regulatory arena.

NGOs ought to be hiring scientists, and scientifically literate people, in large numbers. And the scientific community ought to be inclusive, welcoming the "barbarian" scientists into their culture (as I was usually welcomed when in that role) with the expectation that the norms of the scientific culture itself will provide a counterweight to any imagined potential for misbehavior.

If as scientists we trust our culture, we should use it as a weapon against deception in the public debate. This aspect is particularly important because the NGO sector is not uniform: a small number of NGOs have been established to function as extensions of business interests, and while an open system cannot discriminate, it can try to tame them. Two ways to enforce scientific standards evenhandedly are to demand transparency on funding sources for all sides (something that academic scientists are just learning to do) and help journalists ask the right questions: Were your facts peer reviewed, who reviewed them (if not a journal), and what are the credentials of the reviewers?

Unfortunately, there will remain a serious imbalance because the resources of environmental NGOs (those advocating for regulation) will always be much more limited than those of the business community. Furthermore, many NGOs themselves simply do not recognize the need for scientific skill. Building intellectual infrastructure always takes a back seat to fighting today's fights. Unfortunately, the same attitude is prevalent, with a handful of sterling exceptions, among most of the foundations that support NGOs.

Additionally, all scientists need to recognize that none of us is immune from views, values, and biases that result from workplace cultures and economic pressures. But despite such bias, scientists are also influenced by the separate cultural norms, codes of ethics, and collegial relations of science itself, as outlined in detail by Merton, Kuhn, and many others. It is important for science and scientists to nurture and strengthen this separate component of their identity, this separate domain. In that way, the influence of the corporate, NGO, or government culture can be leavened or resisted to the extent it interferes with scientific judgment. Such leavening is important even if scientific judgment itself is not always perfect.

This is not a pipe dream. Some of the most insightful and fair-minded scientists I have met while participating in scientific assessments—such as the Intergovernmental Panel on Climate Change (IPCC)—are employed by companies with poor reputations among environmentalists. But it is simply not possible to distinguish their judgments from those of other participants.

A favorable development is that the various interests competing to influence environmental policy are not entirely separable entities because people flow more readily among them than before. I hope my own career becomes a model rather than a weird exception. In addition to me, the careers of David Wilcove, Gus Speth, Ellen Silbergeld, and a few others provide examples of advocates crossing the barrier into academia. The fact that I was replaced at Environmental Defense by Bill Chameides, a member of the National Academy of Sciences with a long and highly respected academic record is encouraging since it shows that the flow can go both ways. Whether more porous boundaries are a growing trend or not is unclear, but such a trend ought to be encouraged. Scientists and others in academia and in the other three sectors (NGO, government, and business) ought to facilitate the flow of people and expertise across sector boundaries over the course of individuals' careers. This mixing is one avenue for diffusing the scientific ethic. Academia in particular has been remiss in this respect.

In addition to helping to diversify career paths, the scientific "community" has an obligation to facilitate the diversification of influence over regulatory decision making by assuring adequate participation by NGO-based scientists in its community advisory mechanisms, like the NAS panels, an important objective that has often been resisted.

As noted before, the standard by which the National Academy of Sciences panels judge risk has not always been sensible. It could benefit from more NGO input.

Institutions that work to develop collegial activities among the sectors, or at least are open to equal participation by experts from all sectors, ought to be encouraged because (recent developments in cloning notwithstanding) the scientific ethic is often attractive enough and strong enough to dominate in group interactions and this is one mechanism for assuring that this ethic continually infects all participants. The relative inclusiveness, breadth and success of the IPCC provide an encouraging example.

Involvement in the IPCC or other community activities that service the policy arena, or even taking matters into one's own hands as Jim Hansen has done, is a time-consuming headache that diverts energy. But I am among those who believe that scientists have an obligation to do so.

That said, we ought to bear in mind that a strong public interest/NGO sector is no guarantee that effective and efficient policy based on science will emerge from the policy process. Nor is it a guarantee that the policy process itself will be sensible, fair, and effective. For example, no matter how many NGOs were in place with no matter how much scientific standing, it is doubtful that US climate change policy would be any different in the current government.

In a democracy like ours, the process of turning science into policy ought to be broadly participatory. In many other countries, the policy process on science and technology is an affair limited to narrow elites. This is an undemocratic approach that does not fit with the American style of policy, politics, and government, and we ought to guard against its incursion here.

I am dismayed by the condescending attitude often expressed here and abroad that somehow the average person is not smart enough or is too ignorant of statistics and probability, or is too biased by various psychological heuristics to be trusted with influence over decisions that are heavy in technical content. In fact, as my colleagues in psychology at Princeton and others (Tetlock, 2005) will tell you, experts are subject to these very same biases, and there is precious little evidence that their judgment is much more reliable than a lay person's when applied to policy-relevant questions with large uncertainty.

Exclusionary attitudes are often nothing more than an excuse to narrow the decision base so as to further serve special interests. The NGO community's claim to legitimacy with the public is based on the fact that these organizations do what they can to prevent such narrowing of the decision making process. In a world that may become ever more specialized, where there may be ever more pressure to hand decisions to elites, NGOs and activist scientists can serve as a bulwark against undemocratic and unrepresentative government. It is a capability that scientists in particular, who too often see their findings distorted and ultimately disregarded in the policy process, ought to embrace.

REFERENCES

Jasanoff, Shelia. *The Fifth Branch: Science Advisers as Policymakers*. Cambridge: Harvard University Press, 1990.

Mooney, Chris. *The Republican War on Science*. New York: Basic Books, 2005.

National Academy of Sciences. *Changing Climate*. Washington, D.C.: National Academy Press, 1983.

Oppenheimer, Michael, and Petsonk, Annie. "Article 2 of the UNFCCC: Historical Origins, Recent Interpretations." *Climatic Change* 73 (2005): 195-226.

Tetlock, Philip E. *Expert Political Judgment*. Princeton: Princeton University Press, 2005.

Union of Concerned Scientists. *Scientific Integrity in Policymaking*. Washington, D.C.: Union of Concerned Scientists, 2004.

Steven F. Hayward
Environmental Science and Public Policy

> The method of science depends on our attempts to describe
> the world with simple models. Theories that are complex
> may become untestable, even if they happen to be true.
>
> —Karl Popper (1982: 44)

IN SURVEYING THE CONTENTIOUS NATURE OF POLITICAL CONTROVERSIES
surrounding environmental science today it is tempting to adapt the
episode of *The Simpsons* called "Lisa the Skeptic," in which a judge issues
an injunction requiring that "politics is to stay at least 500 yards away
from religion at all times." Many scientists and policy analysts would
probably like to see a similar injunction issued for the separation of
science and politics, as this relationship is equally contentious and
problematic. Of course, this is not going to happen.

Clarity in understanding this hardy perennial can benefit from
disaggregating three aspects of the issue. The first aspect concerns
the hoary problem of policymaking amidst scientific uncertainty. The
second concerns institutional problems that arise from the necessarily
bureaucratic nature of both large-scale scientific research and policymaking. The third concerns a bundle of factors that complicates the
task of prediction, including the limits on a synoptic understanding of
"the environment" as well as unstated competing principles or values
that the various actors—including scientists—bring to the discourse.

The problem of "uncertainty" in science has become especially
acute in the arena of climate change science and policy today, although

controversy over uncertainty shows up in many other areas of environmental policy—especially in risk assessment of human exposure to environmental chemicals. Even though the term "uncertainty" is perfectly valid and appears frequently in scientific literature—in fact, a reference to uncertainty appears in nearly every climate science article—it has become tendentious in its everyday usage, taken often as a sign of bad faith.

Legitimate scientific uncertainty becomes magnified in the political arena for several reasons. The first is that environmental *policy* is as much as social science as it is a physical science, in large part because our understanding of "the environment" is as much social as it is scientific, insofar as it involves human beings and deeply embedded social and institutional practices. Second, environmental policy is one of the last areas of politics and policy that still proceeds according to the naïve Progressive Era hope that contentious political problems could be converted into administrative problems and managed in a noncontroversial way by highly trained experts. We still govern ourselves as much as possible according to this Wilsonian model, but in areas of purely social policy such as welfare, education, and crime, for example, we can see a consensus across the political spectrum about the sharp limits of social science to understand and prescribe policy in these matters, and therefore the limits of treating these issues in a purely administrative way. Interestingly, when it comes to the environment this view finds agreement among some environmentalists. Michael Schellenberger and Ted Nordhaus noted in their controversial essay, "The Death of Environmentalism," that the movement's political vision is severely constricted because it "became defined around using science to define the problem as 'environmental' and crafting technical policy programs as solutions" (Schellenberger and Nordhaus, 2004: 7).

Third, the magnitude of scientific uncertainty in policymaking is directly proportional to the political and especially economic stakes involved, which means that it is unlikely that legitimate uncertainties of environmental science can ever be definitively resolved to the satisfaction of all the policymakers and stakeholders. One easy way of grasping this is to compare the level of controversy over the climate science assessments of the UN's Intergovernmental Panel on Climate Change (IPCC) with the UN's parallel effort, the Millennium Ecosystem Assessment (MA), a five-year project involving the efforts of more than 1,000 scientists around the world released in March 2005. (MA, 2005.) The MA received little media coverage, and no political interest, in the United States, and fared little better overseas, even though it has a wider scope and much more sweeping policy implications than the IPCC's climate science reports. The relative quiescence greeting the MA owes to its complete disconnection from any specific policy proposal analogous to the Kyoto Protocol. Had the MA been connected with an ongoing diplomatic process as is the IPCC and with a proposal for binding international environmental treaty of some kind, it would have been front-page news and the subject of intense controversy in Washington and other national capitals (Hayward, 2006).

None of these observations are meant to imply that science and policy should be regarded as irreconcilable and therefore granted a divorce or restraining order, and still less that additional scientific research on climate or any other environmental issue is irrelevant. One problem is perhaps that science is too good at what it does. Daniel Sarewitz, director of the Consortium for Science, Policy, and Outcomes at Arizona State University, focuses the point admirably in a 2004 article in *Environmental Science and Policy*:

> [S]cience does its job all too well. . . . [N]ature itself—the reality out there—is sufficiently rich and complex to support a science enterprise of enormous methodological, disciplinary, and institutional diversity. . . . [S]cience, in doing its job well, presents this richness through a proliferation of facts assembled via a variety of disciplinary lenses, in ways that can legitimately support, and are causally indistinguishable from, a range of competing, value-based political positions. . . . In areas as diverse as climate change, nuclear waste disposal, endangered species and biodiver-

sity, forest management, air and water pollution, and agricultural biotechnology, the growth of considerable bodies of scientific knowledge, created especially to resolve political dispute and enable effective decision-making, has often been accompanied instead by growing political controversy and gridlock (Sarewitz, 2004: 386).

Consider a small-bore example of the problem Sarewitz brings to our attention: in 1985 scientists with the US Geological Survey (USGS) estimated a 95 percent probability of a midsized earthquake occurring along the San Andreas fault near Parkfield by 1993. A number of peer reviewers and other geological experts endorsed the statistical analysis that prompted this prediction, which is one reason the USGS, which seldom allows its scientists to issue earthquake predictions, did so in this case. It did not happen. It did not matter that it did not happen. Parkfield is located in a very sparsely populated region of California. (Maybe, by the way, the prediction was sound, and the nonoccurrence of the predicted quake fell within the 5 percent probability of error.) We cannot be certain. The political and economic stakes of the prediction were low, so the uncertainty, small thought it seemed, did not matter.

Imagine, however, if the USGS had issued a prediction with 95 percent certainty of a midsized earthquake in San Francisco or Los Angeles instead. All hell would have broken loose. The "certainty" of the prediction would have come under heavy fire; the research would have been reviewed by a wider circle of seismologists and scientists in other disciplines, and it is likely that the unanimity of opinion would have evaporated, or that the USGS scientists would have been much more reticent about their certainty, and, finally, that the USGS might not have let the scientists make their prediction public.

With this in mind let us turn to the whiplash quality of some of the discussion about uncertainty in climate science, and the problem this poses for policymakers confronting mitigation policy costs running well into the trillions of dollars. This best comes to sight not on the larger scheme of climate models and range of temperature predictions, but on some of the tertiary aspects that have policy relevance for any number of prospective adaptive responses to a warmer world. Consider, for example, the well-known El Niño Southern Oscillation (ENSO) phenomenon. Will El Niño occur more frequently and with more severe effects with global warming, or will the phenomenon lessen in severity? This question has significant policy relevance for different regions of the United States. If severe El Niño were to become a frequent occurrence, California and the southwestern United States would need to make major adjustments to cope with the threat of flooding, though it should be mentioned that, on balance, the increased precipitation of El Niño years has net benefits for the Southwest, chiefly a more ample water supply. But some expensive adaptations would need to be made for flood control, erosion, and water storage. On the other hand, if El Niño diminishes with a warmer world, then these expensive adaptations would be largely wasted. Conversely, high El Niño years typically correlate with diminished hurricane and tropical storm activity in the Atlantic, because El Niño increases Atlantic wind shear that thwarts the organization of strong tropical storms. (El Niño also tends to make conditions warmer and drier in Africa.) An increasing frequency of El Niño would mean a reduced risk of hurricane activity for the eastern and gulf coasts of the United States. On the other hand, a suppressed El Niño would mean the opposite, and the resources spent adapting to potentially higher El Niño activity on the West Coast would be better spent on the gulf coast.

With this binary outcome in mind, consider British climate scientist Mark Maslin's summary of the matter:

> Most computer models of the El Niño Southern Oscillation are inconclusive; some have found an increase and others have found none. This is, therefore, one part of the climate system that we do not know how global warming will affect. Not only does ENSO have a direct impact on global climate but it also affects the numbers, intensity, and pathways of

hurricanes and cyclones, and the strength and timing of the Asian monsoon. Hence, when discussing the potential impacts of global warming, one of the greatest unknowns is the variation of ENSO and its knock-on effects on the rest of the global climate system (Maslin, 2004: 93-94).

One of the frustrations of the climate change issue is how fast our understanding of different aspects are superseded or modified by the rapid pace of published research, often a statement like Maslin's, from a book that is only two years old, is overtaken by events. And sometimes the science simply deepens rather than resolves the uncertainty. In July 2005, *Science* reported on a paleoclimatology study that attempted to discern changes in ENSO in the Pliocene era (roughly 3 million years ago), when the world's average temperature was about 3 degrees centigrade warmer than it is today (and therefore close to what future temperature might be a century from now). The relevance is obvious: "By showing how the tropical Pacific worked the last time the world got hot," *Science* reported, "climatologists hope the Pliocene will help them forecast what to expect next time." Climatologists and policymakers alike are going to have to wait longer for the answer, as *Science* explained: "Two teams of researchers, studying the same evidence with the same techniques, have painted diametrically opposite pictures of a key period in the history of the Earth's climate." After discussing how the two research teams managed to reach conflicting conclusions, *Science* correspondent Richard Kerr hits the macro-keystroke for the common theme: "Researchers say only more research can settle what really happened during the Pliocene" (Kerr, 2005: 687).

The same kind of confounding findings can be found in *Nature* as well, also sometimes within the same issue or single article. One hot topic—no pun intended—in the field is possible changes of Atlantic ocean currents (often called the "global conveyer belt"; the technical term is "thermohaline circulation"). A disruption of the warm northward flow of the Gulf Stream from melting arctic and Greenland ice could have the ironic effect of much cooler temperatures in Europe and the northeastern United States. (This essentially is the scenario portrayed in the feature film *The Day After Tomorrow*, although sped up to the time frame of a single week rather than the decades the process would actually require.) In December 2005, *Nature* published a paper presenting new data that suggests that circulation in one key equatorial segment of the Gulf Stream had slowed 30 percent between 1957 and 2004, a change the authors characterize as "robust" (Bryden, 2005). The authors were careful to point out, however, the wide range of "uncertainty" in their data, noting that "the observed changes are uncomfortably close to these uncertainties." It will be a surprise to most readers that systematic ocean monitoring to gather large-scale data about the matter has only recently begun. *Nature* editorialized that "more measurements are clearly needed if we are to fill the enormous gaps in our knowledge of ocean behavior," and *Nature*'s climate correspondent Quirin Schiermeier observed that, "Even in a new age of constant monitoring and improved modeling, it will be some time before the likelihood, and the probably effects, of a thermohaline circulation slowdown can be predicted with accuracy" (Schiermeier, 2006b: 260). This kind of confounding and contradictory research appears in the mass media almost daily. The May 30, 2006, issue of *USA Today*, for example, carried the headline "A Warmer World May, Or May Not, Be Wetter."

At this point a policymaker might begin to throw up her hands and repair to an axiom of the philosopher of science Karl Popper: "The method of science depends on our attempts to describe the world with simple models. Theories that are complex may become untestable, even if they happen to be true." Add the complications of political decision-making on top of this, and the wonder is that any policy gets made at all.

THIS IS NOT INTENDED AS A BRIEF FOR CLIMATE SKEPTICISM; RATHER, IT is intended to suggest why uncertainty matters to policymaking. This is better understood by shifting attention to the second main theme, which is the difficulty our necessarily bureaucratic policy process has dealing with scientific controversy and dissent even on small points, let alone large ones. Here it is best to avert our gaze from the IPCC and climate change and consider the simpler case of the California Air Resources Board (CARB) and the regulation of ozone—a comparatively modest enterprise from a policymaking point of view.

A strange thing is happening in California at the moment: a disproportionate number of high ozone days are occurring on weekends, which on the surface is counterintuitive since emissions on Saturday and Sundays, especially from cars and trucks, are about 40 percent lower than on weekdays. This "weekend effect," as it is obviously called, is well known among environmental scientists, who have long understood that ground-level ozone formation is a nonlinear process, in which different ratios of nitrogen oxides (NO_x) and volatile organic compounds and hydrocarbons (VOCs) yield wildly different levels of ambient ozone, depending on conditions. The phenomenon is not fully understood, however, as can be seen by the fact that the weekend effect does not happen uniformly across the country. It is not seen in Atlanta or in Texas cities, for example.

A number of scientists with the CARB predicted some years ago we would begin to see this, ironically, as emissions fell, and as the phenomenon began to appear, some of these scientists made the heterodox suggestion that CARB's emissions reduction strategy was wrongheaded. Right now California, along with other parts of the nation, is embarked on a vigorous program to reduce NO_x emissions, ultimately by more than 90 percent from current levels. Question: What will happen to weekday ozone levels a few years from now when the emissions profile on weekdays looks just like the emissions profile of weekends right now? Ozone levels are likely to get worse for a time, even as emissions fall. Eventually a downward trend of ambient ozone will resume when NO_x emissions fall very low, but in the meantime what are we likely to hear about this spike in ozone from environmental activists and politicians? As the "weekend effect" anomaly was coming into focus a small group of CARB scientists recommended that the phasing of emissions reduction strategy ought to be reserved, such that NO_x reductions would take a back seat to VOC reductions. But CARB steadfastly refuses to entertain any second thoughts.

All of those scientists have left CARB—most for other government science jobs—because of their frustration with what they see as CARB's refusal to undertake an open reconsideration of the policy implications of this anomaly. CARB's attitude seems to be, as one observer put it, "Damn the science—full speed ahead." And the scientific consensus seems to be moving more and more against CARB's intransigence. The *Journal of the Air and Waste Management Association*, the peer-reviewed journal of practitioners in the field, put together a special issue devoted to the weekend effect in 2003, and invited the CARB to submit a paper defending its scientific perspective on the issue. The *Journal's* reviewers rejected CARB's paper as insufficient (Lawson, 2003; Schwartz and Hayward, 2004.)

There is another side to CARB's scientific intransigence, however, that should be considered. For CARB in California, like the Environmental Protectiona Agency (EPA) in Washington, it can take sometimes up to 10 years or longer to get a large new regulatory rule adopted and implemented. Between the required notice, hearings, consultations with the stakeholders, and the inevitable litigation, our environmental policy resembles the proverbial supertanker: slow to get going, hard to turn, and difficult to stop once under way. If CARB had to pause and entertain a fundamental reconsideration of its basic science and its regulatory sequencing every time a group of its scientists raised an anomaly and an alternate interpretation, the already slow and excruciating process would grind to a halt. It would introduce an element of seeming capriciousness that would be intolerable. Among others, the private sector—the "regulated community," as it curiously calls itself—would scream bloody murder.

Now let us return to the IPCC, which, while not a policymaking body like the EPA or CARB, has nonetheless some of the same kind of difficulties that beset the EPA and CARB. In the abstract the IPCC deserves its due. The effort to get to the bottom of climate change is perhaps the largest scientific inquiry in human history. It requires the coordination of thousands of specialists, the development of whole new scientific techniques, and the refinement of elaborate computer models that need weeks to run on the most powerful supercomputers. Even accounting for the inherent weaknesses of computer models for any subject, this kind of sustained effort is going to generate valuable knowledge in the fullness of time. Producing a coherent report every few years that combines all of this work is an extraordinary feat.

The difficulty is that a massive effort at synthesis and consensus will be frustrating to those scientists who hold heterodox but possibly valid views. The process cannot accommodate this very well, and still finish its work or say something useful. It is therefore a reasonable criticism that the scientists and experts participating in each iteration have become increasingly self-selected in a manner that overstates the consensus. Heterodox scientists qualified to participate have found the consensus-oriented IPCC process too frustrating and have dropped out; for example, Richard Lindzen, the Sloan professor of meteorology at MIT, a participant and principal chapter author in the IPCC's Third Assessment Report (TAR) in 2001, is not participating in the Fourth Assessment Report (FAR), and has said some very harsh things about the IPCC in recent years. NOAA hurricane researcher Chris Landsea quit the IPCC in 2005 because of what he saw as its increasing politicization, followed not long after by Roger Pielke, Sr.

It is in the nature of large bureaucracies to become echo chambers over time, chiefly because they develop a culture commensurate with their mission. "Every organization has a culture," political scientist James Q. Wilson reminds us in his lengthy study of bureaucracy; "that is, a persistent, patterned way of thinking about the central tasks of and human relationships within an organization. Culture is to an organization what personality is to an individual" (Wilson, 1989: 91). It should not be surprising to find that an organization set up to determine what might be the threshold level of greenhouse gases beyond which the world might experience catastrophic consequences will acquire a bias toward scientific findings that confirm its organizational premise, and discount confounding findings. Such organizations also become resistant to honest criticism.

The IPCC has not merely rejected criticism; it has also, in the fashion of environmental activists, sometimes demonized its reasonable critics. The case of David Henderson and Ian Castles is a good example. Henderson, the former chief economist of the Organization for Economic Cooperation and Development, and Castles, a highly regarded Australian economist, noticed a serious methodological anomaly in the IPCC's 100-year greenhouse gas emission forecasts that are the primary input for the computer climate models (Castles and Henderson, 2003). Henderson and Castles made a compelling argument that many of the emissions forecasts (a suite of 40 different forecasts is used in climate modeling) were unrealistically high. Everyone recalls the first day of computer science class: garbage in, garbage out. If future greenhouse gas emissions are badly overestimated, then even the perfect computer climate model will spit out a false temperature prediction. If the emissions forecasts are unrealistically high, it would mean the problem of climate change may unfold much more slowly (if at all) than current scenarios predict. In any case, the controversy highlights the methodological difficulties of combining social and physical sciences into a single analytical framework.

Since Henderson's and Castles' initial critique, the IPCC's emissions forecasts have been subject to withering criticisms from dozens of other reputable economists, including a number of climate action advocates who, to their credit, argue that this crucial question should be got right (McKibbin, Pearce, and Stegman, 2004.) Moreover, despite the cascade of criticism of the IPCC's emissions forecasts, the FAR is going to use the same set of emissions forecasts for its next round of climate models, assuring that the argument over emissions forecasting will go on for several more years. The IPCC says it would take too long to do a fresh set of forecasts. Despite the IPCC's wall of resistance, the consensus view is coming around to the Castles and Henderson view that the IPCC has done a poor job of handling this important aspect of the issue. *Nature* magazine, normally more closely aligned with climate activists, editorialized in January 2006 that the IPCC's "macroeconomic assumptions . . . ought really to be discarded," and criticized the IPCC for not incorporating "economists' latest thinking" in their next assessment. "There is a growing feeling," *Nature*'s climate correspondent Quirin Schiermeier wrote, "that the economic assumptions on which [the IPCC's] work is based are outdated and unreliable" (Schiermeier, 2006a).

Yet the IPCC's reaction to Henderson and Castles was startling. It issued a vituperative press release blasting Henderson and Castles for peddling "disinformation." The economists and scientists who developed the emissions scenarios that Castles and Henderson criticized tacitly acknowledge the cloistered culture of the IPCC in a reply: "IPCC is not a debating society. It is an assessment body. It does not normally produce responses to individual researchers outside the context of a document review process, or, except out of courtesy when member governments have requested special attention for a particular issue or comment" (Nakicenovic et al., 2003). A few scientists and economists connected with the IPCC had the decency to say publicly that the press release was a regrettable error.

And then consider the case of Bjorn Lomborg, who assembled a panel of eminent economists, including four Nobel Prize winners, to produce the calculation that near-term greenhouse emissions reductions make little economic sense. They were not the first to do this, and the whole exercise turns on the well-established economic principle of discounting future costs and benefits. Now, traditional economic discounting can be criticized on a number of grounds when applied to climate change. However, the IPCC's chairman, Rajendra Pachauri, reacted instead by deploying the *reductio ad Hitlerum*. Pauchuri told a Danish newspaper in 2004 that, "What is the difference between Lomborg's view of humanity and Hitler's? If you were to accept Lomborg's way of thinking, then maybe what Hitler did was the right thing." It doesn't do much to build confidence in an organization whose chairman can say something that self-evidently offensive and keep his job.

THERE IS PROBABLY NO REMEDY FOR THE IPCC'S INSULARITY AND SELF-selection bias that has led inevitably to its politicization short of a full-scale competitive effort at climate science assessment similar to the famous CIA "Team B" exercise in the mid-1970s ("Team B" was the rival CIA assessment of the Soviet Union's military strength conducted in 1976). Given the scale of climate science inquiry, however, such a parallel competitive process is probably not practical.

The credibility and acceptance of science-based policy inquiry like the IPCC is vitally important because of the widespread public perception that many past efforts at broad scale environmental forecasting have been so erroneous. There are inherent limitations to what "better science" can hope to accomplish. It is an oversimplification to say that the core of science consists of replicable experiments; moreover, how can you replicate an experiment about something that has not happened yet, which is the case when we are trying to forecast the future? We are getting better at looking ahead—the Millennium Assessment represents a break with some past attempts at large-scale futurology, for example—though for epistemological reasons there remains a strong case for skepticism that we can ever achieve complete mastery in our understanding of the future course of nature. Politicians and policymakers are rightly cautious about embracing potentially expensive policy regimes based on exercises in synoptic futurology.

The problem, politically, is that, as *New York Times* columnist Nicholas Kristof put it in a column in 2005: "Environmentalists have an awful track record, so they've lost credibility with the public. . . . I was once an environmental groupie, and I still share the movement's broad aims, but I'm now skeptical of the movement's 'I Have a Nightmare' speeches. . . . [E]nvironmental alarms have been screeching for so long that, like car alarms, they are now just an irritating background noise" (Kristof, 2005). Kristof is referring to predictions that were once front-page news of the population bomb, imminent resource scarcity, or even—in the 1970s—the idea that earth was on the brink of a new ice age. Fellow columnist George Will recently pointed out the extensive media coverage of the idea:

Science magazine (Dec. 10, 1976) warned of "extensive Northern Hemisphere glaciation." *Science Digest* (February

1973) reported that "the world's climatologists are agreed" that we must "prepare for the next ice age."

The Christian Science Monitor ("Warning: Earth's Climate is Changing Faster than Even Experts Expect," Aug. 27, 1974) reported that glaciers "have begun to advance," "growing seasons in England and Scandinavia are getting shorter" and "the North Atlantic is cooling down about as fast as an ocean can cool."

Newsweek agreed ("The Cooling World," April 28, 1975) that meteorologists "are almost unanimous" that catastrophic famines might result from the global cooling that *The New York Times* (Sept. 14, 1975) said "may mark the return to another ice age."

The *Times* (May 21, 1975) also said "a major cooling of the climate is widely considered inevitable" now that it is "well established" that the Northern Hemisphere's climate "has been getting cooler since about 1950" (Will, 2006).

It is sometimes considered bad form to cite these not-so-distant embarrassments, and mention of the ice age alarm is dismissed today as a minor sideshow that few scientists took seriously. This is convenient revisionism. The EPA, for example, was sufficiently worried about the idea in the early 1970s that it figured into their thinking about the urgency of regulating sulfate aerosols as rapidly as possible.

The past record of environmental false alarms raises directly the specter of the old moral fable of crying wolf, such that, when we read that many climate scientists believe we only have a decade to turn the tide against catastrophic climate change, even if this time it is correct, the public and policymakers have applied a steep discount to these kind of claims because they have been heard so often in the past in almost identical language.

For example, consider this warning of the secretary general of the United Nations: "Members of the United Nations have perhaps 10 years left in which to subordinate their ancient quarrels and launch a global partnership . . . to improve the human environment, to defuse the population explosion, and to supply the required momentum to development efforts." The secretary general who made this comment was not Kofi Annan, but U Thant, in 1971. Likewise, James Gustave Speth, one of the prime movers behind the *Global 2000* report released in 1980 whose predictions for resources trends and environmental conditions in the year 2000 proved to be hugely inaccurate, is unchastened, writing in his recent book, *Red Sky at Dawn,* that right now "may be our last chance to get it right before we reap an appalling deterioration of our natural assets."

The environmental movement has squandered much of its moral authority with grandiose statements of this kind. This recurring cast of mind forces to the surface the deeper question of why the neo-Malthusian framework of most environmental meta-analysis generates a pessimistic answer before the specific questions are even asked. Why are all potential climate surprises assumed to be negative, even though the IPCC TAR includes substantial material on the benefits of moderate warming? More fundamentally, why is all environmental change, especially if traceable to human intervention, presumed to be adverse? The tacit scientific premise seems to be that the earth's environment should be a steady-state equilibrium, under which any human disturbance is harmful. But this has never been the case, and such a premise is as much an ethical or philosophical judgment as it is a scientific judgment, because the answer turns in part on one's opinion of humankind's place in the hierarchy of nature. This is seldom argued out, in part because it falls on the wrong side of the fact-value dichotomy in modern thought.

A more precise scientific query is why broad-scale environmental forecasting seems to have undergone no reforms or substantial revisions on account of the earlier forecasting errors. A good example of this phenomenon is the *Limits to Growth: The 30-Year Update:* "We are *not* predicting that a particular future will take place. . . . We do not believe that available data and theories will ever permit accurate predictions of what will happen to the world over the coming century." So far, so good. But like an Alcoholic Anonymous member on the fifth of the 12 steps who succumbs when walking by a well-lit tavern, two paragraphs later the authors go on a bender: "Sadly, we believe the world will experience overshoot and collapse in global resource use and emissions much the same as was the dot.com bubble—though on a much larger time scale" (Meadows, Rander, and Meadows, 2004: xix, xxi).

A handful of prominent environmentalists have acknowledged the mistakes of the earlier generation of environmental forecasters. This occurred most notably during the controversy over Bjorn Lomborg's *The Skeptical Environmentalist*, when some environmentalists complained that Lomborg's "litany" of environmental doom amounted to a "straw man." Allen Hammond of the World Resources Institute, for example, argued at a public forum in October 2001 that Lomborg's litany "paints a caricature of the environmental agenda based on sometimes mistaken views widely held 30 years ago, *but to which no serious environmental institution subscribes today*" (Hammond, 2001. Emphasis added.). Michael Grubb of Cambridge University, one of Britain's leading environmental figures, wrote in a *Science* magazine review of Lomborg that "to any professional, it is no news at all that the 1972 *Limits to Growth* study was mostly wrong or that Paul Ehrlich and Lester Brown have perennially exaggerated the problems of food supply" (Grubb, 2001).

But self-criticism has also appeared more recently. *Nature* magazine, which is normally friendly to conventional environmentalism (Ehrlich publishes frequently in *Nature*), published a harsh review of Speth's *Red Sky at Morning*. *Nature*'s reviewer wrote: "It is perhaps surprising to find a man with Speth's record resurrecting the doctrine of the doomsters of the 1970s that we will soon exhaust Earth's limited resources. Such forecasts have proven wildly inaccurate. . . . Remedies prescribed by doctors who continually misdiagnose diseases should not be swallowed uncritically. Speth shows as little regard for contemporary evidence as he does for the reliability of previous forecasts of doom. . . . Speth raises serious issues, but they deserve a more balanced treatment than the prescriptions in his book" (Taverne, 2004).

These acknowledgements of past prediction error remain the distinct minority, however. The reason there has been little discernible revision to the Malthusian outlook that informs most environmental projections is that it has not entertained any second thoughts about the fundamental equation used to approach environmental meta-analysis. This is Paul Ehrlich's famous I = PAT formula, where I represents the adverse human impact on the earth, with P standing for population, A for affluence, and T for technology. Speth explicitly embraces this formula, as does the IPCC (the Millennium Assessment, as noted above, is a partial exception to this general phenomenon). Few environmentalists seem to be aware of the strong criticisms of I = PAT (Goklany, 2001, 2003). While environmentalists have grudgingly come to accept the necessity of economic growth (the "A" term of the equation) and recognize that the population bomb ("P") is turning into more of a wet firecracker, there remains a constant skepticism of technology. "Technology will not save us," both Speth and Ehrlich write. Maybe so, but can this be said to be a *scientific* judgment? How do we *know* that there will be no scientific breakthroughs in energy, genetics, or nano-technology that may enable us to mitigate or reverse environmental damage?

Instead of wrestling with the defects in and criticisms of I = PAT, scientists and the advocates of a supposed "scientific perspective" on environmental problems self-referentially repair to the argument of authority, such as the 1992 "World Scientists' Warning to Humanity" report. This statement was signed by 1,600 scientists, including 102 Nobel laureates, so it must be true:

> Human beings and the natural world are on a collision
> course. Human activities inflict harsh and often irrevers-

ible damage on the environment and on critical resources. If not checked, many of our current practices put at serious risk the future that we wish for human society and the plant and animal kingdoms and may so alter the living world that it will be unable to sustain life in the manner that we know. Fundamental changes are urgent if we are to avoid the collision our present course will bring about (Union of Concerned Scientists, 1992).

The opinions of scientists in their particular fields are surely worth heeding, but when they offer synoptic judgments about the future of the world, are their judgments inherently better than, say, economists? (And if Nobel Prizes were de facto certifications of general authority, then why did we dismiss the social prognostications of Nobel physics laureate William Shockley?)

Moreover, even if the synoptic predictions could be judged to have scientific validity, science does not automatically prescribe what political strategies should be adopted, let alone offer any insight into the economic and social trade-offs that all policy involves. Too often scientific concern for the environment comes to sight as special pleading that the superior intelligence and authority of science should have special recognition, along with a disdain for the ordinary features of democratic consent.

Indeed, scientists may be less well equipped than ordinary citizens when it comes to having common sense about social and political problems. The Harvard geneticist Richard Lewontin wrote in the *New York Review of Books*: "Most scientists are, at a minimum, liberals, although it is by no means obvious why this should be so. Despite the fact that all of the molecular biologists of my acquaintance are shareholders in or advisers to biotechnology firms, the chief political controversy in the scientific community seems to be whether it is wise to vote for Ralph Nader this time" (Lewontin, 2004). This does not inspire a lot of confidence in the political judgment of scientists.

The political responses of most scientists tend to come in two varieties: hopelessly vague, and hopelessly naïve. One good example is Jared Diamond's magisterial recent book *Collapse: How Societies Choose to Fail or Succeed*. After hundreds of pages of remarkably intricate detail about the problems of past collapsed civilizations, Diamond concludes with a load of windy generalities about the "failures of group decision-making on the part of whole societies or other groups." After a tour of factors that contribute to this problem, Diamond reduces the matter to a problem of *values*: "Perhaps the crux of success of failure as a society is to know which core values to hold on to, and which ones to discard and replace with new values when times change." This is merely a restatement of the rationalist fallacy, and supposes that "society" is a collective entity that can pick and choose its values as easily and authoritatively as a consumer might shop for a faucet at a hardware store. There follows an utterly conventional tour of all the clichés of "groupthink" and the importance of outstanding national leaders, about having the "courage to practice long-term thinking, and to make bold, courageous, anticipatory decisions at a time when problems become perceptible but before they have reached crisis proportions." Don't forget also the "courage to make painful decisions about values." Not much specific advice for a policymaker to go on. This is portrayed as a matter of simple *will*; there is no consideration of institutional problems let alone any acknowledgement of trade-offs. What, exactly, would Diamond recommend as between a carbon tax or a tradable emissions system?

Diamond might quite reasonably say—I am not a political scientist, and this is beyond my range. That is fine, though we should note that even the politicians who view our environmental future with deep alarm often strike a pose that suggests that they really do not have any idea of what to do either. The case of former Vice President Al Gore is fascinating in this regard; in his famous book *Earth in the Balance*, he describes our civilization as "deeply dysfunctional" and calls for a "wrenching transformation" of society. Again, these can hardly be considered scientific judgments. Similarly Gus Speth in *Red Sky at*

Morning calls for "the most fundamental transition of all, a transition in culture and consciousness."

Paul Ehrlich actually tries to grasp the nettles of this problem in a serious way in his most recent book, *One with Nineveh*. Ehrlich favors junking the EPA in favor of a Federal Environmental Authority (FEA) modeled after the political independence and power of the Federal Reserve—precisely because the Fed is "insulated from day-to-day politics" (Ehrlich and Ehrlich, 2004). Never mind the purely cognitive problem of making wise resource allocation decisions in such an institutional arrangement; the more troublesome feature of this idea is Ehrlich clarity that his agenda of governmentally imposed "constraint" (his term) cannot succeed in a free democracy.

Gus Speth similarly points to "U.S. regulatory agencies like the Federal Trade Commission and the Food and Drug Administration, which, operating under broad 'public interest' mandates from Congress, set rules and norms in their areas. A small group of appointed officials is, in effect, writing laws for the country, subject, to be sure, to congressional oversight and reversal. *One could imagine a world environment agency like these federal agencies*" (emphasis added). No, actually, one cannot imagine such a thing on a global scale.

This leads to one of Gus Speth's general complaints about the state of environmental politics and policy today: "I often ask myself why more American conservatives do not more actively seek to conserve America. Part of the answer, I suspect, lies in the point made by Benjamin Barber. Environmental challenges threaten the ascendant pro-market, antigovernment ideology. They require major governmental responses, including action at the international level. They require 'interference' with the market to ensure that social and environmental goals are served." This is exactly correct; stripped of Speth's pejorative construction here, Speth is right: conservatives understand that the solutions Speth and the other authors on display here propose would be worse than the problems they purport to solve. There are worse things than a warmer world, and one of them is an entirely cavalier attitude toward the huge expansion and reach of government power such schemes propose. It is one thing to have intelligent disagreement with the conservative philosophy of limited government (see, for example, the thoughtful criticisms of Cass Sunstein or Michael Sandel). Speth clearly does not have any respect for, or understanding of, conservative points of view.

The *Limits to Growth: The 30-Year Updated* team is a little more realistic that "a world of strict, centralized government control" of the environment is not possible, but they still indulge in some wishful thinking about how the world should be changed:

> It doesn't take much imagination to come up with a minimum set of social structures—feedback loops that carry new information about costs, consequences, and sanctions—that would allow evolution, creativity, and change, and permit many more freedoms than would ever be possible in a world that continues to crowd against or exceed its limits. One of the most important of these new rules would fit in perfectly with economic theory: It would combine knowledge and regulation to "internalize the externalities" of the market system, so that the price of a product would reflect the full costs (including all environmental and social side effects) of making the product. This is a measure every economics textbook has called for (in vain) for decades. It would automatically guide investments and purchases, so people could make choices in the monetary realm that they would not later regret in the realm of material and social worth (Meadows, Randers, and Meadows, 2004: 257).

Never mind whether this idea is truly consistent with "economic theory"; clearly none of these authors has ever set foot inside a federal regulatory agency. It is ironic that these prophets of our lack of perception of environmental reality have so little perception of political and policy reality.

As democratic citizens, scientists should be encouraged along with all other citizens to speak their views on important matters, though, as equal citizens, their views deserve no more or no less weight than their fellow citizens merely by the fact of their being scientists. If that were the case then political scientists would rightly rule. Sustainable environmental policy can only be formed with the popular consent of the governed, and taking account of a number of institutional and economic realities that cannot be wished away merely because they are uncongenial.

REFERENCES

Bryden, H., H. Longworth, and S. Cunningham. "Slowing of the Atlantic Meridional Overturning Circulation at 25 Degrees N." *Nature* 438 (Dec. 1, 2005): 655-657.

Castles, I., and D. Henderson. "The IPCC Emission Scenarios: An Economic-Statistical Critique." *Energy and Environment* 14:2-3 (2003): 159-185.

Diamond, Jared. *Collapse: How Societies Choose to Fail or Succeed*. New York: Viking, 2005.

Ehrlich, Paul, and Anne Ehrlich. *One with Nineveh: Politics, Consumption, and the Human Future*. Washington, D.C.: Island Press, 2004.

Goklany, Indur. *Economic Growth and the State of Humanity*. Bozeman, Mont.: Political Economy Research Center, 2001.

———. "The Future of the Industrial System." *Perspectives on Industrial Ecology*. Eds. D. Bourg and S. Erkman. Sheffield, UK: Greenleaf Publishing, 2003: 194-222.

Grubb, Michael. "Relying on Manna from Heaven?" *Science* (November 9, 2001): 1285.

Hammond, Allen. Remarks delivered at forum of the American Enterprise Institute-Brookings Institution Joint Center for Regulatory Studies, October 3, 2001. Transcript on file with author.

Hayward, Steven F. "Fate of the World Redux: Assessing the Millennium Ecosystem Assessment." *Environmental Policy Outlook* 1 (March 20, 2006) <http://www.aei.org/publications/pubID.24076/pub_detail.asp>.

Kerr, Richard A. "El Niño or La Niña? The Past Hints at the Future." *Science* (July 29, 2005): 687.

Kristof, Nicholas D. "I Have a Nightmare." *New York Times*, March 12, 2005.

Lawson, D. L. "The Weekend Effect: The Weekly Ambient Emissions Control Experiment." *Environmental Manager* (July 2003).

Lewontin, Richard. "Dishonesty in Science." *New York Review of Books* (November 18, 2004): 39.

Maslin, Mark. *Global Warming: A Very Short Introduction.* London: Oxford University Press, 2004.

McKibbin, Warwick, David Pearce, and Alison Stegman. "Can the IPCC SRES Be Improved?" Working Paper, Lowy Institute for International Policy, 2004 <http://www.lowyinstitute.org/Publication.asp?pid=129>.

Meadows, D., J. Rander, and D. Meadows. *Limits to Growth: The 30-Year Update.* White River Junction, N.H.: Chelsea Press, 2004.

Millennium Ecosystem Assessment. March 2005 <http://www.millenniumassessment.org/en/index.aspx>.

Nakicenovic, N., et al. "IPCC SRES Revisited: A Response." *Energy and Environment* 14:2-3 (2003): 210.

Popper, Karl. *The Open Universe.* London: Hutchinson, 1982.

Sarewitz, Daniel. "How Science Makes Environmental Controversies Worse." *Environmental Science and Policy* 7 (2004).

Schiermeier, Q. "The Costs of Global Warming." *Nature* 439 (Jan. 26, 2006a): 374-375.

———. "A Sea Change." *Nature* 439 (Jan. 19, 2006b): 260.

Shellenberg, Michael, and Ted Nordhaus. "The Death of Environmentalism" (2004) <http://www.thebreakthrough.org/images/Death_of_Environmentalism.pdf>.

Schwartz, Joel, and Steven F. Hayward. "Emissions Down, Smog Up. Say What?" *Environmental Policy Outlook* (January-February 2004) <http://www.aei.org/publications/pubID.19746/pub_detail.asp>.

Speth, James G. *Red Sky at Morning.* New Haven: Yale University Press, 2004.

Taverne, Dick. "When Greens See Red." *Nature* (November 25, 2004): 443-444.

Will, George F. "Combating 'Warming' Is Still Up for Debate." *Washington Post,* April 2, 2006.

Wilson, James Q. *Bureaucracy: What Government Agencies Do and Why They Do It.* New York: Basic Books, 1989.

"World Scientists' Warning to Humanity." Union of Concerned Scientists. 1992 <http://www.ucsusa.org/ucs/about/page.cfm?pageID=1009>.

Paul R. Ehrlich
Environmental Science Input to Public Policy

AN EARLY VERSION OF THE AGENDA OF THE CONFERENCE ON POLITICS
and science at the New School stated: "Public policy is determined
through careful balancing of various interests, including science." The
meaning of this statement was somewhat obscure—what, for example,
is the "interest" of science and what sort of entity is "science"? But I
suppose it represents the view that a balancing of inputs from scientists
or a consensus of the scientific community and those of other interested parties enters at an appropriate level into the formation of policy.
That level, in my view, is as far as possible supplying a factual background that should be taken into account when values enter the mix in
the formulation of policy. But if that is the case, it is crystal clear that
in the area of environmental policy the statement is very often dead
wrong. Indeed, it is easy to come up with examples in which scientific
input has not been given remotely the attention it deserves in policy
formation, while there are other cases in which such input, at the very
least, has pointed policy in the right direction. I will first look in some
detail at a sample of what I and most of my colleagues would consider
the many failures to consider the scientific input and draw appropriate
conclusions, such as in population policy. Then I will examine briefly
some successes and partial successes, such as the Clean Air Act. Finally,
I will see what might be said about why the failures have been worse
in some areas than others, and why in some circumstances the level of
scientific input was recognized and taken seriously.

SCIENTIFIC INPUT IGNORED OR UNDERVALUED

Egregious examples where the inputs of science to environmental policy have been given too little weight or were totally overwhelmed by other inputs are easy to come by. Perhaps most dramatic is the total lack of population policy in what might be considered the world's most overpopulated nation, the United States of America (Ehrlich and Ehrlich, 1989b; 1990; 1991). A nation of 300 million people (third largest in the world), with by far the highest level of per capita consumption of any large nation and heavily dependent on imports, should have population policy at the top of its list. The life support systems around the world being destroyed to support that consumption, of course, are also those that will be required to support future generations—including those in the United States.

Population size and growth rate are largely absent not only from policy but from public discourse, even though virtually every environmental problem nationally and globally is exacerbated by population growth, as the scientific community has repeatedly pointed out (Brown, 1954; Daily et al., 1998; Ehrlich, 1968; Ehrlich and Ehrlich, 2005; Ehrlich and Holdren, 1971; National Academy of Sciences USA, 1993; Union of Concerned Scientists, 1993; Vogt, 1948). Of course, one does not need to be a rocket scientist to see the connection. More people, *ceteris paribus*, mean more greenhouse gases released to the atmosphere (and thus more rapid climate change), more natural ecosystems paved over, more tropical forests cut down, more toxic substances injected into the environment, more extensive and intensive agriculture, more water needed for households, industry, and irrigation, and so on.

But all is *not* equal. Human beings are bright apes—they bring the richest land under agriculture first, get water from the nearest, most convenient sources first, mine the most concentrated ores before those that have only traces of the desired metal, exploit the shallowest, most extensive oil deposits that will flow naturally before drilling down thousands of feet, opening fields under shallow seas, and injecting steam to thin recalcitrant oil so it can be pumped to the surface. So, on average, each person added to the population has *disproportionate* negative impacts on the environment as poorer soils are cultivated to feed her, water is brought from more distant, more polluted sources to supply her, poorer ores are mined to manufacture things for her, and oil wells are drilled deeper and the oil transported farther to power her SUV. All of these activities require additional energy, and the level of energy use is the best quick and dirty measure of a person's (or a society's) impact on the environment (Ehrlich and Ehrlich, 2005; Ehrlich and Holdren, 1971; Holdren and Ehrlich, 1974). Yet the disproportionate environmental costs associated with population growth virtually never enter the policy discussion.

Furthermore, ecologists and epidemiologists are very concerned as a growing, ever denser human population, is pushed into closer contact with animal reservoirs of novel infectious diseases. Such contacts greatly increase the odds of more novel epidemics (such as that of AIDS) occurring as it becomes more likely that diseases that "jump" from animal to human populations will establish themselves in Homo sapiens. The chances of horrendous epidemics are also increased by the existence of high-speed transport systems (remember, 10 generations ago the fastest any human being had traveled was the speed of a galloping horse) and huge absolute numbers of hungry, and thus immune-compromised people (Daily and Ehrlich, 1996). Only recently, with the SARS outbreak and increasing publicity about bird flu, have issues like the importance of transport speed started to become part of general discourse.

Population is an area where pundits often work against allowing science to influence policy. Typically they neglect the severe negative externalities of population growth (Ehrlich et al., 1992; Ehrlich and Ehrlich, 1990) and focus instead on increases in wealth and health in the last century, while the population has quadrupled in size (for example, Eberstadt, 2006). They either ignore or do not realize that this has been achieved by depleting humanity's natural capital, likely mortgaging our future. And they do not focus on the role population control has played in underpinning the growth in average prosperity (which may turn out to be temporary). Could the "Asian tigers" have reached their present level of prosperity if they had not first reduced their once-high birthrates? Would China be achieving such remarkable economic expansion without its prior success in curbing population growth? Might India have achieved more if its family planning programs had been more successful? Can the population Pollyannas name any country with a high birthrate (other than a few oil-rich oligarchies) that has attained a high level of well-being for the majority of its population? Two billion people are living in misery today—as many as the entire world population when I was born in the 1930s. Almost 900 million are now severely or chronically hungry, and over 2 billion people suffer from "hidden" hunger—micronutrient deficiencies (Sanchez and Swaminathan, 2005)—not much support for Nicholas Eberstadt's claim (2006: 29-30) that the incidence of severe poverty has "been markedly reduced over the past 100 years."

The Pollyannas ignore that health and real prosperity would quite likely have *increased* but for the retarding effect of rapid population growth—highest in rate about 35 years ago and, in absolute numbers added annually, about 15 years ago. To argue that our economic development has made more of us "better off" is not to argue that it was done in the most beneficial way. We could have done it better. Valuing and protecting environmental assets would have been a much safer and more sustainable way to develop—and it is not too late to move toward that path.

The area where the consensus of the scientific community is most publicly being undervalued today in the United States is environmental, and it results in part from a failure to value an asset. Specifically, the area is climate change. The asset is the pollutant-absorbing capacity of the biosphere, its ability to serve as a "sink" for human waste products. While there are always uncertainties in something as complex as climate change, the evidence assembled by the objective and well-balanced Intergovernmental Panel on Climate Change (IPCC) or the assessments of the US National Research Council point strongly to the climate being significantly warmed by human activities, primarily by the addition of carbon dioxide and other greenhouse gases to the atmosphere (IPCC,

2001). Indeed, a mass of more recent evidence (Emanuel, 2005; Pounds et al., 2006; Root et al., 2004, 2003; Webster et al., 2005) has led scientists increasingly to decry the lack of action on reducing greenhouse gas emissions. For example, Walther et al. (2005: 649) state clearly: "There is an urgent need to not only enhance the visibility of science, but also actively communicate scientific knowledge on climate change (and other human-caused global change) to the public, and to point out to what degree it is (not) taken up in policy. Scientists need to get more closely involved in opinion-forming to influence more effectively future climate-change decisions made by politicians and policy makers."

Fortunately, despite the position of the Bush administration on this issue (in which it is virtually alone in the world), other bodies, from the government of California and other states to a wide variety of businesses (including some forward-looking oil companies), are paying attention to the scientific community. The *New York Times*' coverage of the science of climate change has been relatively good (a stunning contrast to its otherwise weak overall coverage of environmental issues). The electronic and print media are finally beginning to catch on (see, for example, Ignatius, 2006). It is about time—2005 was just announced to be the warmest year on record.

In the realm of policy generation, perhaps the greatest single gap between scientists and some American political decision makers and ordinary citizens is in the area of evolution. Understanding evolution is essential to understanding any important aspect of biology, including environmental biology. It is particularly critical at the most practical level in establishing appropriate policies in public health and agriculture as well as environmental protection in general—for example, buffering our crucial life-support systems against the impacts of climate change. Evolutionary theory helps us to predict how organisms will respond to such change (Bradshaw and Holzapfel, 2001; Hellmann, Pelini, and Prior, 2006). It has long been essential for designing strategies for controlling epidemic diseases (Anderson, May and Anderson, 1992), fighting bacterial infections, and suppressing crop pests (Naylor and Ehrlich, 1997). But only rarely is evolutionary theory appropriately injected into the policy process, even though evolution is one of the most solidly supported theories—by myriad observations of nature—in science. Policymakers should regard it as an underlying principle when making all kinds of decisions relative to biology.

Science, the premiere American science journal, recently declared "evolution in action" as the 2005 "breakthrough of the year" (Culotta and Pennisi, 2005). The authors stated in part, "Today evolution is the foundation of all biology, so basic and all pervasive that scientists sometimes take its importance for granted" (1878).

That statement points to the massive evidence showing the efficacy of natural selection in theory, in the laboratory, and in nature. It rests in part on tens of thousands of examples of populations evolving into new species in both plants and animals—something observable in geographic patterns all over the globe. It is supported by an increasingly detailed fossil record showing the course of evolution in numerous groups. Not the least of these is in the history of *Homo sapiens,* where the discovery of "missing links" galore has shown that the human family tree, once thought to be a rather simple evolutionary sequence, was actually a complex evolutionary "bush." And in recent years all of this has been magnificently supported by the use of new molecular techniques that get at the very basis of genetic change.

But, supported by right-wing and fundamentalist interests, creationism—or its pseudoscience doppelgänger, "Intelligent Design" or "ID"—increasingly is a public issue in educational policy (Judge Jones, 2005). In part, ID has gained prominence because right-wing operatives have resurrected the discredited, centuries-old idea (Paley, 1803) to use as a political wedge issue. Some regions of the United States provide fertile ground for this dangerous retrograde trend. Eighty-seven percent of the American public (in contrast with a minority of opinion in most developed nations) believe either that a deity created human beings more or less in their present form within the last 6,500 years (44 percent) or that a deity guided the evolutionary process (39 percent), while only 10 percent believe humanity evolved without supernatural guidance ("Public Beliefs, n.d.; based on 1997 data).

Among scientists, the equivalent numbers are 5 percent, 40 percent, and 55 percent. And the gap between the knowledgeable scientific community and the general public is certainly even greater than this indicates, since the category "scientist" presumably includes chemists, physicists, engineers, and others who do not necessarily have any expertise in evolutionary theory. Of course, one need not be very familiar with evolutionary theory, or even a scientist, to know that creationism/ID cannot be considered "science" in any case.

The numbers on religiosity just cited suggest that one major barrier to involving science in the policy process is a preference of much of the American public for a "believe-and-obey" form of political discourse (as opposed to private conviction) rather than a "question-and-test" mode (Ehrlich and Ehrlich, 2005: 338; Harris, 2004), although many religions (including the Roman Catholic Church) believe we need to understand the results of scientific inquiry and see no basic science-religion conflict. But the preference for "believe-and-obey" seems to be growing, fertilized by the extreme anti-science posture of the Bush administration (Union of Concerned Scientists, 2004) and many other conservative politicians. It led Donald Kennedy, editor of *Science*, to remark that "when the religious/political convergence leads to managing the nation's research agenda, its foreign assistance programs, or the high-school curriculum, that marks a really important change in our national life. Twilight for the Enlightenment? Not yet. But as its beneficiaries, we should also be its stewards" (Kennedy, 2005). The Bush administration most recently attempted to keep the government's top climate scientist from warning the public about the catastrophic potential of climate change (Revkin, 2006), the censor being a 24-year-old rapturist with a faked résumé. By frequently distorting the results of science, allowing no sound environmental science advice to penetrate the White House, and trying to intimidate scientists, the administration is greatly reducing the value of science to the American public.

One of the most dangerous environmental areas where independent scientific input to the policy process has been largely ignored is that related to the potentially catastrophic ecological effects of nuclear war (Ehrlich, 1968; Ehrlich and Ehrlich, 1970; Ehrlich et al., 1983; Turco et al., 1983), which would enormously amplify the impacts on humanity. Despite the end of the cold war, the United States and Russia still have substantial numbers of nuclear-tipped intercontinental ballistic missiles that could all too easily be used in a full-scale exchange. Technically they are no longer targeted on once "enemy" countries, but in reality, the target sets that have been removed electronically from the guidance systems could be restored in a matter of minutes in a time of crisis. Something on the order of 2,000 weapons on each side are on short reaction-time alert and pose a risk of launch through malfunction, misinformation, or misinterpretation. Worse yet, the Russian command and control system has deteriorated since the days of the Soviet Union, and that nation no longer is able to keep its force of missile submarines at sea. That makes their submarine deterrent much more vulnerable to nuclear attack and means that Russian nuclear forces are on a relatively hair-trigger alert. Thus the chances of accidental nuclear war could be greater than ever (Holdren, 2002; National Academy of Sciences, 1997). This problem is exacerbated by the growing chance of terrorist or rogue nation use of nuclear weapons—a situation long warned against by the scientific community (Brown, 1946; Ehrlich et al., 1977; Willrich and Taylor, 1974).

A related issue is the continued funding of the missile defense system by the Bush administration. Advertised as a way of preventing nuclear attack by rogue nations and its concomitant human and environmental devastation, missile defense actually tends to further destabilize the shaky international arms control structure, making a nuclear (and environmental) disaster *more* likely. As scientists have pointed out, the excuse that such a system would guard against attack from rogue nations approaches the absurd: a ballistic missile unambiguously identifies its source and invites retaliation (Glaser and Fetter, 2001: 55). Sending a nuclear weapon to the United States by submarine, tramp steamer, private airplane, shipping container, or suitcase (among many other possible "vehicles") carries much less chance of source detection.

Indeed, one scientist, when asked by President Bill Clinton how a nuke might be sneaked into the United States, said it could be concealed in a bale of marijuana—since we only intercept a tiny fraction of those.

Furthermore, tests of the missile defense system under development suggest it is highly unlikely ever to work. Moreover, if "rogue" nations develop substantial nuclear missile capability, another scientific issue would arise: it is generally far cheaper and easier to increase numbers of warheads and dummy warheads than to keep up the production of defensive missiles sufficient to assure the nearly 100 percent kill rate of incoming warheads that public policy appears to require. As in the case of global climate change, scientists to dispute these views can be found—sometimes (in this case) in the pay of those with a financial stake in the policy. This dilemma highlights the problem of educating both the public and decision makers on how to evaluate divergent "scientific" views.

FAILURE OF GOVERNANCE

In some cases the reason science is not properly integrated into policy formation is obvious—the power of corporate dollars in buying politicians. The case of the scientifically flawed, failed, and provocative missile defense system is a good example. The technical failure, widely recognized in the scientific community, led to an *increase* in Bush administration budgets—from $4.2 billion in fiscal year 2001 to $7.7 in 2002 and a proposed $8.8 billion in 2006. The reason is clear—pork for defense contractors with an interest in manufacturing components of the missile defense system, despite their dismal performance in a dangerous cause. Boeing, Lockheed Martin, Northrop Grumman, and Raytheon received 77 percent of missile defense prime contracts between 2001 and 2004; overall, 75 companies received $10 million or more, and more than 250 contractors were allotted at least $1 million (Hartung and Berrigan, 2005). And guess what? The top missile defense contractors shelled out $4.1 million to 30 key congresspeople between 2001 and 2006 in return for the billions in pork—a real bargain.

Similar stories could be developed around the pressures to cause further environmental deterioration by such political acts as allowing drilling for oil in the Alaska National Wildlife Reserve and numerous protected areas throughout the American West, strengthening the legal position of private landowners to impose high social costs on all of us through environmentally damaging acts (for example, by exterminating endangered species), relaxing regulations on pollution and toxic substances, dispensing national assets for grazing and mining ventures at far below cost, and on and on.

An important aspect of the interplay of politics and science in making public policy was dramatically illustrated by the environmental policies of the Clinton administration, one vastly better informed and much more honest than its successor. Vice President Al Gore was and is brilliant and perhaps knew more about environmental issues than any leading politician of his time. During the "nuclear winter" meetings held by the scientific community in the early 1980s, he was the only congressman to attend the scientific briefings personally rather than simply send staff. When Tim Wirth decided to leave the Senate in 1992, Gore personally told Anne Ehrlich and me that he would "pick up Tim's mantle on population issues." He also published a well-reviewed book on environmental issues (Gore, 1992). He was elected and reelected vice president on a ticket with another brilliant, well-read man, Bill Clinton, and they sought (and listened to) some of the best science advice available.

Nonetheless, the listening did not provide the results environmental scientists were hoping for. For example, issues of America's population size and consumption levels never made it into political discourse generated by the White House, and without Wirth and with the 1994 Republican takeover of Congress, the population issue disappeared from the congressional agenda. When Gore was running for president in 2000, one of the main topics of discussion among environmental scientists was whether he would feel it *politically* possible to raise key environmental issues—especially to discuss political poison-pills such as a substantial increase in the gasoline tax. Would any initiatives in such an area really lead to sure electoral defeat, as some of his advisers argued? And would that be a worse consequence for the human future than continuing to neglect key issues? Gore turned out to be near absolute proof that simply getting knowledgeable politicians into positions of power will not automatically produce scientifically sensible policy results.

There are clearly multiple reasons for this. One is the extreme stochasticity of cultural microevolution (Ehrlich, 2000: 228)—the "for want of a horseshoe nail" events that can have such a dramatic effect on the future course of society. (These contrast with cultural macroevolutionary factors such as differential access to fossil fuels or animals that could be domesticated [Diamond, 1997]). Brilliant as he is, Gore suffered from weak staff work in the area of the environment and obviously was also poorly advised politically on his presidential run. He almost certainly would have been elected president were it not for another "minor" glitch—the Lewinsky affair. Clinton's loss of effectiveness as a result may have altered the course of human history in significant ways. Had Gore been elected, unlike Bush he certainly would have actively worked to preserve the environment, not to destroy it for short-term profit. He certainly would never have started an ill-conceived war in part to gain control over oil, a resource humanity should be transitioning away from (Ehrlich and Ehrlich, 2005; Klare, 2004). And he might have paid attention to warning intelligence and prevented the 9-11 attacks.

The Clinton-Gore debacle was hardly a unique extremely influential "minor" event. Bad luck and perhaps bad politics earlier led to the defeat of a scientifically knowledgeable and environmentally sensitive president, Jimmy Carter, opening the door to the environmentally disastrous Reagan administration. If the helicopter collision in the Iranian desert in late April 1980 had not occurred, the American hostages in Iran might have been freed and Carter reelected. The role of science in policy formulation (indeed, perhaps the fate of civilization) may well have been changed dramatically for the worse by that one incident, just as it almost certainly was by Clinton's lying under oath about his ill-advised sexual activity.

THE FAILURE OF EDUCATION

Environmental policy obviously suffers from a failure of education both within science and in the general community. Within departments of biology and medical schools in particular, not enough attention is paid to epidemiology, and especially to the epidemiological environment, which I discussed earlier. The education of scientists, much like that of everyone else, has become increasingly specialized and discipline-bound. More serious is the failure of many scientists, including not a few biological scientists, to have a thorough grounding in evolutionary theory. There is also the failure of many scientists to participate in the process of policy formation—they have not been trained to do so. A start has been made in correcting this through the Aldo Leopold Leadership Program (http://www.leopoldleadership.org/content/index.jsp), which trains midcareer scientists to address lay audiences: the general public, business, and Congress. One of the problems that I and many scientists who talk to the public have had to solve is how to separate personal views from consensus science. The approach we employ is first to try to honestly represent the views of the scientific community. Then, if necessary, we can state where our own scientific judgment differs from the consensus. Finally, we can give our opinion, as informed observers, on the nonscientific normative aspects of policy formation. It is sometimes difficult to make those distinctions, but I and others do try.

More generally, what education there is on environmental issues at all levels in the educational system tends to focus on prominent symptoms of environmental damage and miss or barely touch on a wide variety of other crucial topics. Most products of our higher education system cannot sensibly discuss even half of such things as the mechanisms and risks of rapid climate change; the relationships between population growth, emerging viruses, and pandemics; risk analysis or Bayesian statistics; how the agricultural system works; the role oil plays in the global environmental situation; ecosystem services; or the IPAT relationship (Ehrlich and Ehrlich, 1990). Very bright people usually have little access to information in such areas because the educational system skirts these and many other topics essential to formulating sound environmental policy.

MEDIA FAILURE

Of course, education does not take place only in schools. The media provide potentially superb channels for informing the public on policy issues, environmental or otherwise. To say that it fails at that job is to state the obvious. In some cases, as in that of Fox News, the failure appears deliberate—the intention seems to be to downplay environmental and other critical issues and circulate disinformation in order to serve the short-term interests of the network's owner and his or her ideological associates. In other cases, there is a problem of circularity. People in the media are a sample of the "educated" portion of the American public but, as I noted, in many areas pertinent to environmental policy, the educational system does a pathetic job. The media, at the moment, are not educational instruments and do not pretend to be. But considering the state of our educational system and the speed at which the environmental situation is evolving, the media must play a bigger educational role.

One obstacle is the journalists' "truth-in-the-middle tradition"— the idea that there are two sides to every question, and that the truth lies somewhere in the middle (Schneider, 2002). This may be sensible for many social or political issues, but science does not work by producing compromise solutions to differences of opinion. Science suffers from a particular kind of "elitism"; better explanations replace poorer ones. It is an elitism based on experiment and systematic observation, theory, intense internal debate and competition, and the testing of conclusions against the real world. In scientific debates the truth almost never lies in the middle. The earth goes around the sun, they do not both go around each other; there is no phlogiston, or even phlog; as Michelson and Morley showed, there is no "ether" filling space whereby earth could cause an ether wind as it travels (and no compromise "ether breeze" either!); and "scientific creationism" is an oxymoron.

I was once involved in an argument with Ben Bradlee when he was executive editor of the *Washington Post*. He claimed that his reporters should be ignorant of science—and certainly not friends of scientists—so they could be more objective. He added that, after all, "any good reporter could learn what he needed in a day." Hardly; many cannot learn it in a year! In areas critical to environmental policy, though, he has largely gotten his wish, and one result is a frequent "balancing" of scientific consensus on issues with comments from uninformed or bought-and-paid-for critics. Most reporters learned enough during their education not to feel they must balance every space flight story with a contrary view from a representative of the Flat Earth Society, but environmental science has been so poorly taught to most reporters that they will cite scientifically ignorant mail-order marketers, obscure statisticians, and even physician-novelists as contrary scientific "experts."

Gross political and media failure is not restricted to the United States. In Australia, Prime Minister John Howard's government is pursuing an anti-scientific environmental agenda similar to that promoted by the Bush administration. In 2002 a report from the Commonwealth Scientific and Industrial Organization (CSIRO) pointed out some of the problems that would need to be faced if Australia's population grew until 2050: deteriorating water quality, the disappearance of "iconic" resources such as plentiful seafood, depleted oil and gas stocks, and the possibility of 90 new cities the size of Canberra (CSIRO, 2002). Australian scientists have long recognized that even with some 20 million people, Australia is already overpopulated. Those who view future population growth there positively should at least demonstrate that today's population can manage the continent sustainably. Professor Charles Birch, one of the world's most distinguished ecologists, stated he believed "the maximum sustainable population for Australia with anything like today's patterns of behavior would be about 10 million people." Harry Recher, one of Australia's leading conservation biologists, expressed his continuing distress at the negligible attention many Australian politicians pay to the information made available by the scientific community: "They and the government bureaucracy are more interested in elections and power groups than the future of Australia's children. Disgracefully, they often even try to censor the reports of the scientists they pay to discover and tell the truth." Other leading Australian scientists agree (for references, see Ehrlich and Ehrlich, 2005: 203).

Until the Bush administration, such censorship was more severe in Australia than in the United States. In Australia, government ecologists normally must give their scientific papers to their bosses for political approval before they are permitted to publish them. And, unlike in the United States, most ecologists there work for the government. Environmental problems within Australia (as opposed to those created elsewhere by Australian activities) are more serious because the carrying capacity of that continent is dramatically lower than that of the United States and most other nations of comparable size. And there the press tends to be even more supine and in the service of industry and the economy tuned to the export of natural resources than that of the United States. For example, the CSIRO population report was greeted by much ignorant commentary in Rupert Murdoch's newspaper *The Australian* (for details of this incident, see Ehrlich and Ehrlich, 2005: 198ff). But, showing that not all Australian leaders are stuck in the antique "growth at any price" rut, the then premier of New South Wales, Bob Carr, stated that the idea of growing to 50 million people was "nonsense." Fortunately, there are numerous other Australian politicians who grasp the risks posed by population growth.

Still, in fairness to Oz and its press, at least there *is* a public debate about population size and carrying capacity. In contrast, when the *New York Times* (Roberts, 2006) announced that the United States was approaching the 300 million mark, there was no commentary on what a threat the continuing growth of the world's most overpopulated nation posed for the rest of the world. But what political leadership the United States has for dealing rationally with environmental issues today is largely found at state and local levels; the Bush administration, in contrast, leads the world in trying to destroy the environmental services we all depend upon.

SCIENTIFIC FAILURE

As a starter, while the declining ability of the biosphere to sustain civilization approaches free fall, too many ecologists, evolutionists, systematists, and other environmental scientists go about their work as if nothing were happening—often doing sophisticated analyses applied to trivial problems (Ehrlich, 1997: 34). For example, the field of taxonomy, which should be at the forefront of working to preserve biodiversity, with some outstanding exceptions suffers from a dreadful stasis (Ehrlich, 2005).

The situation in the social sciences is on the whole worse. The best environmental news on the academic front in the past 15 years has been the accelerating involvement of world-class economists in confronting the human predicament (see, for example, Arrow et al., 2004a; Dasgupta, 2001; Hanna et al., 1996; Heal, 2000) and collaborating with other environmental scientists (Arrow et al., 2004b; Daily et al., 2000). But most economists remain embedded in a defunct paradigm that tells them that limits are far off or nonexistent and that innovation and substitution will save us all (Ehrlich, 1989). There is a general need for economists, political scientists, anthropologists, sociologists, and other social scientists to work hard and cooperatively on how culture evolves and how that evolution could be directed, among other routes, toward a better integration of science into public policy (Ehrlich and Ehrlich, 2005). But that need is not being met, in part because of an antique disciplinary structure that haunts the social sciences (Wallerstein, 2003; Wallerstein et al., 1996), and in part because most social scientists have not seen the desperate need to become engaged on environmental issues. It is high time that universities were generally restructured to meet the challenges of the twenty-first century, dissolving many antique and stultifying departmental fiefdoms. Stanford has a start with its new Stanford Institute for the Environment (SIE), but *all* universities have a long way to go (Ehrlich and Ehrlich, 2005: 261-262). In short, they must learn to value the interdisciplinary highly, and not put disincentives in its way.

A difficult and troubling exception is that, being human like everyone else, some scientists can be bought. There is a well-funded antiscience movement designed to denigrate environmental problems and prevent any effort to ameliorate them that might hurt the interests of the funders. That movement is most active in the area of climate change. There a handful of mostly third-rate scientists and a famous medical novelist with no credentials in climate science strive to blunt the warnings emanating from the hundreds of scientists involved in the IPCC. These climate contrarians are called the "climate monkeys" because they "see no warming, hear no warming, speak no warming" (the name is based on the famous carving of the three wise monkeys from the Sacred Stable in Nikko, Japan). The monkeys and their views are promoted by politicians like Senator James N. Inhofe (R., Oklahoma), who actually had Michael Crichton testify as a climate "expert" in a congressional hearing (Janofsky, 2006).

Thus, while it is easy to point the finger at venal and ignorant businesspeople and corrupt politicians, a fair amount of the blame for the failure of environmental science to influence public policy rests with scientists themselves.

CULTURAL EVOLUTION

I think that substantial conscious cultural evolution (Ornstein and Ehrlich, 1989) will be required if environmental science is to be injected appropriately into policy in time to stave off disaster. The need for cultural change in ways to think about environmental policy was brought into focus by the 2004 Indian Ocean tsunami tragedy and the flooding of New Orleans by Hurricane Katrina in 2005. Instead of seeing the disasters as primarily failures of human behavior, most people and the media treated them as "acts of God." In the case of the tsunami, people bore responsibility in part because the natural shoreline shields of coral reefs and mangrove forests had been greatly reduced. According to the Millennium Ecosystem Assessment, about 27 percent of the earth's coral reefs and 35 percent of its mangroves have been destroyed in the last few decades, and much of this destruction had occurred in the region impacted by the tsunami. At the same time massive coastal development, population growth, and a coastal movement of populations had occurred. The result was a loss of natural protection coupled with a greatly increased vulnerable population. Despite this, immediately after the tragedy no newspaper was interested in publishing an op-ed written by me and my ecologist colleague Harold Mooney—an article that simply pointed out the need to take such factors into account when rebuilding tsunami-devastated areas. That, of course, further underlines press incompetence in dealing with environmental issues, since these considerations only slowly later worked their way into the press.

The New Orleans situation was hauntingly similar. Channelization of the Mississippi had led to loss of much protective land in the delta, in essence moving New Orleans closer to the sea (Eilperin, 2005). Throw in inadequate levees (due to either corruption or incompetence), human-induced sea-level rise, and warmer gulf waters possibly contributing to bigger hurricanes (Kerr, 2005), and New Orleans was and will remain a sitting duck—something many observers in addition to scientists had long warned about (Gyan, 2003). But most of the press coverage of the event focused on government failures to help the survivors and clean up the mess—not on government failures to implement policies that would have ameliorated or avoided the disasters in the first place. Human cultures comfortably deal with short-term events; preparing for even the midrange future goes against our genetic and cultural dispositions (Ornstein and Ehrlich, 1989).

Our culture also teaches us to look for the simple explanation and the quick solution—even when the latter may hinder finding and implementing a permanent solutions (Sterner et al., 2006). An important environment-related example of the failure of scientific findings to penetrate the policy process can be seen in the suppression of terrorism (defined restrictively here as "actions carried out by militarily weak subnational or transnational groups from developing nations against private citizens, public property, or occupying troops of militarily powerful developed nations" [Ehrlich and Liu, 2005]). There is little appreciation of the complex issue of the origins and recruitment of terrorists. Some possible terrorist acts (exploding fission weapons, various forms of bioterrorism) could have widespread deleterious environmental impacts, and others ("dirty" bombs, chemical weapons) substantial regional ones. Any of these could have widespread indirect environmental impacts through disruption of economic and political systems. It would therefore be important for the public and decision makers to be clear on what social scientists know about conditions that favor recruitment of terrorists. For instance, many leaders and laypeople believe poverty and lack of education are at the base of terrorism, but social science research (Krueger and Laitin, 2003; Krueger and Maleckova, 2003; Stern, 2000) suggests that international politics, political oppression, and other factors may be more important.

Cultural lack of appreciation of complexity in the US policy process is dramatically demonstrated by the fact that most US politicians have bought the meretricious argument that the nation is in a "war on terrorism." As former national security adviser Zbigniew Brzezinski pointed out, "America's role in the world . . . is not served by an abstract quasi-theological definition of the war on terrorism. That definition oversimplifies a complex set of challenges that needs to be addressed. It talks about a phenomenon, terrorism, as the enemy while overlooking the fact that terrorism is a technique for killing people. It doesn't tell us who the enemy is. It's as if we said that World War II was not fought against the Nazis but against blitzkrieg" (2003). Since he said that, the administration has used this "war"—with no defined enemy, no strategy for fighting or standard for winning—to pursue a real war for an advantageous position with regard to maintaining flows of Middle East Oil (Klare, 2004). This is a policy that will be environmentally disastrous in the long run. It has also used it in support of a wide range of other short-sighted environmental and other policies, domestic and international.

While many citizens now have figured out that the administration lied its way into the Iraq invasion (lies that were transparent to well-informed people at the time), many still seem to believe that the Bush government's actions are increasing US security—when nothing could be further from the truth with regard to both environmental (Ehrlich and Ehrlich, 1989a; Myers, 1989) and military security. No issue in the policy arena is more essential to the future possibility of having adequate scientific input to the national policy process than electing a more honest and competent government. Divining how that might be done would be an important advance in scientific understanding of cultural evolution, which despite many decades of attention from social (and some natural) scientists lags far behind the understanding of genetic evolution (Ehrlich and Levin, 2005).

WHEN SCIENCE IS SUCCESSFULLY INTEGRATED WITH POLICY

Lest I give the impression that all US national environmental policy is set with too little scientific input, let me summarize some (at least partial) counterexamples. There are many examples of relative success, albeit almost all achieved in slow motion. One, of course, must balance a necessary conservatism in policy formulation (society cannot always go off in hot pursuit of solutions to poorly understood or even nonexistent problems) with careful benefit-cost risk analyses to determine at what point erring on the side of premature action is balanced by the potential consequences of not acting soon enough. The Clean Air Act (starting with the Air Pollution Control Act of 1955, amended in 1970), Clean Water Act (Federal Water Pollution Control Act, first enacted in 1948 and completely reorganized in 1972), and the National Environmental Policy Act (NEPA, 1969) all had significant scientific input in their formulation and have substantially abated air and water pollution; in the United States, NEPA assured that federal agencies develop environmental impact statements before undertaking major projects. By 1980, a remarkably innovative body of laws was in place to protect America's environment and public health—laws that have been admired and emulated by many other countries around the world.

In addition, although imperfect, the United States does actually have some remarkable and, I believe, globally and historically unique institutions in place to provide scientific advice to government. Most prominent is the nongovernmental National Research Council/National Academy of Sciences (NRC/NAS) system, which can have as many as 600 scientific committees operating. All are essentially striving to provide the best possible scientific advice on huge variety of issues, large and small, and to apply the strictest controls to avoid conflict of interest. A vast range of other advisory committees and boards operate across agencies and levels of government (international, national, state), although unlike the NRC/NAS, they are not independent and are appointed by the agencies they advise. In any case, for the most part, our planes do not crash, our drugs work, our food is not poisoned, our curricula teach, our boilers do not explode, our power systems do not fail, our computers talk to each other, and even our wildland management often succeeds. That is a credit to the scientists and other technical professionals who participate in these activities, often without pay.

Implementation of the advice, of course, often is far from ideal, but here the NGO community is most valuable, pushing government through legal or media channels to do what the science says is needed to meet stated public policy goals. Rather than working to expand the use of the government advisory apparatus to deal with the difficult environmental and social issues now at hand, however, the trend of the Bush administration and Congress today is to downgrade and defund these scientific advisory activities and, in some cases, to actually subvert, contravene, curtail, and circumvent them. A major dismantling, should it go much further, would be a huge loss for the nation and the world.

In the environmental arena, many questions remain about whether the scientific input to pathbreaking laws was adequate, and whether it has been adequate during many revisions and reauthorization of these acts. For example, the 1973 Endangered Species Act has helped to stem the loss of biodiversity; while not ideal it is vastly better than comparable legislation in other nations (Goble et al., 2005). At the moment attempts are under way, not to give it the needed revision and strengthening that environmental scientists think critical, but to constrain public comment and keep science out of the political process, under the aegis of Republican Representative Richard Pombo of California (Bontrager, 2005).

Furthermore, much of the environmental regulatory structure has been weakened or lost in political battles and simple neglect. At the same time, the gravity and scope of environmental problems have enormously escalated, such as the unanticipated early arrival of indications of global warming and the gradual realization of the bird flu threat, which is driving home the growing menace of global epidemics. Action on one of the potentially most serious of those problems, limiting the flux of chlorofluorocarbons (CFCs) into the atmosphere, may have reversed the potentially lethal trend of stratospheric ozone depletion in the nick of time (Benedick, 1991; Roan, 1989). It certainly had substantial and probably adequate scientific input. But appropriate action was not taken until first, an ozone hole over Antarctica was shown nightly in living color on the evening news, and second the main manufacturers of CFCs realized they could make even more money producing substitutes, which they worked on for a decade while publicly opposing any action against their existing products. And the results of attempts to evade the ban on CFCs that continue to this day in some areas of the world are still not clear.

If there is any generality to be extracted from these failures and successes in the environmental area, it seems to me that the successes are largely concentrated on abating prominent, well-understood symptoms—the health consequences of heavy smog, filthy rivers (some so polluted they could burn), the sad decline of a national symbol such as the bald eagle, significant illness and high mortality unambiguously tied to the use of tobacco and directly affecting people and their close associates (Biglan and Taylor, 2000). Scientific input is less likely to be given adequate weight in consideration of the *drivers* of environmental deterioration or problems with less obvious (especially less visible) symptoms. This is particularly true where the causal chain is more complex than most citizens are trained to follow, as in the connections between population size, climate change, and the chance of emerging global epidemics or between overconsumption among the rich and food insecurity among the poor (Ehrlich and Ehrlich, 2005).

WHAT NEEDS TO BE DONE

It is time that such connections be widely recognized, something that might have automatically occurred if there were a standard mechanism in place for assessing the roles of individual and institutional behavior in creating our environmental and social predicaments, and for promoting appropriate action. Developing such a mechanism, as a joint effort between natural and social sciences, may be the most important scientific venture of the twenty-first century and an absolute requirement for achieving a sustainable society. It would not be appropriate for science to set the agenda, but it is crucial that the value judgments inherent in policy be informed by the best (and most dispassionate) possible scientific information.

Such a mechanism was proposed in *One with Nineveh* (Ehrlich and Ehrlich, 2005). The nations of the world, through the United Nations, might be persuaded to inaugurate a Millennium Assessment of Human Behavior (MAHB). Anne and I proposed this name to emphasize that it is human *behavior* toward the environmental systems that sustain all of us, and our behavior toward one another, that require rapid modification. The scientific community has developed more than enough information to show in what directions humanity should be moving, but we're not on those courses. The idea is that an MAHB might help cure this by becoming a basic global mechanism to expose people to scholarly thought on the full range of population-environment-resource-ethics-power issues (and eventually *all* behavioral issues of significant social import) and thus be one tool for getting policymakers to pay more attention to what scientists know about key issues. It could help move humanity toward integrating that knowledge into policies and thus moving us toward a sustainable society.

The Intergovernmental Panel on Climate Change (IPCC) could serve as a partial model for the MAHB. The IPCC involves hundreds of scientists from nearly every nation, representing diverse disciplines from atmospheric physics, chemistry, and ecology to economics and other social sciences. They are conducting an ongoing evaluation of the current and projected effects on the world's climates of increasing greenhouse gas concentrations in the atmosphere, and attempting to reach consensus on the related technical, economic, and policy issues. A major role of the IPCC is to sort out the scientific validity of claims and counterclaims of competing interests. It also puts a strong emphasis on finding *equitable* solutions, which may be one reason members of the Bush administration are not fans of the IPCC's efforts, even though the institution was started by President Bush's father to provide a sound factual basis for setting policy on climate change. The sessions are open and transparent, and representatives of various governments, interested industries, and environmental organizations also participate as observers.

The endeavor that might serve as another partial model for an MAHB is the Millennium Ecosystem Assessment (Millennium Ecosystem Assessment, 2003), which was carried out by scientists to assess the condition of earth's life-support systems. Some 1,300 leading ecologists and earth scientists, along with economists and other social scientists, from 95 countries gathered information for a major report that was released in April 2005. The report is intended to be useful at the global, regional, and local levels. It includes not only a detailed assessment of the current state of the world's ecosystems but also projections of alternative future trends and consideration of related policy choices.

Like both the IPCC and the Millennium Ecosystem Assessment, the MAHB would work best if it included broad participation from a variety of nonscientists, ranging from ethicists and businesspeople to politicians and representatives of public interest groups. It would especially need to recruit social scientists from diverse fields such as sociology, psychology, economics, and political science, as well as experts in resource and environmental law, into its global effort to assess and seek ways to escape the human predicament. Such an effort should, among other things, have a positive effect on integration of the social sciences. Most important, the MAHB would have communications capability built in from the start, and could use that capacity to generate support or authorization from one or more governments, government bodies, or international institutions, and help create the climate where solutions to environmental problems would be plausible.

Stanford University's Woods Institute for the Environment has just begun a pilot MAHB focused on the question of how the state of California, which has been a pioneer in trying to reduce greenhouse gas emissions, should further react to climate change. Should the state adopt policies that will embarrass the Bush administration into taking sensible steps at the national level? Would it be ethical to impose more costs of slowing climate change on Californians than citizens of other states? Stanford's

MAHB already involves not only natural scientists but ethicists, law professors, engineers, political scientists, economists, anthropologists, psychologists, specialists in communications and members of the humanities faculty—and was organized by Walter Reid, who played a major role in the success of the Millennium Ecosystem Assessment. The MAHB hopes to use techniques of deliberative polling (asking members of the general public for their opinions before and after fully informing them on all sides of the issue) as a device for disseminating the MAHB's results.

A full MAHB, if it ever comes into being, could be kicked off with a world megaconference like the United Nations Conference on Environment and Development (UNCED), which was held in Rio de Janeiro in 1992. The purpose of this conference would be to initiate a continuing process; the MAHB should be created as a semi-permanent institution. It should be designed as an umbrella forum for integration of information and insight from many smaller forums. One of its primary roles would be public education. The MAHB would be a way of washing *Homo sapiens*' dirty linen in public and trying to reach agreement on how to live within increasingly tight environmental constraints. The forum would explicitly review and support modern research on the behavior of complex systems subject to irreversible change. In light of historical precedents, it would develop scenarios to examine possible fates of the emerging global civilization, to provide guidance in creating an environmentally sustainable and socially and economically equitable global society. A broad base of support already exists worldwide for individual elements of such a strategy, including support for maintaining environmental quality (usually too narrowly defined); meeting basic needs for food, health, and education; ending gross economic, racial, and gender inequities; providing family planning services to those who want them; and stopping economic globalization from making poor people even poorer. In summary, I think we need to make a more organized and determined effort toward conscious cultural evolution—to discuss openly the directions in which our society is moving and possibilities for changing those directions.

Another approach to preserving our life-support systems and improving the visibility of science to policymakers is to search for ways to make the government of the United States less of a corporate-controlled democracy—and to do that by placing more of the process in the hands of carefully selected and monitored specialists, including scientists, distasteful as that may be to some. Many issues require technical knowledge, long-term attention, and freedom from day-to-day political interference if the best interests of the public are to be served. This is not a novel idea. As Alan Blinder pointed out (1997), several areas of our government have already been to one degree or another insulated from the vagaries of politics. Blinder's main example is the Federal Reserve System, in which "the pace is deliberate, sometimes plodding. Policy discussions are serious, even somber, and disagreements are almost always over a policy's economic, social, or legal merits, not its political marketability." The Fed is not completely beyond political control—its seven-member board of governors is appointed by the president of the United States and confirmed by the Senate, and in an extreme case its decisions can be overturned by Congress. Perhaps its biggest failing is a considerable lack of transparency in documenting the reasoning behind its decisions. But it is an excellent instance of what Anne and I called "delegated delegation" (Ehrlich and Ehrlich, 2005: 306ff, on which this discussion is based)—the people elect representatives, who then, in the name of the common good, delegate some of their delegated authority. The hope is that relatively insulated bodies might have the time and interest to become informed on the scientific consensus on an issue and do a better job of considering it when the political process of determining policies takes place.

The Fed is by no means the only government unit that was designed to be at least somewhat insulated from day-to-day politics. In addition to the Supreme Court, other permanent entities include the Food and Drug Administration, the Federal Trade Commission, the Securities and Exchange Commission, and the Environmental Protection Agency (although in the Reagan and second Bush administrations, the EPA's independence was sorely eroded). There have also been temporary examples of delegated delegation that might help in designing better ways to deal with difficult environmental policy-making, such as the

Base Realignment and Closure Commission. In that case, the commission recommended a number of military bases to close, and Congress had to vote yes or no on the list as a whole.

Nowhere could delegated delegation be more important, and spare politicians more pain, than in areas of fundamental constraints. One can think of the messiness of politics as a sort of market in which ideas, interests, and jurisdictions compete with one another. Just as financial markets need government constraints, so does the chaotic political market need institutional limits set on the impacts of the human enterprise. Our society needs laws that will establish such limits, and institutions similar to the Federal Reserve System or a series of commissions could be created to set and monitor them. For example, to constrain America's use of fossil fuels, one tactic might be for Congress to set up a commission to determine a reasonable gasoline tax and, as it did with the base-closing commission, bind itself to simply vote up or down on the commission's conclusions. Elected representatives should be delighted to be distanced from many of the tough decisions required by what the World Scientists' Warning to Humanity (Union of Concerned Scientists, 1993) called "humanity's collision course with the natural world." Exactly what the constraining mechanisms should be is beyond the scope of this paper. So is the difficult problem of bringing large multinational corporations under social control, which I have discussed in detail elsewhere (Ehrlich and Ehrlich, 2005: 299ff).

WHAT SCIENCE CANNOT DO FOR POLICY

More careful consideration of the available scientific evidence on environmental problems is clearly highly desirable. But more scientific input is no panacea. Above all, science cannot be much help with the ethical decisions that are often central to policy issues—environmental or other. The scientific community can project the environmental results of a large-scale nuclear war, but it cannot tell society what kinds of risks of nuclear war it is ethical to take. It cannot decide what level of illness from air pollution is "acceptable" when balanced against the costs, financial and human (for example, job loss), of achieving that level, but it can give a good estimate of the economic and health impacts of the pollution. It cannot tell whether or not abortion should be legal, and under what circumstances, but science can unambiguously state that human life is continuous—it does *not* begin at conception. As my colleague Steve Schneider puts it, environmental science is often "about risk (what can happen and what are the odds), and policymaking is about what risks are acceptable, who should pay and how losers can be compensated by winners—in short, the normative stuff." Those are the sorts of issues I wish a MAHB would tackle in transparent forums, in the hope that they would focus attention on what science can add to the debate. Then, in combination with the normative aspects of political decision making, it could aid in the formulation of policies that would help to solve the human predicament. This is very Pollyannaish, but as I have said many times before, *Homo sapiens* appears to have reached a crossroads where idealism has become necessity.

NOTES

* I am grateful to Gretchen Daily, Anne Ehrlich, John Holdren, Don Kennedy, Tom Lovejoy, Michael Oppenheimer, Peter Raven, Walt Reid, Steve Schneider, Kirk Smith, and Senator Tim Wirth for tough and insightful criticism of the manuscript. I am indebted to the Mertz-Gilmore Foundation, which made this work possible. Needless to say, all errors and bizarre ideas are mine.

REFERENCES

Anderson, R. M., R. May, and B. Anderson. *Infectious Diseases of Humans: Dynamics and Control.* Oxford: Oxford University Press, 1992.

Arrow, K., P. Dasgupta, L. H. Goulder, G. Daily, P. Ehrlich, G. Heal, S. Levin, K. G. Mäler, S. H. Schneider, D. Starrett, and B. Walker. "Are We Consuming Too Much?" *Journal of Economic Perspectives* 18 (2004a): 147-172.

Benedick, R. E. *Ozone Diplomacy: New Directions in Safeguarding the Planet.* Cambridge: Harvard University Press, 1991.

Biglan, A., and T. K. Taylor. "Why Have We Been More Successful in Reducing Tobacco Use Than Violent Crime?" *American Journal of Community Psychology* 28 (2000): 269-302.

Blinder, A. "Is Government Too Political?" *Foreign Affairs* 76 (Nov.-Dec. 1997): 115-126.

Bontrager, E. "In Senate, Endangered Species Act Faces Overhaul." *Wall Street Journal,* Dec. 27, 2005.

Bradshaw, W. E., and C. M. Holzapfel. "Genetic Shift in Photoperiodic Response Correlated with Global Warming." *Proceedings of the National Academy of Sciences, USA* 98 (2001): 14509-14511.

Brown, H. *Must Destruction Be Our Destiny?* New York: Simon and Schuster, 1946.

———. *The Challenge of Man's Future.* New York: Viking, 1954.

Brzezinski, Z. "Another American Casualty: Credibility." *Washington Post,* Nov. 9, 2003.

Commonwealth Scientific and Industrial Organization (CSIRO). "Future Dilemmas: Options to 2050 for Australia's Population, Technology, Resource and Environment" (2002) <www.dwe.csiro.au>.

Culotta, E., and E. Pennisi. "Breakthrough of the Year: Evolution in Action." *Science* 310 (2005): 1878-1879.

Daily, G. C., P. Dasgupta, B. Bolin, and P. Crosson. "Food Production, Population Growth, and the Environment." *Science* 281 (1998): 1291-1292.

Daily, G. C., and P. R. Ehrlich. "Global Change and Human Susceptibility to Disease." *Annual Review of Energy and the Environment* 21 (1996): 125-144.

Daily, G. C., T. Söderqvist, S. Aniyar, K. Arrow, P. Dasgupta, C. Folke, A.M. Jansson, B.O. Jansson, S. Levin, J. Lubchenco, K.G. Mäler, D. Starrett, D. Tilman, and B. Walker. "The Value of Nature and the Nature of Value." *Science* 289 (2000): 395-396.

Dasgupta, P. *Human Well-being and the Natural Environment.* Oxford: Oxford University Press, 2001.

Diamond, J. M. *Guns, Germs, and Steel: The Fates of Human Societies.* New York: Norton, 1997.

Eberstadt, N. "Doom and Demography." *The Wilson Quarterly* 30 (2006): 27-31.

Eckstrom, K. "Poll: Belief in Angels, Devil on Rise." Religion News Service 26 May 2004.

Ehrlich, P. R. *The Population Bomb*. New York: Ballantine Books, 1968.

———. "The Limits to Substitution: Metaresource Depletion and a New Economic-Ecological Paradigm." *Ecological Economics* 1 (1989): 9-16.

———. *A World of Wounds: Ecologists and the Human Dilemma*. Oldendorf/Luhe: Ecology Institute, 1997.

———. *Human Natures: Genes, Cultures, and the Human Prospect*. Washington, D.C.: Island Press, 2000.

———. "Twenty-First Century Systematics and the Human Predicament." *Biodiversity: Past, Present and Future*. Ed. N. G. Jablonski. San Francisco: Proceedings of the California Academy of Sciences, 2005.

Ehrlich, P. R., G. C. Daily, and L. H. Goulder. "Population Growth, Economic Growth, and Market Economies." *Contention* 2 (1992): 17-35.

Ehrlich, P. R., and A. H. Ehrlich. *Population, Resources, Environment: Issues in Human Ecology*. San Francisco: W. H. Freeman and Co., 1970.

———. "The Environmental Dimensions of National Security." In *Global Problems and Common Security: Annals of Pugwash 1988*. Eds. J. Rotblat and V. Goldanskii. Berlin: Springer Verlag, 1989a: 180-190.

———. "Too Many Rich Folks." *Populi* 16 (1989b): 20-29.

———. *The Population Explosion*. New York: Simon and Schuster, 1990.

———. "The Most Overpopulated Nation." *The NPG Forum* (1991): 1-4.

———. *One with Nineveh: Politics, Consumption, and the Human Future*. Washington, D.C.: Island Press, 2005.

Ehrlich, P. R., A. H. Ehrlich, and J. P. Holdren. *Ecoscience: Population, Resources, Environment*. San Francisco: W. H. Freeman and Co., 1977.

Ehrlich, P. R., J. Harte, M. A. Harwell, P. H. Raven, C. Sagan, G. M. Woodwell, et al. "Long-Term Biological Consequences of Nuclear War." *Science* 222 (1983): 1293-1300.

Ehrlich, P. R., and J. Holdren. "Impact of Population Growth." *Science* 171 (1971): 1212-1217.

Ehrlich, P. R., and S. A. Levin. "The Evolution of Norms." *Public Library of Science* 3 (2005): 943-948.

Ehrlich, P. R., and J. Liu. "Socioeconomic and Demographic Roots of Terrorism." *The Making of a Terrorist: Recruitment, Training and Root Causes.* Ed. J. Forest. Westport, Conn.: Praeger, 2005.

Eilperin, J. "Shrinking La. Coastline Contributes to Flooding." *Washington Post*, Aug. 30, 2005.

Emanuel, K. "Increasing Destructiveness of Tropical Cyclones over the Past 30 Years." *Nature* 436 (2005): 686-688.

Glaser, C. L., and S. Fetter. "National Missile Defense and the Future of U.S. Nuclear Weapons Policy." *International Security* 26 (2001): 40-92.

Goble, D. D., J. M. Scott, and F. W. Davis, eds. *Endangered Species Act at Thirty: Renewing the Conservation Promise.* Washington, D.C. Island Press, 2005.

Gore, A. *Earth in The Balance: Ecology and The Human Spirit.* Boston: Houghton Mifflin, 1992.

Gyan, J., Jr. "South La. Warned Shrinking of Coast Raises Risk in Storms." *State-Times/Morning Advocate* (Baton Rouge), Nov. 22, 2003.

Hanna, S. S., C. Folke, and K.-G. Mäler, eds. *Rights To Nature: Ecological, Economic, Cultural, and Political Principles of Institutions for the Environment.* Washington, D. C.: Island Press, 1996.

Harris, S. *The End of Faith: Religion, Terror, and the Future of Reason.* New York: Norton, 2004.

Hartung, W. D., and F. Berrigan. "Missile Defense Is Mainly about Pork." *Disarmament Times* 28 (2005): 1, 3.

Heal, G. *Nature and the Marketplace: Capturing the Value of Ecosystem Services.* Washington, D. C.: Island Press, 2000.

Heckman, J. J., and A. B. Krueger. *Inequality in America: What Role for Human Capital Policies.* Cambridge: MIT Press, 2003.

Hellmann, J. J., S. L. Pelini, and K. M. Prior. "The Local Adaptation of Contrasting Butterfly Species at the Edge of Their Geographic Range." *Ecology* (submitted 2006).

Holdren, J. P. "Beyond the Moscow Treaty." Testimony before Foreign Relations Committee of the United States Senate. Hearings on

Treaty on Strategic Offensive Reductions, Sept. 12, 2002.

Holdren, J. P., and P. R. Ehrlich. "Human Population and the Global Environment." *American Scientist* 62 (1974): 282-292.

Ignatius, D. "Is It Warm in Here? We Could Be Ignoring the Biggest Story in Our History." *Washington Post,* Jan. 18, 2006.

Intergovernmental Panel on Climate Change (IPCC). *Climate Change 2001: Synthesis Report.* Cambridge, Eng.: Cambridge University Press, 2001.

Janofsky, M. "6 Ex-Chiefs of E.P.A. Urge Action on Greenhouse Gases." *New York Times,* Jan. 18, 2006.

Judge Jones. *Memorandum Opinion: Tammy Kitzmiller et al. Plaintiffs v. Dover Area School District, et. al.* United States District Court for the Middle District of Pennsylvania, Case 4:04-cv-02688-JEJ, Document 342. Filed Dec. 20, 2005: 1-139.

Kennedy, D. "Twilight for the Enlightenment?" *Science* 308 (2005): 165.

Kerr, R. A. "Is Katrina a Harbinger of Still More Powerful Hurricanes?" *Science* 309 (2005): 1807.

Klare, M. T. *Blood and Oil: The Dangers and Consequences of America's Growing Dependency on Imported Petroleum.* New York: Henry Holt and Company, 2004.

Krueger, A. B. "Inequality: Too Much of a Good Thing." *Inequality in America: What Role for Human Capital Policies.* Ed.s J. J. Heckman and A. B. Krueger, Cambridge, Mass.: MIT Press, 2004.

Krueger, A. B., and D. D. Laitin. "Kto Kogo?: A Cross-Country Study of the Origins and Targets of Terrorism." Ms., 2003.

Krueger, A. B., and J. Maleckova. "Education, Poverty and terrorism: Is there a causal connection." *Journal of Economic Perspectives* 17 (2003): 119-144.

Millennium Ecosystem Assessment. *Ecosystems and Human Well-being: A Framework for Assessment.* Washington, D. C.: Island Press, 2003.

Myers, N. "Environmental Security: The Case of South Asia." *International Environmental Affairs* 1 (1989): 138-154.

National Academy of Sciences (Committee on International Security and Arms Control). *The Future of U.S. Nuclear Weapons Policy.* Washington,

D.C.: National Academy of Sciences, 1997.

National Academy of Sciences USA. "A Joint Statement by Fifty-Eight of the World's Scientific Academies." *Population Summit of the World's Scientific Academies.* New Delhi: National Academy Press, 1993.

Naylor, R., and P. R. Ehrlich. "Natural Pest Control Services and Agriculture." *Nature's Services: Societal Dependence on Natural Ecosystems.* Ed. G. C. Daily. Washington, D. C.: Island Press, 1997.

Ornstein, R., and P. Ehrlich. *New World/New Mind: Moving toward Conscious Evolution.* New York: Doubleday, 1989.

Paley, W. "Natural Theology: or Evidences of the Existence and Attributes of the Deity." Collected from the *Appearances of Nature.* 5th ed. London: Faulder, 1803.

Pounds, J. A., M. R. Bustamante, L. A. Coloma, J. A. Consuegra, M. P. L. Fogden, P. N. Foster, E. La Marca, K. L. Masters, A. Merino-Viteri, R. Puschendorf, R. R. Santiago, G. A. Sánchez-Azofeifa, C. J. Still, and B. E. Young. "Widespread Amphibian Extinctions from Epidemic Disease Driven by Global Warming." *Nature* 439 (2006): 161-167.

"Public Beliefs about Evolution and Creation" <http://www.religioustol-erance.org/ev_publi.htm)>.

Revkin, A. C. "Climate Expert Says NASA Tried to Silence Him." *New York Times,* Jan. 29, 2006.

Roan, S. *Ozone Crisis: The 15-Year Evolution of a Sudden Global Emergency.* New York: Wiley, 1989.

Roberts, S. "Come October, Baby Will Make 300 Million or So." *New York Times,* Jan. 13, 2006.

Root, T. L., D. P. MacMynowski, M. D. Mastandrea, and S. S. Schneider. "Human-Modified Temperatures Induce Species Changes: Joint Attribution." *Proceedings of the National Academy of Sciences* 102 (2004): 7465-7469.

Root, T. L., J. T. Price, K. R. Hall, S. H. Schneider, C. Rosenzweig, and A. Pounds. "'Fingerprints' of Global Warming on Wild Animals and Plants." *Nature* 421 (2003): 57-60.

Sanchez, P. A., and M. S. Swaminathan. "Cutting World Hunger in Half." *Science* 307 (2005): 357-359.

Schneider, S. H. "Keeping Out of the Box." *American Scientist* 90 (2002): 496-498.

Stark, R., and R. Finke. *Acts of Faith: Explaining the Human Side of Religion.* Berkeley: University of California Press, 2000.

Stern, J. "Pakistan's Jihad Culture." *Foreign Affairs* 79 (2000): 115-126.

Sterner, T., M. Troell, S. Aniyar, S. Barrett, W. Brock, S. Carpenter, K. Chopra, P. Ehrlich, M. Hoel, S. Levin, K-G Mäler, J. Norberg, L. Pihl, T. Söderqvist, J. Wilen, J. Vincent, A. Xepapadeas. "Natural Disasters and Disastrous Policies." *Science* (submitted 2006).

Thurow, L. *Generating Inequality: Mechanisms of Distribution in the U.S. Economy.* New York: Basic Books, 1975.

Turco, R., O. Toon, T. Ackerman, J. Pollack, and C. Sagan. "Nuclear Winter: Global Consequences of Multiple Nuclear Weapons Explosions." *Science* 222 (1983): 1283-1292.

Union of Concerned Scientists. "World Scientists' Warning to Humanity." Cambridge, Mass., 1993.

———. "Preeminent Scientists Protest Bush Administration's Misuse of Science." UCS Press Release, Feb. 18, 2004.

Vogt, W. *Road to Survival.* New York: William Sloan, 1948.

Wallerstein, I. "Anthropology, Sociology, and Other Dubious Disciplines." *Current Anthropology* 44 (2003): 453-460.

Wallerstein, I., C. Juma, E. F. Keller, J. Kocka, and D. Lecourt. *Open the Social Sciences: Report of the Gulbenkian Commission on the Restructuring of the Social Sciences.* Stanford: Stanford University Press, 1996.

Walther, G. R., L. Hughes, P. Vitousek, and N. C. Stenseth. "Consensus on Climate Change." *Trends in Ecology and Evolution* 20 (2005): 648-649.

Webster, P. J., G. J. Holland, J. A. Curry, and H.-R. Chang. "Changes in Tropical Cyclone Number, Duration, and Intensity in a Warming Environment." *Science* 309 (2005): 1844-1846.

Willrich, M. and T. Taylor. *Nuclear Theft: Risks and Safeguards.* Cambridge: Ballinger, 1974.

James E. Hansen
Can We Still Avoid Dangerous Human-Made Climate Change?

1. SUMMARY

THE EARTH'S TEMPERATURE, WITH RAPID GLOBAL WARMING OVER THE past 30 years, is now passing through the peak level of the Holocene, a period of relatively stable climate that has existed for more than 10,000 years. Further warming of more than 1°C will make the earth warmer than it has been in a million years. "Business-as-usual" scenarios, with fossil fuel CO_2 emissions continuing to increase approximately 2 percent annually for several more decades, yield additional warming of 2° to 3°C this century and imply changes that constitute practically a different planet.

Multiple lines of evidence indicate that the earth's climate is nearing, but has not passed, a tipping point, beyond which it will be impossible to avoid climate change with far ranging undesirable consequences. The changes include not only loss of the Arctic as we know it, with all that implies for wildlife and indigenous peoples, but losses on a much vaster scale because of worldwide rising seas. Sea level will increase slowly at first, as losses at the fringes of Greenland and Antarctica due to accelerating ice streams are partly balanced by increased snowfall and ice sheet thickening in the ice sheet interiors. But as Greenland and West Antarctic ice is softened and lubricated by melt-water and as buttressing ice shelves disappear because of a warming ocean, the balance will tip to rapid ice loss, bringing multiple positive feedbacks into play and causing cataclysmic ice sheet disintegration. The earth's history suggests that with warming of 2° to 3°C, the new equilibrium sea level will include not only most of the ice from Greenland and West Antarctica, but a portion of East Antarctica, raising sea level of the order of 25 meters (80 feet).

Contrary to lethargic ice sheet models, real world data suggest substantial ice sheet and sea level change in centuries, not millennia. The century time scale offers little consolation to coastal dwellers, because they will be faced with irregular incursions associated with storms and with repeatedly rebuilding above a transient water level.

This grim "business-as usual" climate change can be avoided through an "alternative" scenario in which growth of greenhouse gas emissions is slowed in the first quarter of this century, primarily with concerted improvements in energy efficiency, thus reducing the growth rate of atmospheric CO_2, and a parallel reduction of human-made climate forcings that drive global warming, especially the air pollutants methane, carbon monoxide, and black soot. Before mid-century, advanced energy technologies will be needed to reduce CO_2 emissions faster. The required actions make practical sense and have other benefits, but they will not happen without strong policy leadership and international cooperation. Action must be prompt, otherwise CO_2-producing infrastructure that may be built within a decade will make it impractical to keep further global warming under 1°C.

2. GLOBAL WARMING

I must begin with two caveats. First, the views I present are my personal scientific opinion. They are based on my 39 years of experience at NASA, but I am not representing the agency or the government. Second, I do not attempt to define policy, which is up to the people and their elected representatives, and I do not criticize policies. The climate science has policy relevance, but I let the facts speak for themselves about consequences for policymakers.

I will show that the answer to the question "Can we still avoid dangerous human-made climate change?" is yes, we can, but we are not on a path to do that. And if we do not begin actions to get on a different path within the next several years we will pass a tipping point, beyond which it will be impossible to avoid climate change with widespread undesirable consequences. Why we are not taking actions to avoid climate change is a central issue, which I will consider in due course. But I must first address the climate science, because public understanding of climate change is important and the scientific story has not received the emphasis it deserves during recent discussions about government censorship of scientists.

The earth is getting warmer. Rapid warming in the past three decades coincides with the time in which greenhouse gas climate forcing became much larger than other climate forcings. Global warming in just the past 30 years is about one degree fahrenheit (1°F) or 0.6 degrees celsius (0.6°C), making the earth at least as warm as it has been within the Holocene (Hansen et al., 2006), the current interglacial period of relative climate stability that has existed for the past 10,000 years.

However, it is important to remind people that 1°F, or even 1.4°F, which is the global warming over the past century, is much smaller than day-to-day weather fluctuations or even month-to-month changes of local mean temperature. Figure 1 shows maps of recent monthly temperature anomalies (in degrees celsius, fahrenheit anomalies are a factor 1.8 larger; that is, approximately twice as large). January 2006 was the warmest January in the period of instrumental data in the Midwest United States, about 5°C above normal, but Europe and Western Asia were abnormally cold. Regional temperature fluctuations are normal, although this specific case was unusual, as you can see by comparison with other months.

You can also see (figure 1) that warm anomalies now dominate over cool anomalies. And the notion that European cold weather is due to a slowdown of the Atlantic circulation is a red herring. The

Atlantic Ocean, in fact, has been warmer than normal recently. From a map of the average surface temperature anomaly for the past five years (Hansen et al., 2006), we can see that the earth's surface has been warmer than climatology, the 1951-1980 mean, almost everywhere on the globe. Warming has occurred over the ocean as well as over land, with the largest warming in remote regions. It is obviously a real global warming, not an artifact of thermometers being located close to urban centers.

3. CLIMATE SENSITIVITY

Let us now address the topic of climate sensitivity—that is, the question of how much the global temperature changes in response to a given climate forcing. A climate forcing is an imposed change of the earth's energy balance with space—for example, a change of the amount of solar energy impinging on the earth, or a change of the amount of greenhouse gases in the atmosphere. Our most precise knowledge about climate sensitivity comes not from climate models per se, but from empirical information on climate change interpreted with the aid of climate models.

Figure 2 shows records of atmospheric carbon dioxide, methane, and temperature for the past 400,000 years that have been extracted from Antarctic ice cores. The temperature difference between the warmest (interglacial) periods, and the depths of the ice ages is about 10°C in Antarctica, about 5°C on global average, and about 3°C over the equatorial oceans. We can evaluate climate sensitivity by comparing the present interglacial period, which has existed for about 10,000 years, with the ice age that peaked 20,000 years ago.

We know the change of surface conditions on earth between the ice age and the current interglacial period quite well. During the ice age an ice sheet covered Canada and parts of the United States. The brighter surface during the ice age reflected more sunlight, so there was less heating of the earth, which reduced climate forcing by about 3½ watts per square meter (W/m^2). The atmosphere was also different, with a smaller amount of greenhouse gases during the ice age. The total forcing of about 6½ W/m² (figure 3) maintained a global temperature difference of 5°C, implying a climate sensitivity of ¾ ± ¼ °C for each W/m² of forcing. This value for climate sensitivity is similar to estimates obtained from climate models.

One might question whether the climate sensitivity derived from two points in time has more general validity. We can now investigate that question and obtain additional important inferences about climate change with the help of detailed data for sea level change during the past 400,000 years (Siddall et al., 2003). Sea level changes by about 100 meters between ice ages and interglacial periods (figure 4A). For reasonable assumptions about the shape of ice sheets, we can approximate the area covered by ice sheets, and thus the ice sheet climate forcing, as being proportional to the sea level change to the ⅔ power. Given the ice sheet forcing of 3½ W/m² 20,000 years ago, when sea level was about 110 meters lower, we obtain an ice sheet forcing for the entire 400,000 year period (figure 4B).

We can calculate the greenhouse gas climate forcing accurately, using the ice core records of CO_2 and CH_4 amounts as a function of time. Detailed temporal variations of N_2O are not available, but we approximate its smaller contribution to the greenhouse gas climate forcing by increasing the CO_2 and CH_4 forcing by 15 percent. This approximation is based on the magnitude of the maximum glacial-to-interglacial N_2O change and the fact that temporal changes of N_2O sometimes follow those of CO_2 and sometimes follow CH_4. Dating errors in comparing the sea level records and the greenhouse gases can be as much as several thousand years.

The earth must be in radiation balance on these millennial time scales. If the planet were out of balance by even 1 W/m² for a thousand years, it would melt all the ice on the planet or raise the ocean temperature an implausible amount. Therefore, we can calculate an estimate of expected global temperature change by simply multiplying the climate forcing by climate sensitivity, ¾°C per W/m², thus obtaining the blue curve in figure 4C. An estimate of observed global temperature change (figure 4C) is obtained by taking one-half of the Vostok Antarctica temperature change.

The good agreement of observed temperature with that calculated from known forcings, without making any time scale adjustments that might improve the fit, has important implications, in addition to showing that the climate sensitivity ¾°C per W/m^2 fits the entire record. These implications can be understood with the help of two more pieces of information.

First, we note that, although CO_2, CH_4, and temperature changes over the past 400,000 years are reasonably congruent, when looked at carefully we find that the temperature changes usually lead the gas changes by of the order a thousand years (Petit et al., 1999; Hansen and Sato, 2004). Second, we note that the human-induced increases of greenhouse gases in the past century are far outside the range that has existed for hundreds of thousands of years (figure 2), and they will continue to be so for centuries because of the long lifetime of some of these gases.

The greenhouse gas and ice sheet changes on the paleoclimate time scales are thus feedbacks, although they also can be described as indirect forcings. These feedbacks, or indirect forcings, cause almost the entire paleotemperature change, as shown by figure 4C. Therefore, climate on these long time scales is *very sensitive* to even small forcings. The *instigators* of climate change (that is, the *pacemakers*), include especially earth orbital variations, which change the latitudinal distribution and seasonality of sunlight on the planet, but also any other small forcings, and chaos.

Given that humans have taken control of atmospheric CO_2, CH_4 (figure 2), N_2O, and CFCs (chlorofluorocarbons), another implication of figure 4 is that another "ice age" cannot occur unless humans become extinct. Humans now control global climate, for better or worse.

4. CLIMATE CHANGE IN THE INDUSTRIAL ERA

Global temperature change in the past century is shown on a greatly expanded time scale on the right side of figure 2. In this recent period, unlike the earlier part of the graph, the planet is not in energy balance with space, because human-made greenhouse gases are being added to the atmosphere so rapidly that the planet has not yet had time to fully respond.

Climate change in the industrial era differs from paleoclimate in another way: in recent times it is necessary to account for several human-made climate forcings in addition to the well-mixed greenhouse gases (CO_2, CH_4, N_2O and CFCs). The largest of these other forcings are caused by aerosols (fine particles). Most aerosols, such as sulfates originating from sulfur in fossil fuels, have a direct cooling effect by reflecting sunlight. They also have an indirect cooling effect by modifying cloud cover and cloud brightness. Black carbon aerosols (black soot) have a net warming effect since they absorb sunlight and darken snow surfaces. Deforestation also has multiple climate effects, but in most cases the dominant regional effect of deforestation is probably cooling due to an increasing reflectivity of the planetary surface.

When our best estimates for the human-made and natural forcings are used in our global climate model, which has a sensitivity of 2.7°C equilibrium warming for doubled CO_2, (Hansen et al., 2005), the model yields global warming over the period from 1880 to 2005 that is in good agreement with observations (figure 5). Comparably good agreement probably could be achieved by using a larger forcing in a model with smaller climate sensitivity, or vice versa. However, the sensitivity of our model is consistent with that indicated by paleoclimate data.

One inference from the climate simulations is that the planet must now be out of energy balance if the forcings and model sensitivity are approximately correct. The energy imbalance is a direct result of greenhouse gases blocking outgoing radiation and the large thermal inertia of the ocean, so it provides a fundamental test and confirmation of the greenhouse effect. The magnitude of the energy imbalance fluctuates from year to year. In our ensemble of model runs the present imbalance ranges from 0.5 to 1.2 W/m², implying that there is an additional warming of approximately 0.5°C "in the pipeline" that will be realized in the future even without any further increase of climate forcings.

We note that the coarse resolution ocean in the climate model used by Hansen et al. (2005) does not simulate the El Niño phenomena and does not produce the large interannual variability of heat storage in the upper layer of the ocean suggested by observations including recent analyses of J. Willis et al. (priv. comm.). The absence of this variability does not significantly affect the derived magnitude of the planetary energy imbalance, which is a function mainly of the multidecadal rate of heat storage.

5. FUTURE GLOBAL CLIMATE CHANGE

Now let's consider future climate. Fifteen years ago all nations, including the United States, agreed to the Framework Convention on Climate Change (FCCC). The goal of the FCCC is to stabilize greenhouse gas emissions at a level that prevents dangerous human interference with climate. But what level of global warming constitutes dangerous interference?

I have suggested that we are near a tipping point, a point of no return, beyond which the built in momentum arising from warming already in the pipeline and climate feedbacks will carry us to levels of climate change with staggering consequences for humanity and all of the residents of planet earth. Investigation of this issue requires a combination of information from the history of the earth and climate models. Paleoclimate data and climate models each have severe restrictions, but they can be effectively used in combination to tell us a great deal about the likely effects of continuing increases of greenhouse gases.

We tested the ability of our climate model to simulate past climate change, so now lets extend the simulations into the future for different scenarios. IPCC scenarios A2 and A1B have a growth rate for CO_2 emissions of about 2 percent per year over the next 50 years, similar to the actual growth rate of the past 10 years, so A2 and A1B both constitute "business-as-usual" scenarios. The "alternative scenario," in contrast, assumes slowly declining emissions, so that the added CO_2 forcing is about 1 W/m² in 50 years and 1.5 W/m² over 100 years. The alternative scenario climate forcing, and a climate sensitivity consistent with paleoclimate data, yields additional warming (above that in year 2000) that peaks in the early twenty-second century at less than 1°C. In the business-as-usual scenarios, added warming is more than 2°C and still rising rapidly at the end of century.

How much more "dangerous" is 2° to 3°C global warming, as opposed to less than 1°C? The most important global issue for humans, in my opinion, is sea level. Discussion of sea level change can be usefully divided into two parts: the equilibrium change of sea level for a given magnitude of global warming, and the question of how long it takes the ice sheets to respond to global warming.

The warmest interglacial periods in the past 400,000 years were about 1°C or so warmer than today, and in one or two cases sea level may have been higher by as much as about 5 meters. On the other hand, to find a temperature 2½° or 3°C warmer than today, we must go back to the Middle Pliocene, 3 million years ago, when sea level was about 25 meters (80 feet) higher than today. There is a geological feature along the East Coast called the Orangeburg Scarf, which was the coastline at about that time. It is typically 100 kilometers inland now, about 25 to 35 meters above sea level. Most of Florida was under water then.

The principal uncertainty is how long it will require for ice sheets to respond to warming. There is now evidence indicating that ice sheets respond substantially to warming within centuries. In one period during the last deglaciation, about 14,000 years ago, sea level went up 20 meters in 400 years, which is *an average* of one meter every 20 years. There is also evidence that rapid sea level changes of 10 meters or more have occurred many times in the past.

It requires millennia for ice sheets to grow, because their growth is limited by the rate of snowfall in cold parts of the planet. However, ice sheet disintegration can occur more rapidly, because it is a wet process. On Greenland the area of the ice sheet with summer melt fluctuates from year-to-year with the weather, but the area has increased by about 50 percent over the past two decades. The summer of 2005 broke the prior record for melt area.

Meltwater descends through crevasses and lubricates the base of the ice sheet. The largest ice streams on Greenland have doubled their speed in recent years and their flux of icebergs to the ocean. If the Earth were to warm another 2° to 3°C, which implies warming about twice that large in the high latitude regions of Greenland and Antarctica, it is inconceivable to me that the ice sheets on either Greenland or West Antarctica would survive. Indeed, the history of the earth indicates that they would not, and part of East Antarctica would go with them.

As was noted earlier, sea level will increase slowly at first, as losses on the fringes of the ice sheets due to accelerating ice streams are partly balanced by increased snowfall in the ice sheet interiors. But as the ice is softened and lubricated by melt-water and as buttressing ice shelves disappear due to a warming ocean, a point of no return will be reached when multiple positive feedbacks take over and cause cataclysmic ice sheet disintegration. And contrary to ice sheet behavior in some old lethargic ice sheet models, real world data imply that sea level would change substantially in centuries, not millennia. The century time scale for ice sheet disintegration is probably the worst case for coastal dwellers, because the damage occurs irregularly in conjunction with storms, so they would be faced with repeatedly rebuilding above a transient water level.

6. REGIONAL CLIMATE EFFECTS

Let us consider regional climate change. For that purpose, I will first make a general statement and then examine some specific cases.

We have used our global climate model to calculate the change of seasonal mean temperature by the end of the present century for two IPCC business-as-usual scenarios and for the alternative scenario. The model has climate sensitivity consistent with paleoclimate data and observed climate change of the past century; indeed, the climate simulations (figure 5) were extensions of the runs that fit well the observed climate in the prior century.

We compared the local seasonal mean warming in these simulations with the local standard deviation of seasonal mean temperature in the twentieth century. This standard deviation thus includes the effect of both year-to-year variations and long-term change; this is, it is a measure of the total variation in the past century. The business-as-usual simulations yield changes in the mean by 5 to 10 standard deviations, which I submit represents prima facie evidence of dangerous change. Changes of 5 to 10 standard deviations would mean that the environment and its inhabitants would face *average* local conditions that they had never experienced, even in the most extreme years. People, with the help of technologies that allow control of living environments, may adjust readily to such changes, but the ecology will have a more difficult time adjusting (Hansen et al. 2006).

The Arctic provides an example of regional climate change that is already becoming noticeable. As in the case of ice sheets and sea level, Arctic regional climate has a potential tipping point, because of positive feedbacks. In particular, as sea ice melts, the ocean absorbs more sunlight and becomes warmer. This process is not a runaway feedback or instability, but it is very sensitive, so a moderate increase in climate forcings could melt all of the summer ice, thus destroying the habitat of many species and the way of life of indigenous peoples.

We are getting dangerously close to this tipping point for the Arctic, as summer sea ice has already decreased about 25 percent since the late 1970s. At this point, it is still possible to save the Arctic, because even though there surely will be increased CO_2 forcing this century, there are other forcings that are very effective in the Arctic, specifically methane, tropospheric ozone, and black soot. A focused effort to reduce these pollutants might suffice to stabilize Arctic climate, provided that the growth rate of CO_2 decelerated as in the alternative scenario.

Tropical storms, specifically potential changes in the intensity and frequency of such storms, are another important regional climate issue. In our climate model we calculate that human-made climate forcings cause an ocean surface warming in the region of hurricane formation over the past few decades that is equal to a large fraction of observed warming there. Therefore, the categorical contention of the National Oceanic and Atmospheric Administration (NOAA) National Hurricane Center that hurricane intensification in recent years is due to a natural cycle of Atlantic Ocean temperature, and has nothing to do with global warming, seems irrational. How could a hurricane distinguish between a natural warming and greenhouse gas warming? It is conceivable, but it would require an explanation that has not been proffered. On the contrary, I suggest that greenhouse gases are responsible for a substantial fraction of the ocean warming that has fueled stronger hurricanes.

I bring up the topic of tropical storms because during last year's hurricane season NOAA took an official position that global warming was not a cause of hurricane intensification. The public, glued to television watching reports from the National Hurricane Center, was repeatedly given that message. This scientific topic is a complex one that the research community is still working on, but it seems to me that the public, by fiat, received biased information. Furthermore, NOAA scientists were told not to dispute the Hurricane Center conclusion in public. Given the first amendment to our Constitution, I am not certain whether such instructions are legal.

However, what I can say is that an official government position restricting discussion of a scientific matter flies in the face of the scientific method. You will not be successful in science unless you are able to explain and discuss what is bad and what is good about any theory.

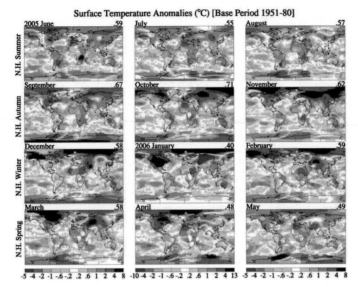

Surface Temperature Anomalies (°C) [Base Period 1951-80]

Fig. 1 Recent monthly surface temperature anomalies (°C) relative to the period 1951–1980, based on Hansen et al. (2001), Reynolds and Smith (1994), and Rayner et al. (2003).

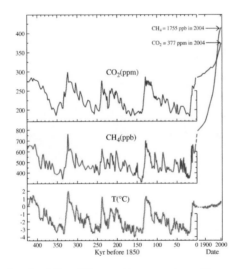

Fig. 2 Time series for CO_2, CH_4, and temperature. The paleoclimate record is based on local Vostok Antarctica ice core data (Petit et al., 1999; Vimeux et al., 2002) and modern temperature on Hansen et al. (2001). The Vostok temperature is divided by two to approximate global temperature anomalies. The zero point for temperature is the 1880–1899 mean.

Ice Age Climate Forcings (W/m^2)

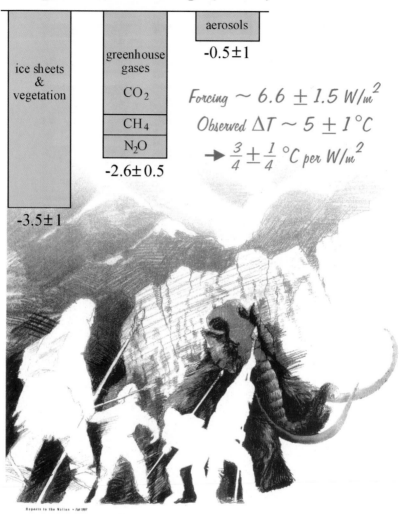

Forcing $\sim 6.6 \pm 1.5\ W/m^2$

Observed $\Delta T \sim 5 \pm 1\,^\circ C$

$\rightarrow \frac{3}{4} \pm \frac{1}{4}\,^\circ C$ per W/m^2

aerosols
-0.5±1

greenhouse gases
CO$_2$

CH$_4$

N$_2$O

-2.6±0.5

ice sheets & vegetation

-3.5±1

Fig. 3 Climate forcings during the ice age that peaked about 20,000 years ago relative to the pre-industrial era. These forcings maintained a 5°C global temperature change, implying an equilibrium global climate sensitivity of about ³/₄°C per W/m² (Hansen et al., 1993).

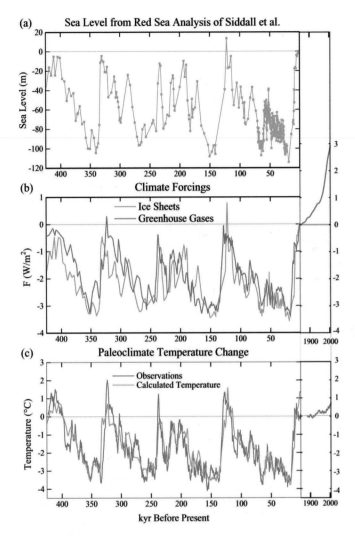

Fig. 4. (A) Global sea level from Red Sea analysis of Siddall et al. (2003) obtained by concatenating Siddall's MD921017, Byrd, and Glacial Recovery data sets, which use AMS radiocarbon dating. (B) Paleoclimate forcings, assuming ice sheet forcing is proportional to (sea level)$^{2/3}$. Greenhouse gases included are CO_2, CH_4 and N_2O, with the N_2O forcing taken as 15% of the sum of CO_2 and CH_4 forcings. (C) Paleoclimate temperature change, the calculated temperature being the forcing, from (B), multiplied by climate sensitivity, $3/4°C/W/m^2$, while the observed temperature is one-half of the Antarctic temperature record extracted from the Vostok ice core.

Surface Air Temperature (°C)

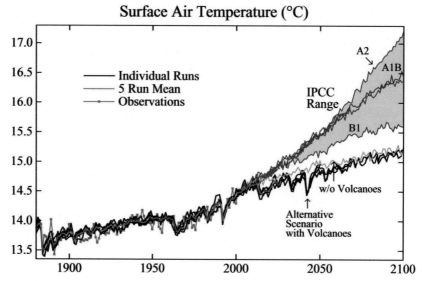

Fig. 5. Simulated and observed global surface temperature. Simulations for the past use 10 climate forcings defined by Hansen et al. (2005). Extensions into the future are driven by IPCC scenarios and the "alternative" scenario. IPCC A2 and A1B scenarios have growth rates of about 2 percent/year for CO_2 emissions in the first half of the present century, which we describe as a "business-as-usual" growth rate since it matches the growth rate of the past decade.

Fossil Fuel CO₂ Emissions

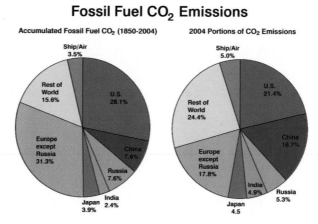

Fig. 6. Fossil fuel CO_2 emissions by source, with accumulated emissions over the period 1850–2004 on the left and apportionment in 2004 on the right.

More broadly, I do not see how any decision making can be successful, if there is not freedom to question.

There has been publicity lately about restrictions on NASA communications with the media. NASA is working on that problem and I have high hopes that NASA will fix its own problem and be a model for other agencies. However, I have been told by NOAA colleagues about conditions that seem worse than those in NASA. NOAA scientists involved in global warming research often cannot speak with a reporter unless there is a "listener" on the line with him or her. It seems more like the old Soviet Union than the United States. The claim is that the "listener" is there to protect the NOAA scientist. If you buy that one, please allow me to show you a bridge in Brooklyn that I would like to sell to you.

There is a good rationale for preventing scientists from intruding in policymaking. The converse is also true. Policy should not intrude in science, or it will destroy the quality of the science and diminish the value of the science to the public.

The ultimate policymaker is the public. Unless the public is provided with unfiltered scientific information that accurately reflects the views of the scientific community, policymaking is likely to suffer.

In summary, with regard to regional climate: as with global climate and sea level, business-as-usual scenarios by the end of the century produce basically another planet. How else can you describe climate change in which the Arctic becomes an open lake in the summer and fall, and most land areas on earth experience mean warming this century that is 5 to 10 times larger than the standard deviation of the past century?

7. CLIMATE CHANGE SCENARIOS

Can we still avoid dangerous human-made climate change? As we have shown, that would require avoiding the business-as-usual scenario, which would yield additional global warming of 2° to 3°C over and above the 0.7°C global warming that already existed in 2000. Definition

of the precise level of global warming that would constitute "dangerous" change may not be possible, but based on present knowledge it is
reasonably clear that we should aim to keep additional global warming
beyond that of 2000 from exceeding 1°C.

A limit of 1°C on additional global warming is still possible, but
just barely. Achievement of this limit on global warming is the goal of
the alternative scenario, which has two requirements. First, the rate of
CO_2 emissions must flatten out soon and decline substantially before
mid-century. Second, we must achieve a moderate absolute decrease
of the present non-CO_2 forcings, primarily CH_4, tropspheric O_3, and
black soot.

These two goals are interdependent, because of positive feedbacks between global warming and atmospheric amounts of greenhouse gases such as CO_2, CH_4 and N_2O. Thus substantial failure on
one of the two goals means that the other is unlikely to be achieved.
As a result, we see a dichotomy of possible scenarios for the future:
either we make the effort needed to achieve both portions of the
alternative scenario or the planet will be faced with a global warming
that extends well above the estimated level for dangerous climate
change.

The most difficult part of the alternative scenario is the needed
decrease of CO_2 emissions. In the past decade global fossil fuel CO_2
emissions have been increasing at a rate of 2 percent per year, which is
the "business-as-usual" growth rate. Is there a feasible energy pathway
that could move us off this course onto a course with declining CO_2
emissions?

Satisfying energy needs while decreasing CO_2 emissions will
require, in the long run, increased emphasis on energy efficiency,
development of renewable energies, sequestration of CO_2 produced
at fossil fuel power plants, and probably a new generation of nuclear
power, unless there are some unforeseen technological breakthroughs.
In the near-term, improved energy efficiency has the greatest potential
to flatten out the rate of emissions. Avoiding growth of near-term emis-

sions is critical for attainment of the alternative scenario and avoidance of dangerous climate change. Continued growth of CO_2 emissions at 2 percent per year until 2015 would yield about a 35 percent increase of CO_2 annual emissions with associated CO_2-producing infrastructure. Given the long life of both atmospheric CO_2 and energy infrastructure, a 35 percent increase of the CO_2 emission rate would make attainment of the alternative scenario impractical.

There are two major sources of CO_2 emissions that must be flattened out in the near-term: vehicles and power plants. Vehicles are the fastest growing source, and power plants have the longest-lived infrastructure, especially coal-burning power plants without sequestration. The best prospects for achieving the needed reductions in the near-term are in energy efficiency. Attainment of the "alternative scenario" for vehicles and power plants can be achieved only if the United States, as a technology leader and as the largest producer of CO_2 in the world, takes a leadership role.

Vehicle efficiency improvements provide the potential to achieve a leveling off or decline in annual CO_2 emissions, even though the number of vehicles on the road increases every year. For example, the National Research Council has recommended requiring an average 30 percent improvement in vehicle efficiency, which is feasible with existing technology. The California Air Resources Board is attempting to impose such a requirement in California, but this requirement is being opposed in court by automobile manufacturers and the federal government. Automobile manufacturers make largest near-term profits on large inefficient vehicles.

The proposed California automobile efficiency requirements, if applied nationally over a 35-year period, would yield a savings of oil equal to more than seven times the amount of oil that the US Geological Survey estimates to be available in the Arctic National Wildlife Refuge. The savings at $50 per barrel of oil would be more than $100 billion *per year*. These savings increase each year, as vehicle population increases, even without likely additional efficiency improvements. There are thus numerous benefits of improved efficiency and there is likely to be a great commercial market for improved efficiency, so it should be pursued more vigorously, for our own good as well as for the planet's well-being.

Climate change is a global problem and CO_2 emissions must be addressed globally. Although the United States has the largest CO_2 emissions, the emissions by China and India are growing more rapidly. Figure 6 (left side) illustrates that, integrated over time through 2004, the United States has emitted more than 28 percent of global fossil fuel emissions. Aircraft and ship emissions of CO_2 are tabulated separately in figure 6, so assigning an appropriate fraction to the United States raises its integrated emissions to nearly 30 percent. The next highest emitters are China and Russia, each at less than 8 percent.

CO_2 emissions by China, India, and other developing nations are increasing rapidly, as can be inferred from comparison of the left and right sides of figure 6. Within the next few years, China will pass the United States as the greatest source of ongoing CO_2 emissions. The continuing need to improve living standards in the developing world makes attainment of the "alternative scenario" for climate forcings a monumental challenge.

However, it should be noted that the global growth rate of emissions has been "only" 2 percent annually in the past decade despite rapid growth in China and India. Actions required to get off the global 2 percent per year growth rate pathway make sense for a number of reasons and they are technically feasible. China and India, overall, are even much less energy efficient than the United States. Also, China, India, and the rest of the developing world are likely to suffer greatly from increased global warming. Clearly, there is a good basis for cooperation in limiting CO_2 emissions, but achievement of that cooperation will require leadership.

There is another reason for optimism that the alternative scenario for climate change may be feasible. Keeping additional global warming under 1°C requires, in addition to a limit on CO_2 emissions, an absolute decrease of non-CO_2 climate forcings. The developing world is a large source of the non-CO_2 forcings and these countries would benefit greatly from a reduction of the non-CO_2 emissions since those emissions are the principal sources of air pollution that cause extensive damage to human health and agricultural productivity.

The non-CO_2 portion of the alternative scenario has been addressed in two workshops held in recent years at the East-West Center in Hawaii. These workshops concluded that it would be practical to reduce tropospheric ozone through feasible reductions of sources of methane and carbon monoxide, with benefits to climate, human health, and agricultural productivity. In addition, focused efforts to reduce the sources of black carbon (black soot) aerosols, would similarly benefit climate, human health, and agricultural productivity. The benefits, although concentrated more in developing countries, extend to developed countries through reduced pollution and to future generations through reduced climate change.

8. DISCUSSION

In summary, is there still time to avoid dangerous human-made interference with climate? The evidence shows with reasonable clarity that additional global warming greater than about 1°C would put us into dangerous territory. Our estimate of the dangerous level will need to be refined as more data comes in, but this estimate cannot be too far off the mark.

The answer to our question is yes: it is technically possible to avoid grim business-as usual climate change. We could follow an alternative scenario in which growth of greenhouse gas emissions is slowed in the first quarter of this century, primarily through concerted near-term improvements in energy efficiency, a parallel reduction of non-CO_2 climate forcings, and longer term advances in energy technologies that yield a cleaner atmosphere as well as a stable climate.

The required actions make practical sense and have multiple benefits, but they will not take place without strong policy leadership and international cooperation. Action must be prompt, otherwise CO_2-producing infrastructure that may be built within a decade could make it impractical to keep further global warming under 1°C. I refer especially to the large number of coal-fired power plants that China, the United States, and India are planning to build without CO_2 sequestration.

If the alternative scenario is practical, has multiple benefits, and makes good common sense, why are we not pursuing it?

There is little merit in casting blame for inaction, unless it helps point toward a solution. It seems to me that special interests have been a roadblock wielding undue influence over policymakers. The special interests seek to maintain short-term profits with little regard to the long-term impact on the planet that will be inherited by our children and grandchildren or the long-term economic well-being of our country.

The public, if well informed, has the ability to override the influence of special interests, and the public has shown that it feels a stewardship toward the earth and all of its inhabitants. Scientists can play a useful role if they help communicate the climate change story to the public in a credible, understandable fashion.

NOTES

* This paper is derived substantially from my presentation to the American Geophysical Union on December 6, 2005 in San Francisco honoring Charles David Keeling. Both presentation draw on research carried out with colleagues at the NASA Goddard Institute for Space Studies and the Columbia University Earth Institute, especially Makiko Sato, Reto Ruedy and Andy Lacis.

REFERENCES

Hansen, J. "A Slippery Slope: How Much Global Warming Constitutes 'Dangerous Anthropogenic Interference?'" *Climatic Change* 68 (2005): 269-279.

Hansen, J., A. Lacis, R. Ruedy, M. Sato, and H. Wilson. "How Sensitive Is the World's Climate?" *National Geographic Research and Exploration* 9 (1993): 141-158.

Hansen, J., L. Nazarenko, R. Ruedy, M. Sato, J. Willis, A. Del Genio, D. Koch, A. Lacis, K. Lo, S. Menon, T. Novakov, J. Perlwitz, G. Russell, G.A. Schmidt, and N. Tausnev. "Earth's Energy Imbalance: Confirmation and Implications." *Science* 308 (2005): 1431-1435.

Hansen, J., R. Ruedy, M. Sato, M. Imhoff, W. Lawrence, D. Easterling, T. Peterson, and T. Karl. "A Closer Look at United States and Global Surface Temperature Change." *Journal of Geophysical Research* 106 (2001): 23947-23963.

Hansen, J., and M. Sato. "Greenhouse Gas Growth Rates." *Proceedings of the National Academy of Sciences* 101 (2004): 16109-16114.

Hansen, J., M. Sato, R. Ruedy, K. Lo, D.W. Lea, and M. Medina-Elizade. "Global Temperature Change." *Proceedings of the National Academy of Sciences*, 2006. In press.

Petit, J. R., et al. "420,000 years of Climate and Atmospheric History Revealed by the Vostok Deep Antarctic Ice Core." *Nature* 399 (1999): 429-436.

Rayner, N. A., D. E. Parker, E. B. Horton, C. K. Folland, L. V. Alexander, D. P. Rowell, E. C. Kent and A. Kaplan. "Global Analyses of SST, Sea Ice and Night Marine Air Temperatures since the Late Nineteenth Century." *Journal of Geophysical Research* 108 (2003): doi:10.1029/2002JD002670.

Reynolds, R. W., and T. M. Smith. "Improved Global Sea Surface Temperature Analyses." *Journal of Climate* 7 (1994): 929-948.

Siddall, M., E. J. Rohling, A. Almoghi-Labin, Ch. Hemleben, D. Meischner, I. Schmelzer, and D. A. Smeed. "Sea-Level Fluctuations During the Last Glacial Cycle." *Nature* 423 (2003): 853-858.

Vimeux, F., K. M. Cuffey, and J. Jouzel. "New Insights into Southern Hemisphere Temperature Changes from Vostok Ice Cores Using Deuterium Excess Correction." *Earth and Planetary Science Letters* 203 (2002): 829-843.

HELP SUPPORT

THE JOURNAL DONATION PROJECT

Begun in 1990 with the collapse of the Soviet Union, the Journal Donation Project (JDP), a *Social Research*, initiative, is an international library assistance program that assists in the rebuilding of major research and teaching libraries in countries that have fallen victim to political and economic deprivation. Through the provision of current subscriptions drawn from over 2,000 of the most important English-language scholarly, professional and current events journals, the JDP has helped to develop significant journal archives at over 300 libraries in 30 countries. The Project has grown substantially over the years, due to the generosity of donors. Gifts from individuals, families, corporate matching programs, grant-giving foundations, and others are deeply appreciated.

Donors may wish to make a one-time donation, pledge an annual gift, give in honor of or in memory of a loved one, or designate monies for a specific project/geographic location. All donations are tax deductible.

To learn how you can help support the JDP, please contact:

Professor Arien Mack, Project Organizer and Director
New School University, Journal Donation Project
65 Fifth Avenue
New York, NY 10003
Tel: 212 229 5789
Fax: 212 229 5476
Email: jdp@newschool.edu
Website: www.newschool.edu/centers/jdp

V. Energy: Technology and Sources of Power

The Journal of Energy and Development, published twice yearly since 1975 on an academic calendar—fall and spring—by the International Research Center for Energy and Economic Development (ICEED), offers articles on energy resources; energy-related topics as conservation, environment, finance, and management; domestic and international energy issues; the producer-consumer relationship, and development linked to energy, as well as book reviews and a listing of books and publications received. *Subscription rates* (surface book post included) per volume: *Student/faculty (personal payment)*, $25; *Library*, $37; *Institutional/General*, $45. Air mail post charges are additional. ISSN 0361-4476.

Occasional Paper Series, each 20-28 pages and $10, begun in 1986. A full listing is available on the web site of the Center. More recent papers include:

- #36: *Green Trading™: The Next Financial Market*, Peter C. Fusaro (2003)
- #37: *Oil and the Iraq War*, John Robert (2003)
- #38: *Oil Supply Security 2004: Does the Song Remain the Same,* Michael C. Lynch (2004)
- #39: *Hedge Funds Change Energy Trading*, Peter C. Fusaro & Gary M. Vasey (2005)
- #40: *Crop Circles in the Desert: The Strange Controversy over Saudi Oil Production*, Michal C. Lynch with Appendix by M. A. Adelman (2006)

34th Annual International Energy Conference and 28th Annual International Area Conference of the ICEED are scheduled for April 15-18, 2007, in Boulder, Colorado. These meetings are the oldest of their type held in the United States, bringing together the public and private sectors world-wide as well as multinational agencies. Emphasis is placed on economic and policy aspects of energy and energy-related topics. In order to facilitate the open exchange of information and contacts, the size of the conferences is kept small, with attendance by invitation only. Those wishing additional information or an invitation should contact the ICEED. CDs of earlier conferences are available and listed with ordering details on the web site.

**International Research Center for Energy and
  Economic Development (ICEED)**
850 Willowbrook Road
Boulder CO 80302 U.S.A.
Telephone: (303) 442-4014 / Fax: (303) 442-5042
E-mail: iceed@colorado.edu
Web site: www.iceed.org

Henry Kelly
Introduction

IF YOU COULD ASK AN ORACLE TWO QUESTIONS ABOUT THE HUMAN
condition a century from now, they might be "Have nuclear weapons
been used?" and "Has a way been found to provide all a comfortable
living for everyone on the planet without a disastrous impact on the
natural environment?" Finding a way to ensure an attractive answer
to these closely related questions will require unprecedented technical and political ingenuity. Technologies must be developed that can
provide amenities such as mobility and comfortable living space using
a third or less of the natural resources needed to provide them today.
Since this is likely to require expanded use of nuclear power and an
accompanying expansion of nuclear-fuel-processing facilities and associated expertise, some way must be found to provide ironclad guarantees that materials and know-how is not diverted to build weapons.

The papers in this section vividly describe the significance of the
task before us, the consequences of failure, and the difficulty of finding practical solutions. As Kurt Gottfried suggests, this is a "political
dilemma of unprecedented complexity and magnitude that faces all
societies and the international community as a whole."

Solutions encounter three major challenges. First, any successful program must lead to real changes in the behavior of individuals,
companies, and governments. But any program that actually forces
change will meet determined resistance from those whose near-term
behavior is being altered while typically receiving lukewarm support
for the vast majority whose long-term interests would be served. The
second is that policies must address the huge inequality in income and
in resource use prevailing in the world today. It is simply not possible

for the world to sustain 7 to 10 billion people if their consumption is like that of today's Americans—let alone the future US consumption rates implied by current trends. As Gottfried's paper puts it, "there is mounting recognition that the worldwide quest for economic growth, and the energy needed to fuel it, are on a collision course with nature."

A workable response to these challenges requires inventing a future more appealing than the widely understood US success story—one that would be attractive both to US investors and developing economies. Finally, concrete action on environmental and energy problems in the past benefited from immediate, visible problems: air so polluted that it was causing acute health problems and long lines at the gas pumps. The risks of climate change and potential price spikes and other disruptions in energy supplies facing us today are long-term and visible only through expert analysis.

One theme linking these formidable tasks is that they are surely insurmountable without active participation by credible scientists and engineers. Our recognition that a problem of climate change or limits to inexpensive energy resources depends entirely on foresight gained from technical analysis. Options for attractive solutions depend on defining a range of potential technical solutions and a clear understanding of their costs and benefits. This work should serve to set the framework for the equally difficult political challenge of building consensus and aligning interests behind research programs, fiscal policies, and regulatory strategies required to move away from a "business as usual" trajectory plainly headed for disaster.

William Martin's remarks at the conference—not, unfortunately, included in this volume—suggested, for example, that we badly need to understand technical options and also understand "which ones do the best at reducing carbon and which do the best in reducing oil imports." But he also expressed shock that the federal government has not provided such a fair accounting. As he pointed out, in the absence of widely credible analysis, we have what amounts to a propaganda and political maneuvering contest between "R&D tribes."

Nuclear power is a peculiarly difficult case. It is highly likely that a solid program of research, testing, and regulation can result in nuclear electric power that meets acceptably high standards of safety and reliability. Cost is likely to be the most difficult commercial barrier. But as several of the authors vividly remind us, the most vexing problem in nuclear power is a political one: how to build a fail-safe firewall between legitimate commercial activities and military applications of the same technology. Rapid growth in nuclear power must be accompanied by equivalent growth in commercial facilities for uranium enrichment and fuel processing. Large amounts of fissionable material will need to be transported. And rapid growth of expertise in these technologies will be needed to support these activities. Advances in technology are unlikely to improve the situation and may actually make things worse by, for example, driving down the cost and complexity of uranium enrichment. Only a tight international control regime can succeed—one that will require sacrificing some sovereign control over the fuel cycle by all parties. This includes the United States.

It is obvious that no acceptable solution to world energy challenges can be achieved without close links between the scientific and engineering community and policymakers. Scientists must take great care ensuring that they separate their personal opinions from the facts they present, but it is essential to provide a forum for objective scientific research. The question addressed by papers presented here is whether this sad state of affairs in scientific and technical advice in US policymaking results from simple bumbling or from a conscious effort to block analysis that might result in outcomes ruled unworthy for political reasons. It is unfortunately well understood in political circles that if you know you are likely to lose a debate, it's best not to enter one. It is far better to invent a new game with your own rules and referees. These forces have always been present but seem increasingly difficult to resist.

The problem, of course, is that there is no accepted alternative to the rules that govern scientific debate hammered out over centuries of painful experience. It is painful to restate the obvious but the situation seems to demand it. The selection of theories in science is transparent and continuously competitive. At any given time there are always a range of troubling problems with even the most powerful theories. Most of the time, these difficulties can be resolved by refining experiments or extending existing theories. On rare occasions the applecart gets overturned in a true scientific revolution. Einstein's theory of gravity, for example, attacked one of the most hallowed theories in science—Newton's theory of gravity. Scientists have a powerful incentive to find flaws in existing theories since this is a well-known path to promotion and fame. The burden on anyone proposing to displace an existing theory is, however, enormous. The challenger must find an alternative theory that does a better job of explaining existing observations. An opponent to theories of climate change, for example, must provide an improved way to explain the myriad of observations so convincingly consistent with the prevailing theory.

The lowercase-p politics in science has often played a role in scientific research. No one likes to be proved wrong and established scientists have successfully blocked new ideas for years. In the long run it is difficult to suppress a theory that has valuable explanatory or predictive power. Einstein's theory of gravity explained a detail about Mercury's orbit that simply could not be explained by Newton's theory and critics eventually caved in.

What frustrates scientists about the current debate in energy and environmental policy is not being challenged, but that their proponents are not willing to accept the fundamental premises of scientific debate. It never occurred to Einstein, for example, to ask business leaders or politicians to plead his case.

What is frightening about the current state of affairs is that there may be a systematic effort to undermine the integrity of the scientific process itself and make science simply one more politically motivated interest group. As Martin Hoffert suggests, arguments are being made by climate change deniers that make sense only if there is "a vast conspiracy that involved the editors of all the major scientific journals."

As Paul Gilman's article points out: "Once an issue has become the focus for partisan political debate, the value of scientific and technical information in that debate declines." Nothing could be more damaging to urgent work we have before us in energy and the environment. There is simply no substitute for the open process of scientific debate now operating worldwide.

Science and engineering, of course, have fundamental limitations. While they can tell us we can do, they say nothing about what we should do. But without confidence that there is an objective process for defining risks, developing solutions, and sorting out options, we will surely fail.

Journal of
Industrial Ecology

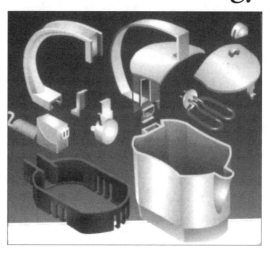

Reid Lifset, Editor-in-Chief

Helge Brattebø and
John Ehrenfeld, Editors

The Journal of Industrial Ecology is the premier journal in the emerging field of industrial ecology—dedicated to the investigation of environmental issues linked to industrial activities and their associated flows of materials and energy. The official publication of the International Society for Industrial Ecology, the Journal is a highly-regarded peer-reviewed quarterly which has been praised for both its readability and its timely relevance to key environmental issues.

Articles in the Journal of Industrial Ecology (JIE) address:

- Materials and energy flow studies ("industrial metabolism")
- Dematerialization and decarbonization
- Technological change and the environment
- Life-cycle assessment, planning, design and management
- Design for environment ("eco-design")
- Extended producer responsibility ("product stewardship")
- Eco-industrial parks ("industrial symbiosis")
- Product-oriented environmental policy and management
- Eco-efficiency

MIT Press Journals
238 Main Street, Suite 500
Cambridge, MA 02142 USA
Tel: 617-253-2889
Fax: 617-577-1545
journals-orders@mit.edu
http://mitpressjournals.org/jie
Published quarterly in
winter, spring, summer and fall.
Volume 10 forthcoming.
ISSN 1088-1980 / E-ISSN 1530-9290

Stay on top of the field!
Sign up for the JIE's FREE table of contents alert service.

Four times a year you will receive an e-mail message highlighting the articles published in the most recent issue of the Journal.

http://mitpress.mit.edu/jie/e-mail

Martin Hoffert
An Energy Revolution for the Greenhouse Century

When there is no vision, the people perish.
                                        —Proverbs 29:18

You see things: and you say, "Why?"
But I dream things that never were; and I say, "Why not?"
          —George Bernard Shaw, *Back to Methuselah* (1921)

We choose to go to the moon in this decade and do the other things, not because they are easy, but because they are hard, because that goal will serve to organize and measure the best of our energies and skills, because the challenge is one that we are willing to accept, one we are unwilling to postpone, and one we intend to win. . . .
          —John F. Kennedy, Rice University, 1962

THE REALITY OF GLOBAL WARMING FROM THE BUILDUP OF FOSSIL FUEL CARBON dioxide in the atmosphere is no longer in doubt. Arctic sea ice, tundra, and alpine glaciers are melting, tropical diseases like West Nile virus and malaria are penetrating higher latitudes, and sea surface temperatures have risen to the point where Katrina-like hurricanes are not only more probable, but actually occur. Also taking place are the extinction of plants and animals adapted to cooler regimes but unable to migrate poleward fast enough to keep pace with a warming climate. Polar bears, already far north, may have nowhere to go. Ominously, the melting of Greenland and Antarctic icecaps is accelerating, threatening worldwide major sea level rise and coastal inundation (Hansen, 2006; Gore, 2006; Kolbert, 2006; Flannery, 2006).

These are well-documented facts, not alarmist predictions by desperate environmentalists in search of funding (Crichton, 2003) or some colossal hoax on the American people (Inhofe, 2003). Atmospheric warming from water vapor, CO_2, and other greenhouse gases is a basic principle of atmospheric science. It is responsible for maintaining earth as a habitable zone for life, and for making Venus, with its pure CO_2 atmosphere 100 times thicker than earth's, hot as metaphorical Hell. Cooling can result from suspended aerosol particles also produced by burning fossil fuels, but aerosols remain in the atmosphere a much shorter time than CO_2 and their cooling effect, so far, has mainly served to mask the full impact of warming from CO_2 emissions. (Some propose "geoengineering" climate by intentionally injecting aerosols to cool regions most threatened by global warming, such as the Arctic; see for example Teller, Wood, and Hyde, 2002). Heat temporarily stored in oceans can also delay or mask committed greenhouse warming, as can variations in the output of the sun and volcanic eruptions. But volcanoes, the sun, and the oceans cause surface temperature to rise and fall in a narrow range. In retrospect, it was inevitable that the explosive growth (on a geological time scale) of human CO_2 emissions, driven by population growth, industrialization and, most of all, by fossil fuel energy use, made it inevitable that human-induced warming would overwhelm climate change from all the other factors at some point. And we are at that point.

That fossil fuel atmospheric carbon dioxide would warm the planet was predicted over a century ago (Arrhenius, 1896). Roughly half the CO_2 input by humans remains in the atmosphere. The rest mostly dissolves in the ocean, creating excess acidity that marine organisms may not be able to tolerate, which is another problem. By the third quarter of the twentieth century, CO_2 buildup in the atmosphere was evident, although greenhouse warming did not emerge from background "noise" until the late 1980s. Hans Suess and Roger Revelle recognized early on that transferring hundreds of billions of tons of carbon in fossil fuels (coal, oil, and natural gas) formed over hundreds of millions of years and locked up in earth's crust to the atmosphere as CO_2 in a few hundred years was "grand

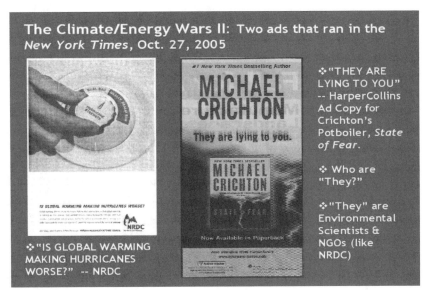

Fig. 1

geophysical experiment" on a scale unseen in human history (Revelle and Suess, 1957). Revelle was to be an influential professor of Al Gore's at Harvard, with ramifications reverberating today (Gore, 2006). By the late 1960s, Syukuro (Suki) Manabe, to my mind, an "Einstein" of atmospheric science, had worked out the detailed physics of how greenhouse gases affect atmospheric temperature from the surface to the stratosphere, including the water vapor feedback that roughly doubles warming from CO_2 alone (Manabe and Weatherald, 1967).

The discovery of global warming is a fascinating chapter in the history of science (Weart, 2003). Many phenomena that we are now seeing—heat going into the oceans, greater warming at the Arctic, volcanic and aerosol effects—were predicted decades ago. One group, including Steve Schneider, Richard Sommerville, Jim Hansen and this author, worked on this problem in the 1970s, primarily as an intellectual challenge in theoretical climate modeling and computer science at the Goddard Institute of Space Studies (GISS), a NASA-funded research institute near Columbia University started by Robert Jastrow while he was still in his twenties.

Back then, global warming was not yet politicized as it is now (figure 1). A "back of the envelope" calculation I did at GISS in the 70s suggested fossil fuel greenhouse warming would emerge from background temperature variations by the late 80s. So I thought it might be a good idea to publish some papers predicting this, which I did, as did colleagues at GISS and elsewhere. That limiting CO_2 emissions to avoid adverse global warming might disrupt consumerist civilization and multinational energy companies while putting a damper on industrialization of China and India was implicit, but academic.

Ironically, in light of the conclusive support for it developed at the research institute he founded (Hansen et al., 2005), Jastrow was highly critical of the global warming hypothesis. He never published peer-reviewed climate research, in stunning contrast to the present GISS director, Jim Hansen; but, on taking early retirement from NASA, Jastrow and Fred Seitz of Rockefeller University founded the Marshall Institute in Washington, D.C., a bastion of climate change deniers allied with the American Enterprise Institute, the Cato Institute, and other conservative think tanks in opposition to US participation in the CO_2-emissions-limiting Kyoto Protocol—the first implementation of the UN Framework Climate Change Convention (FCCC).

The United States, China, and India have not ratified Kyoto. Indeed, 850 new coal-fired power plants to be built in these countries by 2012 will overwhelm Kyoto emission reductions by a factor of five (Clayton, 2004). Avoiding "dangerous human interference with the climate system," the goal of the UN FCCC, is a daunting technological challenge because 85 percent of the world's energy comes from fossil fuel; and stabilizing global temperature at acceptable levels will require a revolutionary change in the world's energy systems (Hoffert et al., 1998; 2002; "Energy's Future," 2006). Although global warming is settled science, a public relations battle continues to rage.

Problems exist on both sides of the red-blue divide. In a searing critique of environmental nongovernmental organizations (NGOs) like the National Resources Defense Council and Environmental Defense, Shellenberger and Nordhaus (2005) argue that, despite major campaigns, environmental lobbies have had little success on the global warming front. The authors discount efforts by states in the United

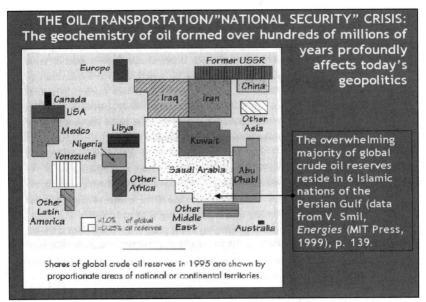

THE OIL/TRANSPORTATION/"NATIONAL SECURITY" CRISIS:
The geochemistry of oil formed over hundreds of millions of years profoundly affects today's geopolitics

The overwhelming majority of global crude oil reserves reside in 6 Islamic nations of the Persian Gulf (data from V. Smil, *Energies* (MIT Press, 1999), p. 139.

Shares of global crude oil reserves in 1995 are shown by proportionate areas of national or continental territories.

Fig. 2

States to create renewable energy portfolios with ambitious targets for alternate energy as so much public relations. They claim, with some justification, that "not one of America's environmental leaders is articulating a vision of the future commensurate with the magnitude of the crisis."

Why? Global warming is not only different in scale from prior environmental challenges (acid rain, heavy metal contamination, DDT, etc.)—its long-term planet-changing nature requires forethought and imagination to a much greater degree than the threats to which Homo sapiens has evolved adrenaline-pumping instinctive responses. The growth of human population, CO_2 emissions, and global warming in the past millennium are very recent from a human evolutionary perspective. For the first time in its history, Homo sapiens has begun to interact more or less as a unit with the global environmental system (Eldridge, 1996). Because modern technology developed *after* we evolved biologically, we lack appropriate instincts to deal with it—these having been unlikely to confer survivability in our evolutionary past. By default, we have to deal with the climate/energy problem cognitively. So far, we are not doing too well. As Carl Sagan observed, our reptilian brains motivate aggressive and tribal, as opposed to thoughtful, responses in ways we barely perceive and across many spheres of human behavior.

In the climate wars, deniers often get more vociferous as the evidence against their views gets stronger (Hoffert, 2003). The so-called hockey stick curve (developed by paleoclimatologist Mike Mann and colleagues) was recently attacked from the floor on Congress by Representative Joe Barton (R-Texas), based on cherry-picked information suggesting their statistics were flawed reported in the *Wall Street Journal*. Would that Rep. Barton, and legislators in general were better educated in statistical and scientific issues. But my experience briefing legislators and aides is that scientific illiteracy and intellectual laziness are rampant. Educated mainly as lawyers, many do not get it that nature does not care about human politics. (Unfortunately, some academics that should know better likewise argue that science is more a "consensual reality" than an objective description of nature deduced by the scientific method.) Too few bright and imaginative students pursue careers in science and engineering today. We need such students badly.

The hockey stick curve that shows a dramatic recent uptick in global temperature with much more to come is easily perceived as a threat not only to Big Oil and Big Coal, but also to election campaign funds. Easier to blame the messenger than think critically about this. The general trend of the Mann et al. (2003) hockey stick was independently verified by other researchers in a recent report by the National Research Council (NRC, 2006). Overwhelmingly, research-active climate scientists know we are entering climatic territory unseen in human history (Hansen, 2006). Our rapidly melting planet is so dominated by humankind's emissions that the present climatic era is being called the anthropocene (Crutzen and Ramanathan, 2003).

Most knowledgeable researchers are very concerned about global warming. Some, including this author, argue for research and development programs on an Apollo space program-like scale to create low-carbon alternate energy supply and demand-reducing technologies in time to make a difference (Hoffert et al., 1998, 2002; Rees, 2006). This effort should include prompt implementation of energy conservation, efficiency, and existing alternate energy sources (Lovins, 1989; Metz et al., 2001; Pacala and Socolow, 2004; Socolow, 2006).

Whatever the deep evolutionary reasons, the climate/energy issue competes for attention with other problems in the mind of the average citizen. A frequently asked question is: "Why even care about global warming and climate change?" The worst effects occur decades to centuries from now. In cost-benefit accounting, many economists strongly discount the present value of adverse future impacts and "externalize" (that is, neglect) the cost of environmentally degrading the global commons (Daly and Townsend, 1994). Economics is, of course, a legitimate branch of behavioral biology dealing with the allocation of scarce resources by Homo sapiens, one of millions of biological species inhabiting this planet. But, so far, in its predictive mode, it resembles astrology more than a hard science. Economist John Kenneth Galbraith went so far as to say, "The only reason for economists to produce forecasts is to make astrology look respectable" (Jaccard, 2005). Undaunted, Bjorn Lomborg, the "skeptical environmentalist" (Lomborg, 2001), convened a group of economists to prioritize investments in various challenges facing humankind. The group concluded in its "Copenhagen Consensus" that climate change, even if real, is near the bottom (Bohannan, 2004). Reading the group's findings, one is struck by how evolutionarily blind our species can be to existential threats. Among the problems with this indifference—noted by Harvard energy policy analyst John Holdren, and in his film and book, *An Inconvenient Truth*, by Al Gore—is that climate change is more an ethical than an economics problem.

An even more basic flaw to this physical scientist is that the environmental constraint of global warming on energy was entirely missed by the Copenhagen group. The late Nobel laureate Rick Smalley astutely observed that, although civilization has many problems, energy is key to them all. Smalley's list of problems encompasses energy, water, food, environment (including global warming), poverty, terrorism and war,

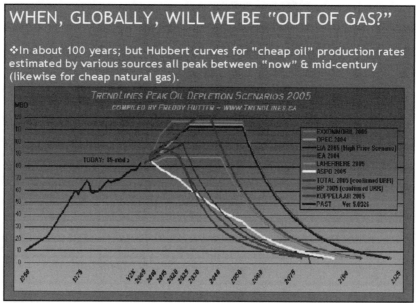

WHEN, GLOBALLY, WILL WE BE "OUT OF GAS?"

❖In about 100 years; but Hubbert curves for "cheap oil" production rates estimated by various sources all peak between "now" & mid-century (likewise for cheap natural gas).

Fig. 3

disease, education, democracy, and population (Smalley, 2005). Energy is key because solving all these problems requires sustainable power on a global scale. Without it civilization collapses. Concentrated fossil fuels are a one-shot boon of nature. Coal being still relatively abundant, humankind might have deferred an energy revolution to another primary power source to the twenty-second century, or even later, were it not for global warming. Coal burned for electricity and even shortages caused by peak oil can be handled at higher cost by making synthetic fuels from coal. But potentially catastrophic global warming is the "canary in the mine." It trumps everything else; moving the climate/energy issue to the front of the list.

To generalize the Shellenberger-Nordhaus thesis, there is little evidence that politicians of *any* persuasion appreciate the magnitude of the problem, or can articulate a vision to address it. The most relevant questions are being asked by energy scientists and engineers: Are there technologies likely to lead to a low-carbon world in time and still allow global GDP to continue growing 2 to 3 percent per year ("Energy's Future," 2006)? What global energy systems should we be aiming at? Can we get there in time? One leading economist put it this way: "The trouble with the global warming debate is that it has become a moral crusade when it's really an engineering problem. The inconvenient truth is that if we don't solve the engineering problem, we're helpless" (Samuelson, 2006).

The issue of "energy security" makes the need for an energy technology revolution a viable policy option even for "red" states and others indisposed see global warming for the threat it is. Two hundred years of innovation—the famous "Yankee ingenuity"—are behind America's ascent to world power (Evans, 2004). Applied science and entrepreneurship enabled by government research and development since World War II (Bush, 1945) are a historically appropriate response for the United States.

The need is clear. Figure 2, from Smil (1999), shows oil reserves around the world, with the lion's share in the Persian Gulf. But Saudi Arabia, Iran, and Iraq are powderkegs of post-9/11 Islamic fundamentalism. Some Al Qaeda ideologues have drawn up a plan aimed at establishing an Islamic caliphate throughout the Middle East, in which attacks against the petroleum industry are critical to the deterioration of American power through constant expansion of the circle of confrontation (Wright, 2006). And because oil is internationally traded, it is irrelevant whether oil imports by the United States originate under a particular Middle Eastern desert. The more oil money that flows to Saudi Arabia, Iran, etc., the more money that flows to Al Qaeda, Hezbollah, and other terrorist groups that we are ostensibly at war with. As Tom Friedman of the *New York Times* has repeatedly emphasized, our addiction to oil combined with lack of any serious policy to develop alternatives is why the United States is funding *both* sides of the "War on Terror."

We know that world hydrocarbon resources are limited. Virtually all major crude oil and natural gas reservoirs have been mapped by seismic probes. Every day, the world consumes about 80 million barrels of oil, a rate that has been increasing with economic growth but is ultimately constrained by geological abundance to peak in coming decades (Deffeyes, 2001). From a global warming perspective, the coming oil peak, accelerated by China and India with booming GDPs, is problematic because it is forcing a transition back to coal for primary energy and thus "recarbonizing" the energy supply since coal emits more CO_2 per unit of energy than oil or natural gas. And, of course, oil prices are rapidly rising, headed for $100 per barrel or more. Figure 3 shows the current range of oil production rate projections. As with the climate change deniers, some "cornucopian" economists say the oil peak is overblown. But consider that oil companies are motivated to inflate, not deflate, their reserve estimates to raise their corporate valuations on Wall Street. Royal Dutch Shell, for example, was recently compelled by the US Security and Exchange Commission to revise its reserve estimate downward 20 percent, suggesting an oil peak sooner rather than later. In any case, most petroleum geologists agree the world will be "out of gas" by the end of the century.

I want to be clear that I am a technological optimist. I believe we can solve the climate/energy problem. But there is no silver bullet and it will not be easy. It will take the greatest engineering effort in history; bigger than the Manhattan project to build the bomb, bigger than the

Fig. 4

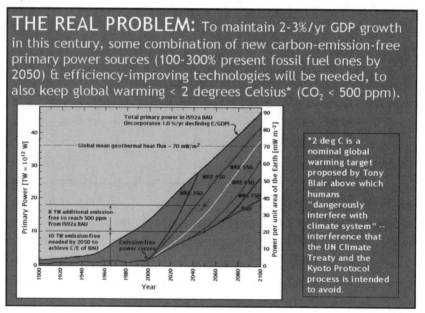

Apollo program to land a man on the moon, bigger than the mobilization to fight World War II. Moreover, the effort has to be international in scope with sufficient inducements for developing giants China and India to sign on. This problem will not solve itself through the invisible hand of the market. Relevant costs and values are not being captured. We are moving rapidly in the wrong direction. Particularly serious is that we are investing in the wrong infrastructures for a sustainable energy world. Vision and imagination are critical. Sooner or later the world will realize this. The longer we wait, the harder the job will be.

Exponential growth cannot be sustained indefinitely on a finite planet. We could, and I believe should, try to maintain 2 to 3 percent per year world GDP growth to the end of the century (a likely minimum for developing nations to attain income equity) as CO_2 emissions are held constant, decreased, and eventually phased out by mid-century. This would—based on our best current models—keep the atmospheric CO_2 concentration below 500 parts per million (ppm) and global warming below 2 degrees Celsius. Higher than 2 degrees could trigger dangerous human interference with the climate system, according to criteria recently adopted by the European Union (Edmonds and Smith, 2006). Two degrees may not sound like much, but more could put us on a planet-changing trajectory with irreversible melting of the Greenland and Antarctic icecaps, which would inundate the world's coastal zones (Hansen, 2006; Gore, 2006). A big job, given that atmospheric CO_2 has already risen to 380 ppm—100 ppm above the preindustrial level from fossil fuel burning and deforestation so far. To do it, some combination of emission-free primary power sources and primary power demand-reduction equivalent to generating 100 to 300 percent of present power from some as yet unidentified set of power systems will be needed by mid-century (figure 4, based of Hoffert et al., 1998; 2002).

How hard is that? Consider that 2050 is nearer in the future than when Fermi's first nuclear reactor (then called an "atomic pile") went critical in December 1942 at the University of Chicago is in the past. We now produce about 5 percent of primary energy worldwide from nuclear power (this is virtually all for electricity; roughly 18 percent

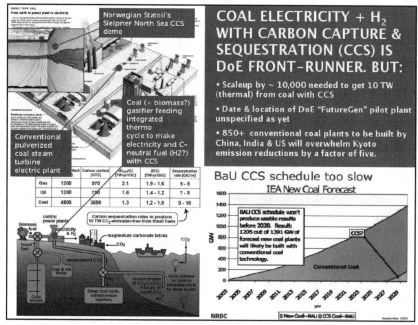

Fig. 5

of electricity generation is nuclear; the rest is from fossil fuels, mostly coal and hydroelectricity). If we need some new carbon-emission free "energy source X" 50 years hence, the implied growth of these new power sources is 20 to 60 times faster than nuclear power, the last revolutionary power source deployed on a large scale. Not impossible, but we do have to concentrate. Below are some ideas that could work if we get serious.

For starters, we could dramatically accelerate what some engineers believe is the most ready for prime time major emission-free energy source: coal with carbon capture and sequestration (CCS). Figure 5 depicts coal gasification plants making electricity and hydrogen with the CO_2 pumped to reservoirs underground, the rationale being that we have large coal resources that can play a role in a transition to a sustainable energy system if we can get the energy out while putting CO_2 (and other pollutants) away in reservoirs underground. One problem is that coal with CCS deployment is unlikely before pilot plants demonstrate that the combined technology works. Iindividual components like coal gasification, combined cycle power plants, and even CO_2 sequestration have been shown, but the technology is too costly without a carbon tax or "cap and trade" emissions policy in place. The United States, China, and India have not agreed on emission limits, and these are precisely the countries with massive coal resources where planned buildup of conventional coal electric power stations is most intense. The lower right panel of Figure 5 shows how conventional coal plants in the works will overwhelm proposed CCS plants. A Department of Energy-funded CCS pilot plant called "FutureGen" was cited by this administration at climate negotiations in Montreal as the US premier effort, in partnership with the coal industry, to combat global warming (Revkin, 2005). But this plant is unlikely before 2012 and its location is still unannounced. Experts believe it may be more expensive to retrofit conventional coal plans with CCS than build gasification plants with CCS from scratch. Suppose global warming got bad—really bad. Will conventional coal plants be abandoned, as the $6 billion Shoreham nuclear plant was after Three Mile Island (TMI) and Chernobyl? Once they are generating electricity from cheap coal, with capital costs "sunk" for 50 to 75 years, it might be so expensive to shut

Fig. 6

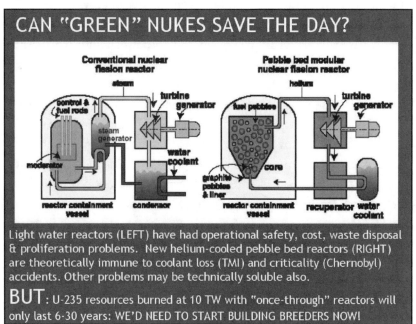

CAN "GREEN" NUKES SAVE THE DAY?

Light water reactors (LEFT) have had operational safety, cost, waste disposal & proliferation problems. New helium-cooled pebble bed reactors (RIGHT) are theoretically immune to coolant loss (TMI) and criticality (Chernobyl) accidents. Other problems may be technically soluble also.

BUT: U-235 resources burned at 10 TW with "once-through" reactors will only last 6-30 years: WE'D NEED TO START BUILDING BREEDERS NOW!

down and build new ones that ratepayers would balk even to slow a global warming juggernaut. This is not a good scenario.

Another class of low-carbon primary power now being reconsidered after a disastrous start is "green" nukes (figure 6). No one has started building a new nuclear reactor in the United States for the past 30 years, though some are planned. Classic problems of nuclear power are operational safety, waste disposal, and weapons proliferation. However, for global warming mitigation, the major constraint may be that planned reactors are "once through" and use the supply-limited uranium 235 (U-235) isotope, which makes up less than 1 percent of natural uranium. The energy content of U-235 in identified deposits is less than natural gas. We would run out of fuel in 30 years employing such reactors at rates sufficient to supply present primary power demand. As with coal, we do not have the luxury of investing in the wrong nuclear power infrastructure. Longer-term, we will need to breed U-238 (99 percent of natural uranium) into plutonium or more abundant thorium to U-233, a fuel I favor for several technical reasons. Why not start now? Infrastructure and weapons proliferations issues need to be faced now if we are serious about green nukes as alternative energy.

The third class of primary power, my own preference, is renewable energy, currently less than 1 percent of primary power (figure 7). Space limitations prevent an adequate discussion, but I and colleagues at the National Renewable Energy Laboratory (NREL) in Golden, Colorado, and elsewhere believe solar and wind power can be scaled up, with a proper infrastructure of transmission and storage, to provide 30 percent or more of primary emission-free power by midcentury (Pew Center, 2004). President Jimmy Carter, a strong advocate of renewables, created the Solar Energy Research Institute, the precursor of NREL. And Jerry Brown, dubbed California's "governor moonbeam" by critics, in the 1970s initiated tax and other incentives leading to the now cost-effective Altamont wind farms. It is hard to overestimate the damage done by Ronald Reagan who, on becoming president, symbolically ripped the solar panels Carter had put on the roof of the White House, likewise dismantling most of Carter's energy research and development initiative. We have not recovered. Carter's administration

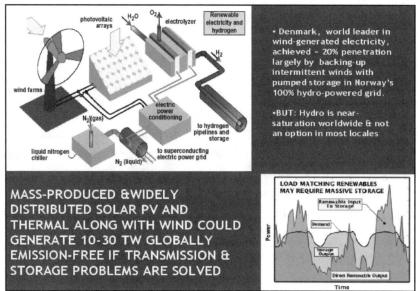

Fig. 7

a quarter century ago was the last time the US had a pro-active alternate energy policy. Unfortunately, the institutional memory of this has dimmed. Whatever the problems of Carter plan, and there were some, the United States, and because of our leadership, the world, was headed toward a sustainable energy future. Not now.

What colleagues and I propose as a goal is that by mid-century, renewables should supply roughly a third of the world's power; clean, safe and sustainable nukes another third; and coal gasification with CCS the final third. The total would amount to 100 to 300 percent of present energy demand. There are major roles for business and talented entrepreneurs, but I do not see how we get there without the stimulus of massive Apollo-like government-funded research and development, perhaps starting with ARPA-E (Advanced Research Projects Agency–Energy; after DARDA, the Defense Research Projects Agency, which gave us, among other things, the Internet) proposed by the National Academy of Science (Committee on Science, 2005).

At the same time, we need to implement everything we have in our alternate energy arsenal immediately. I do this myself as best I can. I drive a hybrid and get my home's electricity from green power, mainly wind power purchased by my utility from upstate New York (Hoffert, 2004). At this point, I pay a premium for this "privilege." I do not claim any special virtue as an early adopter. I do think both ethics and "cool" technology can be early drivers of alternate energy. At least until it become cost-effective to the average person, perhaps stimulated by carbon and gas taxes and/or cap-and-trade schemes. We need work on a broad spectrum of possible solutions; picking technology winners is notoriously uncertain, even by experts (Clarke, 1982).

This is not the forum to elaborate on the most innovative high-tech ideas that could allow us to live sustainably on the planet. Interested readers should consult Hoffert et al. (2002) and the special issue of *Scientific American* on "Energy's Future Beyond Carbon" (2006). Climate and sustainable energy is a political as well a science and engineering problem. With the memory of Rick Smalley's brilliant exposition in mind (he gave a most engaging and accessible public lecture at an Aspen Global Change Institute conference that I co-organized a few years ago), I hold that energy and global warming, not terrorism and mind-numbing dogma, are the appropriate organizing principles for this century. There is no guarantee high-tech civilization will survive into an ever richer future. But I find no solace in joining with the peak oilers to hunker down to a long slow decline with a return to agrarian (and eventually hunter-gatherer?) lifestyles as energy runs down and sea levels rise (Urstadt, 2006). Likewise, keep me away from Ted Kaczynski, the "Unabomber," who would destroy even a solar-powered high-tech world (Kaczynski, 2002).

I am optmistic enough about technology to believe policies based on science and engineering can solve the climate/energy problem; that with enough effort, thoughtful energy policies, instead of the usual pork packaged for public relations, can become part of political party platforms by the next US presidential election. The stakes are high. We owe to ourselves and generations to come to fight for our remarkable technological civilization, with all its imperfections, built on the shoulders of earlier generations. It will be hard. We will need every ounce of creative imagination. If we do make it through the twenty-first century without imploding, perhaps someday we might even find a way to cope with those problems our pre-technology evolutionary history has left us quite unprepared for.

REFERENCES

Arrhenius, S. "On the Influence of Carbonic Acid in the Air Upon the Temperature of the Ground." *Philosophical Magazine* 41 (1896): 237-76.

Bohannan, J. "Economists Rate Greenhouse Gas Curbs a Poor Investment." *Science* 304 (June 4, 2004): 1429.

Bush, V. *Science: The Endless Frontier*. Washington, D.C.: US Office of Scientific Research and Development, July 1945 <http://www.nsf.gov/about/history/vbush1945.htm>.

Cheney, R., et al. *National Energy Policy: Reliable, Affordable and Environmentally Sound Energy for America's Future*. Washington, D.C.: The White House, May 2001.

Clarke, A. C. *Profiles of the Future: An Inquiry into the Limits of the Possible*. New York: Holt, Rinehart and Winston, 1982.

Clayton, M. "New Coal Plants Bury Kyoto." *Christian Science Monitor*, December 23, 2004.

Committee on Science, Engineering, and Public Policy. *Rising above the Gathering Storm: Energizing and Employing America for a Brighter Economic Future*. Washington, D.C.: National Academy Press, 2005 <http://www.nap.edu/openbook/0309100399/html/122.html>.

Crichton, M., "Remarks to the Commonwealth Club." San Francisco, September 15 <http://www.sf.indymedia.org/news/2003/12/1665564.php>.

Crutzen, P. J., and V. Ramanathan, "The Parasol Effect on Climate." *Science* 302 (December 5, 2003): 1679-81.

Daly, H. E, and K. N. Townsend. *Valuing the Earth: Economics, Ecology, Ethics*. Cambridge: MIT Press, 1994.

Deffeyes, K. S. *Hubbert's Peak: The Impending World Oil Shortage*. Princeton: Princeton University Press, 2001.

Edmonds, J, and S. J. Smith. "The Technology of Two Degrees." *Avoiding Dangerous Climate Change*. Eds. H. J. Schellnhuber et al. New York: Cambridge University Press, 2006: 385-392.

Eldridge, N. "The Population Conundrum: Review of *How Many People Can the Earth Support?* by J. E. Cohen." *Issues in Science and Technology* 12 (Spring 1996): 82-84.

"Energy's Future Beyond Carbon: How to Power the Economy and Still Fight Global Warming." Special issue. *Scientific American* (September 2006).

Evans, H. *They Made America: From the Steam Engine to the Search Engine: Two Centuries of Innovators.* New York: Little, Brown and Co., 2004.

Flannery, T. *The Weather Makers: How Man Is Changing the Climate and Weather and What It Means for Life on Earth* Boston: Atlantic Monthly Press, 2006.

Gore, A. *An Inconvenient Truth: The Planetary Emergency of Global Warming and What We Can Do About It.* New York: Rodale Books, 2006.

Hansen, J. "The Threat to the Planet." *New York Review of Books* 53 (July 13, 2006) <http://www.nybooks.com/articles/19131/>.

Hansen, J., et al. "Earth's Energy Imbalance: Confirmation and Implications." *Science* 308 (June 3, 2005): 1431-35.

Hoffert, M. I. "I Planned to Attend, But Now I Cannot . . ." *Tech Central Station* (November 18, 2003) <http://www.techcentralstation.com/111803B.html>.

———. "A Touch of Wind Power Could Go a Long Way." *Newsday* (March 13, 2004).

Hoffert, M. I., et al. "Energy Implications of Future Stabilization of Atmospheric CO2 Content." *Nature* 395 29 (October 29, 1998): 881-884.

———. "Advanced Technology Paths to Global Climate Stability: Energy for a Greenhouse Planet." *Science* 298 (November 1, 2002): 981-987.

Inhofe, J. M. "The Science of Climate Change." Press release, July 28, 2003 <http://inhofe.senate.gov/pressreleases/climate>.

Jaccard, M. *Sustainable Fossil Fuels: The Unusual Suspect in the Quest for Clean and Enduring Energy.* New York: Cambridge University Press, 2005: 32.

Kaczynski, T. "Hit Where It Hurts," *Green Anarchy* 8 (Spring 2002) <http://www.greenanarchy.org/index.php?action=viewjournal&printIssueId=20>.

Kolbert, E. *Field Notes from a Catastrophe: Man, Nature and Climate Change.* London: Bloomsbury Publishing, 2006.

Letters to the editor and authors' response to "Advanced Technology Paths to Global Climate Stability: Energy for a Greenhouse Planet" (Hoffert, 2002). *Science* 300 (April 25, 2003): 581-584.

Lomborg, B. *The Skeptical Environmentalist: Measuring the Real State of the World.* New York: Cambridge University Press, 2001.

Lovins, A. "The Negawatt Revolution: Solving the CO2 Problem." Keynote address, Green Energy Conference. Montreal, 1989 <http://www.ccnr.org/amory.html>.

Manabe, S., and R. T. Weatherald. "Thermal Equilibrium of the Atmosphere with a Given Distribution of Relative Humidity." *Journal of the Atmospheric Sciences* 24 (1967): 241-259.

Mann, M. E., et al. "On Past Temperatures and Anomalous Late-20th-Century Warmth." *Eos: Transactions of the American Geophysical Union* 84:27 (2003): 56-57.

Metz, B., et al., eds. *Climate Change 2001: Mitigation.* New York: Cambridge University Press, 2001.

National Research Council. *Surface Temperature Reconstructions for the Last 200 Years.* Washington, D.C.: National Research Council, June 22, 2006.

Pacala, S., and R. Socolow. "Stabilization Wedges: Solving the Climate Problem for the Next 50 Years with Current Technologies." *Science* 305 (August 13, 2004): 968-972.

Pew Center and National Commission for Energy Policy. "The 10-50 Solution: Technologies and Policies for a Low-Carbon Future." Workshop, Washington, D.C., March 25, 2004. Overview paper <http://www.pewclimate.org/document.cfm?documentID=392>.

Rees, M. "The G8 on Energy: Too Little." *Science* 313 (August 4, 2006): 591.

Revelle, R., and H. E. Suess. "Carbon Dioxide Exchange between Atmosphere and Ocean and the Question of an Increase of Atmospheric CO2 During the Past Decades." *Tellus* 9 (1957): 18-27.

Revkin, A. C. "Pact Signed for Prototype of Coal Plant." *New York Times*, December 7, 2005.

Samuelson. R. J. "Global Warming's Real Inconvenient Truth." *Washington Post*, July 5, 2006: A13.

Shellenberger, M., and T. Nordhaus. "The Death of Environmentalism: Global Warming Politics in a Post-Environmental World." *Grist Magazine*, January 13, 2005 <http://www.grist.org/news/main-dish/2005/01/13/doe-reprint/index.html>.

Smalley, R. E. "Future Global Energy Prosperity: The Terawatt Challenge." *MRS Bulletin* 30 (June 2005): 412-417.

Smil, V. *Energies.* Cambridge: MIT Press, 1999.

Socolow, R. "Stabilization Wedges: An Elaboration of the Concept." *Avoiding Dangerous Climate Change.* Eds. H. J. Schellnhuber et al. New York: Cambridge University Press, 2006: 347-354.

Teller, E., L. Wood, and R. Hyde. *Active Climate Stabilization.* Report UCRL-JC-149012. Livermore, Calif.: Lawrence Livermore National Laboratory, 2002.

Urstadt, B. "Imagine There's No Oil: Scenes from a Liberal Apocalypse." *Harper's* (August 2006): 31-40.

Weart, S. R. *The Discovery of Global Warming.* Cambridge: Harvard University Press, 2003.

Wright, L. "Annals of Terrorism: The Master Plan." *New Yorker* (September 8, 2006): 48-59.

Paul Gilman

Science, Policy, and Politics: Comparing and Contrasting Issues in Energy and the Environment

THE DEGREE TO WHICH SCIENTIFIC AND TECHNICAL INFORMATION IS relied upon in policymaking is related to the perception of the value of that information for the evaluation of options and the degree to which the other factors being evaluated, including political ones, have higher priority. Once an issue has become the focus for partisan political debate, the value of scientific and technical information in that debate declines. Policymakers have valued scientific and technical information differently when considering environmental and energy policy. In some cases, this is because their constituents perceive the effects these issues have on them differently and thus demand different approaches from their elected leaders. In other cases, the issues have taken on a political importance that begins to shape the nature of the scientific debate rather than the technical information shaping the debate. Scientific and technical information has been viewed as more critical for environmental policymaking, often in a regulatory context, and has therefore been the object of more intense debate than in energy policymaking.

Interest in public policy and its interplay with science and engineering takes several forms. In the post-World War II era, as academic researchers have grown increasingly reliant on federal funds for their research, the field of "science policy" has become synonymous with the analysis of federal research and development funding (see the American Association for Advancement of Science website, http://www.aaas.org/spp/rd/> for a good illustration of this). This was inevitable. Federally funded researchers would begin to examine the workings of government and the political process that establishes its leadership for clues as to the likely trends in future research funding. It turns out there is no predictable pattern to funding and the political party in power. Most observers of federal funding for scientific and technical research and development would be hard-pressed, after decades of observation, to find either political party holding that the executive branch of our government is consistently more or less generous toward science and engineering. The patterns are further blurred when one examines congressional actions on funding measures under different political leadership.

Our country's founding fathers appreciated the importance of science and technology for the economy of the country and, therefore, constitutionally provided the system of copyrights and patent protections. James Madison wrote of this power "to promote the progress of science and useful arts, by securing, for a limited time, to authors and inventors, the exclusive right to their respective writings and discoveries" that, "the utility of this power will scarcely be questioned" (Hamilton, Madison, and Jay, 1901).

Later we see evidence of the appreciation of the importance of science and engineering in the running of government; for example, the creation of the National Academy of Science (NAS) in 1863 by an act of Congress. That act went beyond creating an honorific society. It charged the academy to "investigate, examine, experiment, and report upon any subject of science or art" whenever called upon by any department of the government. The purview of these activities was largely related to national defense until more recently (for a brief history, see National Academies, n.d.).

As the number of government scientists and federal funding for nongovernment scientists have grown, interest by federal policymakers in issues related to the "doing" of science has increased. These include questions of scientific misconduct, the use of peer reviews as a tool of quality assurance, and questions of conflicts of interest within the research community.

The use of science and technical information in government decision making is often, in the initial analysis, about whether there is a role for the federal government in the issue and, if so, what should that role be. In our system of government, this initial analysis is often done by the executive branch and then considered by the Congress. Inside the executive branch, staffs engaged in this analysis often have scientific or technical backgrounds and the processes for formulating policy are increasingly transparent (for example, the regulatory process of the Food and Drug Administration). In contrast, the staff of the legislative branch involved in the integration of science and technical information into the policy process are less qualified and the process less transparent. In both venues, the policymaking process is done within a political context. An issue becomes "political" if the options for dealing with it naturally align with differing partisan political philosophies and the issue is perceived by partisans to be of sufficient importance to their constituents that time and attention should be paid to it. Once an issue is "ripe" for politics, the science and technical information underpinning the issue and the analysis of options for dealing with it are also "ripe" for debate.

Debating the science and technical information around an issue can take several forms. The status of the issue is one. For example, a decade ago, there was no debate about whether CO_2 levels were increasing, but there was debate as to whether the earth was warming. The sophistication in these debates has reached such a level that even when there is an emerging consensus on an issue, the debate can change to a discussion of the levels of uncertainty associated with our measurements and the data in general. What to do about changing the state of affairs is another place for debate about the science. For example, how much of the CO_2 increase can be ameliorated by reducing our production of energy using fossil fuels or what role can carbon sequestration play for the future?

If an issue has very strong ideological or partisan political identification, it can become a "litmus" issue. At this point, scientific and technical information may have little to do with the debate. As an issue becomes a litmus test, how you vote on it is all that matters. In the example of drilling for oil in the Arctic National Wildlife Refuge (ANWR), there is no longer a debate on the environmental consequences of the technology that is available or whether or not the effects can be minimized or corrected. Today, people vote either for opening ANWR or not because it is a litmus test as to whether they are for the environment or not. It is a vote on whether one supports energy production or conservation as a solution to our energy situation. Depending on your view, this is a vote about maintaining our way of life, albeit wasteful, or painfully sacrificing our way of life for environmental gain.

In the mid-1970s, the policy approaches for addressing energy and environment issues were similar. On the environment, laws had been enacted providing the federal government with significant regulatory authority. Some of these are technology based. The catalytic converter on our automobiles was a technology based solution. Some are risk based. Our clean air statutes go in this direction. Some of them employ cost-benefit based regulatory approaches (for example, the Safe Drinking Water Act). On energy, coping with the Organization of Petroleum Exporting Countries (OPEC) oil embargo following the Yom Kippur War of 1973 and natural gas shortages during the cold winter of 1973-1974, meant putting in place significant controls on the allocation and price of petroleum and natural gas. Legislating on the environment was contentious because of regional concerns (for example, did cleaner western coal benefit more than dirtier eastern coal), but not on a political basis (for a first hand account, see Baker, 2005). Legislating on energy issues was hampered by disbelief that there were real and fundamental problems with the supply and pricing of petroleum and natural gas, but little partisan politics (Fehner and Hall, 1994).

Through the 1980s, the policy approaches to these two issue areas diverged. In energy, the realization that artificially low pricing for petroleum and natural gas was hurting efforts at conservation and the development of new supplies led to the phase-out of these policies. At the same time, further regulatory efforts did not garner support. Average citizens were not willing to bear the burden or cost of coping with energy shortages. In 1979, Congress overrode the Carter administration's mandatory conservation measures and its "standby" gasoline rationing plan. Instead, informational approaches (the EPA Star Program, for example) for energy efficiency and tax-based incentive programs for the use of alternative energy sources and energy efficiency measures found their way into law.

While energy was still debated and legislated on a nonpartisan basis, there were signs that environment debates were becoming more political. Environmental groups began engaging in congressional elections based on how members had voted in committees of jurisdiction for the Clean Air Act Amendments of 1977 (Senator Pete V. Domenici, personal communication). Today, environmental groups even undertake media campaigns with political action groups (for example, the Natural Resource Defense Council and MoveOn.org; see "First Arsenic," 2004). Issues of the environment like water quality and air quality were recognized as concerns that motivated large numbers of voters. The issues could be portrayed as business interests versus health interests. Early on, in the debates in the late 1970s and early 1980s, environmental regulations, if opposed by industry, were done so on the excessive cost. Often the question was posed, "Is one life worth these many millions of dollars?"

This line of debate proved to be quite fruitless. It seems people perceived that if the life in question was their own, it was worth it. This is where the divergence on energy and environmental issues regarding ripeness for political exploitation has its roots: people's perception of the risks. For many of the environmental statutes, people perceived that it was a risk being imposed upon them, not by their own decision making and the regulatory costs were not falling on them. Industry abandoned the "value of life" approach and adopted an approach of questioning the underlying science that was used to come up with the particular proposed standard or approach to resolving a regulatory

Table 1. Examples and Allegations of the Misuse/Abuse of Science

EPA has had to reverse previous policies found to be scientifically flawed and to amend statistical "errors" it used to argue for new policies. And it has a habit of punishing those who dare to point out flaws. Two years ago, six scientists lost their jobs after writing a letter to the newspaper saying that EPA regulations "stand to harm rather than protect public health and the environment" (*The Cincinnati Enquirer*, December 26, 2000).

EPA has become too politicized in its actions, too eager to pursue narrow political goals, and too willing to ignore Congressional intent in making regulatory decisions. Political motives rather than workable policies based on sound science and reliable data seem to be the driving force behind EPA (Allen James, "Politics Play a Plum Part in FQPA," *Pest Control,* September 1, 2000).

EPA also should reinstitute and strengthen its internal scientific review processes to ensure transparency, account for scientific uncertainty, and improve its analytical bases for its political decisions ("Research Gaps, Legalistic Focus Hinder EPA's Use of Science," Resources for the Future, August 18, 1999).

At least a dozen former EPA officials who played roles in setting pesticide policy now work as industry consultants. "The EPA has become a farm team for the pesticide lobby," says Mike Casey of the Environmental Working Group." (Peter Eisler, "Toughest Decisions Still to Come in Pesticide Review. Congress Wanted Rules Updated, but Politics Slowing Process," *USA Today*, August 30, 1999).

In a scathing opinion, the court stated, "EPA publicly committed a conclusion before research had begun adjusted scientific procedure and scientific norms to validate the Agency's public conclusion. . ." J. R. Clark, "EPA Corrupting Science for Political Purposes" (*Chattanooga Free Press*, October 11, 1998).

> **Table 1 (continued)**
>
> Science is as politicized in America as it was in the Soviet Union and Nazi Germany. And EPA is a prime example. Charlie Reese, "It's a Shame that Americans Can't Trust Their Own Government" (*Orlando Sentinel*, June 30, 1998).
>
> For years, the federal government has known that power plants produce mercury. It knows how technology could be used to reduce that pollution. But the EPA's efforts to regulate the toxic metal have been slowed by industry lobbyists and their allies in Congress. "Coal-Fired Power Plants Spew Mercury but Avoid Crackdown" (*Portland Press Herald*, September 29, 1997).
>
> This is by far the most politicized EPA I've seen in my three decades of working in state governments. . . . It is an agency driven more by sound bites than by sound science. Pranay Gupte and Bonner R. Cohen, "Carol Browner, Master of the Mission Creep" (*Forbes*, October 20, 1997).

problem. The chemistry on environmental issues was right for raising the issues to the partisan political level. Along with it came the debate on the underlying science and technical matters. Indeed, some groups have now adopted the tactics of industry and are debating the quality and use of the underlying science on many major environmental issues.

Peter Isler of *USA Today* posed a hypothesis in conversation with this author. He suggested that science has always been one part of the information weighed in public policy debates. He thought that the notion that it is the science that decides the public policy decision is not the way it has been in the past and not the way it should be. There is always a weighing of, among other things, the ethics, economics, technical facts, and politics of an issue. He hypothesized that this same process was going on in the debate on issues with substantial science and technology content within the Bush administration, but that currently the science was losing more often to the other considerations than it had in the past. An alternate hypothesis is that indeed this weighing of the elements of the issue was going on, and that fundamentally, the balance for wins and losses for science was no different today than it had been in the past. What was different was some of the issues were very good political issues. Charges of misuse of science were no different than in the past, but were getting additional emphasis because it was politically expedient to do so.

A few examples might illustrate the point. A number of headlines like this one, "Advisory Panels Stacked, Scientists Warn" (Environmental News Service, 2003) have appeared in the recent past. Were the candidates unqualified? Were they biased? Was the charge superficial and politically expedient? Take for example Doctor Roger McClellan, "the former Director of the Chemical *Industry* Institute of Toxicology" (emphasis added); he is cited by OMB Watch in this regard for his appointment to the CDC's National Center for Environmental Health Advisory Panel (see OMB Watch, n.d.). No mention is made of the fact that he was elected to the Institute of Medicine (the nation's most prestigious honorific medical body), was a former president of the Society of Toxicology, and has served on advisory panels in at least five federal agencies under many different administrations.

Another example. The Union of Concerned Scientists published "Scientific Integrity in Policymaking: An Investigation into the Bush Administration's Misuse of Science" (February 2004). One of the most egregiously misconstrued statements among the many in the report states that while the Environmental Protection Agency (EPA) had evaluated the Clear Skies Act proposed by Senator Carper as an alternative to the Bush administration proposal, "the EPA has withheld most of the results from the senators." This is in contrast to the remarks of Senator Carper at a hearing of the Environment and Public Works Committee in March 2004 where he said to EPA Administrator Leavitt, "Governor, last summer your staff provided me with the results of their analysis of the multi-pollutant control bill, the bill I just discussed." He went on to say, "Recently, the data in support of that analysis was also provided," and "I appreciate the work of your staff and the timely response in providing that data" (Hearing before the Committee, 2004).

A tabulation of similar sounding charges of the misuse and abuse of science are included in table 1. It is interesting to note that while they sound remarkably similar to recent charges leveled at the Bush administration, all of them precede that administration.

While it may be inevitable that some issues with substantial scientific and technical content will find their way into partisan politics, it behooves scientists and engineers to follow the norms, both ethical and professional, of their training. Remembering that science and technical information is just part of the information upon which policy decisions are made is also essential.

REFERENCES

American Association for the Advancement of Science. R&D Budget and Policy Program <http://www.aaas.org/spp/rd/>.

Baker, Howard H. "Cleaning America's Air: Progress and Challenges," March 9, 2005 <http://digitalmedia.utk.edu:8080/ramgen/11812.rm>.

Environment News Service. "Advisory Panels Stacked, Scientists Warn" (January 23, 2003) <http://www.ens-newswire.com/ens/jan2003/2003-01-23-10.asp>.

Fehner, Terence R., and Jack M. Hall. *Department of Energy 1977-1994: A Summary History.* United States Department of Energy History Series. DOE/HR-0098. November 1994.

"First Arsenic Now Mercury." *The New York Times,* March 26, 2004: A5.

Hamilton, Alexander, James Madison, and John Jay. *The Federalist: A Commentary on the Constitution of the United States,* Number 43. Washington, D.C.: M. Walter Dunne, Publisher, 1901.

Hearing before the Committee on Environment and Public Works. Environmental Protection Agency: Fiscal Year 2005 Budget. March 10, 2004. S. Hrg 108-497: 56

The National Academies. "History of the National Academies" <http://www.nationalacademies.org/about/history.html>.

OMB Watch. "Administration Stacks Scientific Advisory Panels" <http://
    www.ombwatch.org/article/articleview/1384>.
Union of Concerned Scientists. "Scientific Integrity in Policymaking: An
    Investigation into the Bush Administration's Misuse of Science"
    (February 2004).

Kurt Gottfried
Climate Change and Nuclear Power

CLIMATE SCIENCE AND PUBLIC POLICY

SURELY IT IS EVIDENT THAT SCIENCE—AND RATIONAL THOUGHT IN general—has had little influence on the federal government's energy policy recently. That had better change fast, because it is clear that what climate science has been telling us for many years is basically correct. It is climate change and the growing wealth of billions of erstwhile poor that will be the dominant political factors of this century. Many troubling features of globalization can be modified if there is the political will to do so. But the greenhouse gases we have pumped and will continue to pump into the atmosphere cannot be recalled by acts of Congress.

Now, finally, there is mounting recognition that the worldwide quest for economic growth, and the energy needed to fuel it, are on a collision course with nature. We owe this recognition to scientists across the globe who have devoted their lives to reading nature's response to human activity.

Fifty years ago one of climate science's pioneers, Roger Revelle, warned that "human beings are now carrying out a large scale geophysical experiment" on our planet. For most of those 50 years, very few listened. But that has changed. In this country, many states and cities have committed themselves to reducing their emissions. So have many European governments. A growing number of major corporations are adopting plans to exploit the business opportunities presented by climate change.

In short, the climate scientists have had a huge impact on world politics. Thanks to them millions have come to understand that continuing with business as usual is putting us on a collision with nature, and that in such contests nature ultimately wins. Many political and corporate leaders have decided to act on this understanding.

On February 10, 2006, during the New School conference on science and politics, I had said that "Washington, however, is still in denial. It seems unable to see this train coming down the tracks. Nobody was surprised that the words 'climate change' and 'global warming' were not in last week's State of the Union address, but I was astonished to hear them spoken by only one talking head during two hours of comments on the speech."

Now, just three months later, the mental ice in Washington is finally beginning to crack. Many powerful voices in the media and across the political spectrum are recognizing that climate change is real, and that it appears to be coming on more swiftly than expected by most of the experts that were for so long ridiculed by the skeptics.

The White House had not just ignored the climate issue. Thanks to James Hansen, everyone now knows that the administration has gone to great lengths to stifle government climate scientists. His experience is only the latest example. Three years ago the White House tried to distort a climate impact report by the Environmental Protection Agency (EPA) to the point where the EPA decided to squelch the report rather than release a scientifically insupportable document. And in its April 6 issue, *Time* revealed a new case in which the EPA administrator misrepresented his scientific advisory committee's opinion about air pollution.

Climate change and air pollution are not the only issues on which the administration has distorted scientific information and pressured government scientist to stick to the party line or to be silent (UCS, Scientific Integrity, n.d.). This has occurred in the Departments of Agriculture and Interior, at the National Oceanic and Atmospheric Administration, and especially in Health and Human Services—at the

National Institutes of Health, the Centers for Disease Control, and the Food and Drug Administration. These are not irrelevant academic spats; they have serious implications for the health of citizens the government is supposedly serving.

In some quarters it is fashionable to claim that this is nothing new—it happens in all administrations, and that the critics are just partisans. That is not a valid claim. There have been isolated, and sometimes egregious, cases in administrations of both parties, but what we are seeing now is systematic and widespread (Branscomb, 2004). The EPA administrators under the Nixon and Ford administrations have stated for the record that they never encountered White House meddling with science-based reports to the public or the president when they were in office.

CLIMATE CHANGE

I now turn to the climate issue. Here it is important to understand that our global environment is a delicately balanced system. Many large forces that move the system in different ways strike this balance. As a result, if the mean temperature—the average over the whole globe and over a number of years—changes by only a couple of degrees, the system can undergo dramatic change. For the same reason, there are considerable uncertainties in the temperature change that would be caused by a given amount of additional greenhouse gasses.

To establish concrete policies for meeting the climate challenge one needs a credible quantitative target for cutting carbon emissions. Setting such a target, given our state of knowledge, is not an exercise in pure science, although science provides indispensable guidance. Political judgments must be made. Given what is at stake, it is essential to exercise caution and prudence.

All this has led the British government, the European Union and other major actors to adopt the target of a global mean temperature rise of no more than 1.2° C (or 2.1° F) above today's, which translates into a CO_2 composition of the atmosphere no greater than by about a third above the current level (Avoiding Dangerous Climate Change, 2005).

To achieve this goal will require industrialized countries like the United States to reduce annual emissions by 60 to 80 percent by midcentury! Obviously, this is a huge challenge. Furthermore, deep cutting would have to continue during the rest of the century because CO_2 remains in the atmosphere for so long. What is there already would produce considerable warming even if we could, today, halt all further growth in the use of fossil fuels.

CAPPING THE ATMOSPHERIC CARBON CONCENTRATION

At the Union of Concerned Scientists we are taking a comprehensive look at the various alternatives for capping the greenhouse gas (GHG) content of the atmosphere. Here I give a preliminary report on a part of this exercise: the potential role of nuclear power. Whatever you may have thought about nuclear power in the past, the climate change threat is such that all options for dealing with it must be put on the table and examined without prejudice.

A large number of technically realistic measures for reducing GHG emissions exist. Of these, nuclear power carries grave risks that are unique, and which to at least some degree offset its virtue of not emitting GHG. Striking the balance between these pros and cons is, at heart, a societal judgment, not just a technical decision. But this judgment should, of course, be made in light of the best available technical knowledge.

The first task is to identify the full suite of measures, including nuclear power, that could be taken to produce the cut in GHG emissions required to stabilize the atmosphere at the desired level of GHG concentration. A very useful and widely noted examination of this question has been provided by a program at Princeton, sponsored by BP and Ford (Pacala and Socolow, 2004; for subsequent work see <http://www.princeton.edu/~cmi/>). This program has produced a study based on the following logic:

- The CO_2 composition of the atmosphere must rise by no more than about a third above the current level to prevent the temperature from increasing to the point where catastrophic and irreversible impacts become unacceptably probable (destabilization of Greenland and Antarctic ice sheets; reversal of the land carbon sink and the like);
- As a consequence, emissions must, on average, be held at about the current level for next 50 years, and thereafter be reduced further;
- To attain this stabilization in 50 years requires rapid and substantial cutting; therefore, only technologies that already exist and can be rapidly expanded should be given high near-term priority.

The Princeton study introduces the useful concept of a "wedge," defined as any measure that produces a reduction of 1 billion tons of carbon deposited annually in the atmosphere. The growth in energy demand assumed by the study—a doubling in the coming 50 years—implies that a cut of seven wedges, employed steadily, are needed to achieve stabilization in 50 years.

The study then provides a list of measures—technologies, public policy initiatives—that exist today, and which could be scaled up to become one or more wedges:

- Efficiency and conservation: new autos at 60 mpg—50 percent less driving per 30 mpg auto; 25 percent reduced heat loss from buildings; higher power plant efficiency—a total of 4 wedges.
- Decarbonizing of fossil fuel in electricity production: natural gas displacing coal; CO_2 capture and storage; electricity from wind; solar power; biofuels (ethanol, etc.)—a total of 7 wedges.
- Natural sinks: reduced tropical deforestation and better management of forests generally; reforestation; soil management—a total of more than 2 wedges.
- Tripling nuclear power globally (including the United States)—1 wedge.

Including a substantial expansion of nuclear power, there is a total of some 14 to 15 wedges, or about twice the number needed, of which *just one comes from a tripling of nuclear power worldwide.*

This does not mean there is no climate change problem. There are potential problems not captured by the study's assumptions:

▸ Every wedge requires a major expansion, and some may not prove to be cost-effective;
▸ Many face political hurdles even though the technology is proven;
▸ There is some competition between wedges—they cannot just be added;
▸ The GHG concentration target may not prove to be low enough to meet the temperature target sought;
▸ The rise in energy demand may be greater than assumed.

All these cautions, and the signs that global warming is coming on more rapidly than what was anticipated in the Princeton study, imply that it is only prudent to assume that a deeper cut and swifter cutting will be needed to attain the temperature goal.

THE BENEFIT AND RISKS OF NUCLEAR POWER

The wedge depiction of the climate challenge has the merit of clarifying the potential role of nuclear power:

▸ Major expansion of nuclear power is not the indispensable silver bullet that its advocates claim;
▸ A tripling of nuclear power is just one wedge among about 15;
▸ Hence, nuclear power must be evaluated by an unbiased competition with the other options, but taking into account the unique risks that attend nuclear power.

Expansion of nuclear power is a serious proposition because nuclear power does not lead to the emission of greenhouse gases, or to air pollutants (sulfur and nitrogen oxides, mercury, soot). But nuclear power has very serious negatives that have no counterparts in the other options. A nuclear power plant accident or a terror attack on a plant or associated facilities can inflict massive medical and environmental damage. Disposal of spent nuclear fuel is already a vexing problem, and will become much worse if there is a large-scale expansion. And the civilian nuclear-fuel cycle carries an inherent risk of nuclear weapon proliferation.

A major expansion of nuclear power will only be accepted by the American public if it can be assured that the risk of release of radioactivity from an accident, a terror attack, or a waste depository is remote. In principle, that could be done, but the history of nuclear power in this country tells us that this will be very difficult. The proliferation danger is a major international problem, and one that is getting significantly more difficult even without any significant expansion of nuclear power.

Whether nuclear power can compete economically with the other means of generating electricity is a very different matter. This question is left to the end of this paper because it raises fundamental issues that societies must resolve in deciding how much of a commitment to nuclear power they will make.

Accidents and Terrorism

In the last two decades the American nuclear power industry has learned how to operate its plants more reliably, and there have been fewer malfunctions that require the Nuclear Regulatory Commission (NRC) to demand a shutdown. But serious problems persist. The most glaring example is the Davis-Besse plant in Ohio, which came to within 6 months of having a large hole bored through its head by boric acid, which could have led to a catastrophic core meltdown. This was not just a technical near-failure, but a failure by the NRC, as its own post-incident review concluded. Nevertheless, after more than two years the NRC has not implemented a quarter of its "high priority lessons learned."

That terrorism poses a serious threat to nuclear power plants only became widely recognized after 9/11. Not only the nuclear reactors, but the neighboring spent fuel, could wreak havoc if attacked.

Since 9/11, the NRC has upped the "Design Basis Threat" (DBT) that defines the level of attack that the plant operator is responsible for; above this the government is responsible. The DBT is classified, as it should be. It is known, however, to be based on the unrealistic assumption that the risk attending an attack can be reckoned in the same way as the risk of an accident. However, in an accident, backup systems should work, whereas they would also be the target of terrorists. Moreover, testing of readiness, which was ridiculously weak before 9/11, is still too limited, and the Department of Homeland Security does not have the authority or resources to insure that operators can handle the Design Basis Threat.

If nuclear power is to play a major role in addressing the climate challenge, the NRC must undergo fundamental reforms that will make it truly independent of the industry it is supposed to regulate. Congress must provide it with the funding and political authority to strictly enforce the existing regulations pertaining to accidents. Homeland Defense and the NRC must together establish a coherent and effective security regime that can cope credibly with the threats of the post 9/11 world.

Waste

You may be astonished, and even angry, that we do not consider waste to be the showstopper that many believe is the case for even a small-scale expansion of nuclear power in the United States. Hardened interim storage of spent fuel in dry casks is secure and economical viable for 50 years or so. Nevertheless, new plants should not be licensed until a geological depository is licensed. Large-scale expansion of nuclear power should not be considered without a technically sound and politically viable solution of the storage problem. The interim storage option provides a time window in which new storage technologies or new storage sites can be explored and developed.

Proliferation

Both the fuel entering a nuclear reactor and the spent fuel pose serious proliferation risks.

A nuclear chain reaction can take place in suitably configured assemblies of either of the elements uranium or plutonium. Uranium exists in nature, but plutonium does not because it decays with a half-life of some 24,000 years. Both elements can be used in a controlled manner—that is in nuclear power reactors—or as an explosive—in nuclear weapons. That is why nuclear power and nuclear armaments have an inherently deep relationship.

Naturally occurring uranium from uranium ore must be "enriched" before the material can be used as reactor fuel, but that same enrichment technology can, with a relatively small additional effort, produce highly enriched weapons grade uranium.

When the uranium fuel is "burned" in a reactor, a fraction of the uranium atoms are turned into atoms of the preferred weapons materiel, plutonium. The latter can be extracted from the spent fuel by a chemical process called "reprocessing." (The nuclear reactor was invented in the Manhattan Project for the express purpose of producing plutonium from uranium, and this plutonium was then used on the bomb that destroyed Nagasaki. The Hiroshima bomb used highly enriched uranium.)

There is a serious worry that Iran will with time gain a weapon capability by acquiring the ability to enrich uranium for its large civilian nuclear reactor. The reason is that such a reactor needs a very large and steady stream of reactor grade uranium, and that a plant that can produce this "docile" stream can very quickly prepare the rather small quantity of weapons grade uranium needed for a bomb (Albright and Hinderstein, 2004).

The nuclear Non-Proliferation Treaty (NPT) suffers from a serious defect in that it allows a non-nuclear power to acquire essentially all the capabilities for manufacturing weapons material short of actually using this capability for that purpose, and to leave the treaty regime shortly before taking this last step. That was done by North Korea. Removing this defect in the NPT is very difficult politically, mainly because the nuclear powers have for decades put higher priority on satisfying their own, separate national interests than on strengthening the NPT regime. In recent years the United States has put an extra heavy burden on the NPT by adopting nuclear weapons policies that are in conflict with the spirit (though not the letter) of its obligations under the NPT, and by refusing to ratify the Nuclear Test Ban Treaty.

The United States has not carried out any reprocessing to obtain plutonium from civilian reactors for some 30 years. But North Korea did while abiding to the letter though certainly not the spirit of the NPT. Some countries that do not worry us also reprocess. In particular, Japan does, but its accounting system is such that enough plutonium for more than 10 weapons is not accounted for.

The rising concern about climate change, and the heightened interest in nuclear power, has brought with it a campaign in favor of reprocessing in the United States. The nuclear power industry is not behind this because it knows that reprocessing is not even close to being cost-effective. Other private interests, some government laboratories, and segments of the Bush administration are pushing reprocessing, however. They claim that the supply of naturally occurring uranium will eventually run out, and that it is cheaper and safer to deal with the radioactive wastes after reprocessing than with the waste from conventional uranium-fueled reactors. However, the case for reprocessing in the near term (a decade at least) cannot withstand scrutiny on technical or economic grounds.

It seems that nuclear power will acquire a significant share of the global energy menu, even if it does not in the United States. At least some of the new plants will be in politically volatile countries. Unless an effective international regime governing the supply of fissile fuel is established, this will bring with it an unacceptable proliferation risk.

The Bush administration has recently created a new initiative—the Global Nuclear Energy Partnership (GNEP), which would require nations with advanced nuclear knowledge to provide nuclear fuel to newcomers under the aegis of the International Atomic Energy Agency so as to limit the proliferation risk (see Global Nuclear Energy Partnership, n.d.). This is a laudable concept, but it is being advertised in terms of a technology that would in an integrated manner burn and reprocess fissile material. At this time the technology only exists in PowerPoint. It is far too early to claim that GNEP will provide a proliferation-proof *or* affordable means for a major expansion of nuclear power (Garwin, 2006).

WOULD THE MAJOR EXPANSION OF NUCLEAR POWER BE COST-EFFECTIVE AND PRUDENT?

In the United States and in other countries where power generation is not a government function, the market can, in principle, decide whether nuclear power is economically viable. Here "in principle" alludes to familiar conditions required to create an unbiased market, and in addition to the special circumstances that stem from the unique dangers that attend nuclear power.

First, the fact that no new plants have been built in the United States for more than two decades demonstrates that nuclear power has not been an attractive investment. (The claim that this is due to the licensing process is a red herring.) That would change were the US government to impose a sufficiently high price on putting carbon into the atmosphere either by a carbon tax or by creating an obligatory carbon emission cap-and-trade regime. Such restrictions on carbon emission would, of course, be of advantage to all sources of energy that do not add carbon to the atmosphere, and will almost certainly be necessary if the climate challenge is to be met. It remains to be seen whether a regime that would suffice to make other noncarbon and carbon-neutral energy sources competitive will also suffice to do so for nuclear power, but that is a question that the market can, in principle, settle.

Second, the market can only give a legitimate evaluation of the economic viability of nuclear power if the government refrains from favoring it over other energy sources by means of subsidies. Thus far the American nuclear power industry has not been competitive despite the fact that since World War II the US government has spent about half its total energy R&D budget on nuclear power, taken responsibility for nuclear waste, and, through the Price-Anderson Act, has insured the industry against major accidents. Many advocates for an expansion of nuclear power seek a continuation of Price-Anderson and other subsidies. In doing so they are admitting that nuclear power is not competitive now or in the near-term. A sufficiently high price on carbon emission would, of course, change this picture.

In the American setting, therefore, the question of whether nuclear power is an economically viable contributor to cutting GHG emission can, aside from a critical caveat, be settled by the market if all means of reducing GHG emissions are treated equally in terms of subsidies and/or a price on carbon emissions.

The critical caveat stems from the unique dangers posed by nuclear power, which the market cannot adequately assess because the conventional meaning of "cost-effective" does not apply to nuclear power. In the last analysis, any major catastrophe arising from nuclear power would become the responsibility of the government—that is, of the nation as a whole. No matter who bears legal responsibility, only the nation as a whole can deal with a disaster of Katrina or 9/11 proportions, not to mention what could easily be much more dire if a nuclear explosion or a large radioactive release were the cause. The market knows this, and does not count such risks in evaluating the economic viability of any technology that could produce a calamity of catastrophic proportions. Hence the level of commitment to an expansion of nuclear power is a profoundly political and not an economic decision in the United States and other democracies, where the energy supply is governed by an ostensibly free market.

In countries where the energy supply is a government responsibility, only the international market or the nation's overall economic condition checks the wasteful commitment of resources. Therefore unvarnished political power would in such settings be the decisive factor.

Whether and how the climate challenge is to be met is a political dilemma of unprecedented complexity and magnitude that faces all societies and the international community as a whole. The risk of nuclear weapons proliferation that would inevitably accompany a major worldwide expansion of nuclear power would constitute an additional major challenge to the international community—a challenge to which the response has been faltering even prior to such an expansion. Simple prudence and common sense therefore argues in favor of a go-slow approach to nuclear power expansion until international political constraints and proven new technologies have been established that would provide adequate insurance against the proliferation risk, or until it is evident that the other carbon-free and carbon-neutral technologies will not suffice to meet the climate challenge.

REFERENCES

Albright, D., and C. Hinderstein. "The Centrifuge Connection." *Bulletin of Atomic Scientists* (March/April 2004): 61-66.

Avoiding Dangerous Climate Change (2005) <http://www.stabilisation2005.com/outcomes.html>.

Branscomb, L. M. "Science, Politics, and US Democracy" *Issues in Science and Technology* (Fall 2004): 53-59.

Garwin, R. L. "R&D Priorities for the Global Nuclear Energy Partnership." Subcommittee on Energy, Committee on Science, U.S. House of

Representatives, April 6, 2006, Washington, D.C. <http://www.fas.
org/RLG/060406-gnep.pdf>.

Global Nuclear Energy Partnership <http://www.gnep.energy.gov>.

Pacala, S., and R. Socolow. "Stabilization Wedges: Solving the Climate
Problem for the Next 50 Years with Current Technologies." *Science*
305 (2004): 968-972.

Union of Concerned Scientists. Scientific Integrity <http://www.ucsusa.
org/scientific_integrity>.

VI. Roundtable Discussion

States of Inquiry

Social Investigations and Print Culture in Nineteenth-Century Britain and the United States

Oz Frankel

In the mid-nineteenth century, American and British governments marched with great fanfare into the marketplace of knowledge and publishing. British royal commissions of inquiry, inspectorates, and parliamentary committees conducted famous social inquiries into child labor, poverty, housing, and factories. The American federal government studied Indian tribes, explored the West, and investigated the condition of the South during and after the Civil War.

Performing, printing, and then circulating these studies, government established an economy of exchange with its diverse constituencies. In this medium, which Frankel terms "print statism," not only tangible objects such as reports and books but knowledge itself changed hands. As participants, citizens assumed the standing of informants and readers.

This study contributes to current debates over knowledge, print culture, and the growth of the state as well as the nature and history of the "public sphere." It interweaves innovative, theoretical discussions into meticulous, historical analysis.

New Studies in American Intellectual and Cultural History:
Howard Brick, Series Editor

$48.00 hardcover

The Johns Hopkins University Press
1-800-537-5487 • www.press.jhu.edu

Ira Flatow
Introduction

MELTING GLACIERS. RECORD HIGH TEMPERATURES. RISING SEA LEVELS. raging forest fires. Hellish hurricanes. Reemerging diseases. These are all symptoms of a changing climate, scientists tell us, a warming of the earth and a shift in the balance of nature. Scientists say that our consumption of fossil fuels has helped create a climatic shift. We have changed the very planet that has supported life as we know it for the past thousands of years. But what are we as a nation able to do about it? And do we have the political will to make the changes necessary to adjust?

The federal government, including the Bush administration, has come under heavy criticism from scientists—some who work in and for the government itself—for denying the existence of global warming and the impact humans have had on helping to create it. For example, Senator James Inhofe (R., Okla.) has called the idea of human-induced global warming "the greatest hoax ever perpetrated on the American people." President George W. Bush once denounced an internal government report on global warming as just "something put out by the bureaucracy." And as government scientists have attempted to answer these critics with hard scientific evidence, they have had been asked to change their conclusions to fit government policy. One example: NASA scientist James Hansen, whose paper appears in this volume, says the government has tried to censor his public statements about global warming.

In the light of this political turmoil over global warming, the questions before us are:

▸ Can we stop, slow down, or reverse global warming and if so, what must we do?
▸ Does our government have the leadership and the resources to spearhead a national movement, as part of a larger international movement, that can prepare us for the consequences of climate change?

- What role do scientists play in helping convince our national leaders that action is necessary?
- Will our elected officials heed the warnings of researchers and put politics aside? Just why is global warming a polarizing political issue in the United States?
- What new bridges can be created between scientists and political leaders so that they better understand the role science plays in the future of the planet?
- Is our educational system up to the task of informing students about the interplay of science and politics?
- Should scientists be encouraged to speak out on important geopolitical issues or is that overstepping their roles? Do we need more "citizen-scientists"?
- How do we bring the media into the picture? In an age where loud, brash commentators are the rage, how can one make sure complicated issues receive the media coverage they deserve, while avoiding being "dumbed down" to the point of being useless?

How we answer these questions may influence whether our society is equipped to deal with issues that may take many generations to address. Global warming will be with us for the next hundred or more years. Does our society have the ability to create public policy to address a problem that will outlast one presidential administration to another? After all, history shows that one president's pet project is another's bad idea. When Jimmy Carter installed solar panels on the White House to illustrate the need to develop alternative energy sources after the first oil crisis in the '70s, Ronald Reagan made it one of his first official acts to rip out those panels, in defiance, sending the country in a totally different direction.

Science and technology has always been the driving force behind progress; the basis of our economy. They create jobs, heal the sick, and are instrumental for our "life, liberty, and pursuit of happiness." We are now seeing how the industrial revolution is colliding with the "law of unexpected consequences"—that is, the changing of our climate, the warming of the earth.

The brief remarks that follow, originally presented as a panel discussion, address these issues and help define what kind of future we can expect in the coming age of global climate change.

Robert P. George
Ethics, Politics, and Genetic Knowledge

THE DAY MAY COME WHEN BIOTECHNOLOGICAL SCIENCE MAKES IT possible for parents to custom design their offspring, manipulating genes to produce children with the "superior" traits—strength, intelligence, beauty—the parent or parents desire. But that day is still a long way off. The relationship between genes and qualities such as intelligence and athletic prowess turns out to be so complex that the dream or nightmare of "designer babies" may never become a reality. That does not mean we should not worry about the possibility. But, for now, we should not spend too much of our worry budget on it. There are far more urgent things to be concerned about today in the field of biotechnology.

Before discussing these things, however, we should pause to reflect on the blessings that genetic knowledge and the biotechnologies it makes possible have delivered or will deliver soon. Much genetic knowledge has been generated by inquiry aimed at curing diseases, healing afflictions, and ameliorating suffering. Valuable biotechnologies have been developed for the purpose of advancing human health and well-being. This is to be applauded.

Moreover, genetic knowledge, like knowledge in other fields of intellectual inquiry, is intrinsically valuable. Even apart from its utility in medicine, such knowledge is humanly fulfilling and, indeed, fulfilling in a special way since much genetic knowledge is a species of self-knowledge. Advances in genetics help us to explore and understand more fully that greatest of mysteries, namely, the mystery of man himself. These advances, too, deserve our applause.

Now let us turn to the worries—the urgent ones.

The first worry is that we may compromise, or further compromise, in both science and politics, the principle that every human being, irrespective of age, size, mental or physical condition, stage of development, or condition of dependency, possesses inherent worth and dignity and a right to life. Proponents of research involving the destruction of human beings in the embryonic stage for biomedical research began by proposing only that "spare" embryos held in cryopreservation in IVF clinics be sacrificed. These microscopic humans would, they argued, likely die anyway, so nothing would be lost (and no wrong would be done) by destroying them to harvest stem cells. Soon, however, many of these people were calling for the mass production by cloning of human embryos precisely for use as disposable research material. For now, most insist that they desire to use only embryos in the blastocyst (5- to 6-day) stage, and are not proposing to implant and gestate embryos that would then be killed at later stages of development to harvest cells, tissues, or organ primordia. But this is bound to change. Having abandoned the moral norm against deliberately taking innocent human life, many will be carried by the logic of their position to the view that producing human beings to be killed in the fetal and even early infant stages is justified in the cause of regenerative medicine.

The second worry is closely related. It is that many people are coming to view procreation as akin to manufacture. They also regard children not as gifts to be cherished and loved even when "imperfect," but rather as products that may legitimately be subjected to standards of quality control and discarded or killed in the embryonic, fetal, and even infant stages if they do not measure up. Pre-implantation genetic diagnosis (PGD) of embryos in the context of assisted reproduction is increasingly widely practiced. In IVF clinics in the United States, it is common for a larger number of embryos to be produced than can be safely implanted. So, people reason, why not choose the ones likely to be healthiest? Embryonic human beings are considered more or less worthy of life, and sometimes not worthy of life at all, depending on their "quality." And the eugenic ethic embodied in the practice of PGD is not confined to choosing among embryos for implantation. Eugenic abortion—and, in some cases, even infanticide—is regarded as perfectly legitimate by many in the United States and elsewhere. A child in the womb who has been diagnosed with Down's syndrome or dwarfism is likely to be aborted. A newborn may be deprived of a simple life-saving surgery and "allowed to die." Those responsible will, perhaps, tell themselves that they are doing it "for the good of the child." The reality, however, is that they are treating the mentally or physically handicapped child as a "life unworthy of life." And let no one suppose that such decisions, ghastly as they are even when chosen by parents, are or will remain a matter of unencumbered "choice." Social pressures exist and will build for parents to spare society the burdens of caring for, or even encountering, mentally or physically handicapped people. Some years ago, the geneticist Bentley Glass, envisaging a future in which genetic screening would become the routine thing it is today, proclaimed triumphantly that "no parent will . . . have a right to burden society with a malformed or a mentally incompetent child."

The great bioethicist Leon Kass has diagnosed the situation insightfully. Speaking at the United States Holocaust Museum, Kass warned:

> [The] eugenic vision and practice are gaining strength, all the more so because they grow out of sight behind the fig leaf of the doctrine of free choice. We are largely unaware that we have, as a society, already embraced the eugenic principle "Defectives shall not be born" because our practices are decentralized and they operate not by coercion but by private reproductive choice.

One should observe, of course, that many people continue to resist the eugenic ethic and struggle to reverse it; and despite the (sometimes amusing) boasting of the eugenicists, there is no good reason to think that it cannot be reversed in significant measure. Yet a sober assessment of the situation requires us to acknowledge that support for the eugenic killing of human beings in the fetal and infant stages is no longer a "fringe" position, and is particularly strong in elite sectors of the culture.

Groups dedicated to defending the dignity and rights of handicapped persons (even when they take no official position on the ethics of abortion as such) have recognized the dire implications of the eugenic ethic for the people they serve. As Dr. Kass puts it, "persons who happen still to be born with these conditions, having somehow escaped the spreading net of detection and eugenic abortion, are increasingly regarded as 'mistakes,' as inferior human beings who should not have been born." This has produced an alliance between the pro-life movement and advocates of justice for the handicapped or disabled in a number of domains.

The glory of our political tradition is its affirmation of the profound, inherent, and equal dignity of all human beings. The history of our politics and social practice, our law and economics, and even our medicine is in significant measure the struggle to live up to the demands of this affirmation. The trouble, of course, is that individual and collective self-interest are often at war with it. All too often, people will have powerful motives to regard others as less than fully human, or to believe that humanity can be divided into classes—superiors and inferiors, "persons" and subpersonal or nonpersonal members of the human family. It was true in the days of slavery; it is true in the era of eugenic abortion and infanticide. Sometimes people say that the challenges of biotechnological science will require us to invent new principles of ethics and politics. At least when it comes to the immediate dangers we face, that is not true. What we need is fidelity to the principles of human equality and dignity that have always served us well when we have had the wisdom and fortitude to honor them.

David Goldston
Some Thoughts on Politics and Science

MUCH OF WHAT HAS BEEN WRITTEN LATELY ABOUT POLITICS AND SCIENCE suggests that the intersection of the two has become far more treacherous because of the actions and attitudes of the Bush administration. But while this administration has certainly helped keep the issue in the news, the interaction of politics and science is being altered more by fundamental, systemic, and probably long-term political trends than by the policies of a single administration.

The most salient characteristic of contemporary American politics is the increasing polarization of the political elite. (I say the "elite" because, perhaps for the first time in US history, the polarization of the elite is occurring when the general public seems largely apathetic or withdrawn. This is not a time when, to use a phrase from the 1960s, "democracy is in the streets.")

The polarization is causing, among other things, a scramble by politicians to be heard above the noise, to sound like more than just another partisan, to find a line of argument that will both confirm the views of their "camp" and enable them to convince others to move toward their pole on an issue. And "science" fits the bill; indeed, it seems to be just about the only area of human endeavor that does.

In the political arena, "science" still has the air of objectivity, of offering up incontestable facts. For that reason, science may be replacing patriotism as the "last refuge of the scoundrel." Everyone in politics now tries to frame his or her position as the one and only view that is justified by "sound science." This is in some ways a sincere and salutary development, but it also places an enormous and often insupportable burden on science and distorts debates. And while this political trend reflects a kind of reverence for science, it may end up leaving science in tatters. Politicians may end up loving science to death.

The most deleterious result of this embrace of science is that it obscures debates about values—debates that need to occur to make clear and coherent decisions. A case study of this occurred in 1997 when the Clinton administration proposed tighter standards for ground-level ozone. The short-term effects of ozone are not subject to much debate: for a given level of ozone, experts can predict the likely number of excess hospital admissions for asthma and other respiratory illnesses. The issue in setting ozone standards under the Clean Air Act therefore comes down to deciding how many excess hospital admissions are acceptable as public policy. That is not a science question.

Yet, instead of discussing the direct if difficult question of accept-able hospital admissions, partisans on both sides of the debate, inside and outside Congress, tried to argue that their proposed ozone standard was the level backed by "the science." Each side marshaled scientists to make their case, none of whom, to my knowledge, ever suggested that they were not answering a science question.

The stem cell debate is another example of the same phenom-enon. That debate obviously has to be informed by science and by scientists who can offer their assessments of the potential of stem cell research and who can also weigh in on what should be factual ques-tions, such as the number of stem cell lines available to researchers. But on the fundamentals of the stem cell debate—whether stem cell research is ethical—scientific opinion should not be accorded a place of privilege. The ethical questions are not science questions, and no side of the debate should be labeled "pro-" or "anti-" science.

The lines between science and policy are not always clear-cut, of course, but political debate and scientific integrity would both be enhanced if politicians, scientists, journalists, and the public at least made an effort not to frame every issue as one of science—and not to frame science as a fount of certainty.

There are cases in which the political debate is actually about science, although these tend to be the exception rather than the rule. In the US House of Representatives at least, politicians are debating the scientific question of whether climate change is a real phenomenon. In this case, the best that scientists can do is to state what the scientific consensus is, making clear distinctions between areas of certainty (for example, carbon dioxide and temperatures are rising; the greenhouse effect is real) and areas of uncertainty (the precise impacts that rising greenhouse gas levels are likely to have, for example).

This approach has had some effect; the Bush administration's pronouncements on climate, while varied, have stayed within the boundaries set by the 2001 National Academy of Sciences report that was requested by the president. In contrast, the climate change skeptics (or deniers) in Congress have taken a different tack based, in effect, on a skewed understanding of the history of science. Knowing that "scientific revolutions" have sometimes discarded widely held scientific beliefs, the skeptics argue that whoever is the outlier now must be cultivating the kernel of the next scientific paradigm.

This line of "reasoning" is bad history, bad logic, and bad policy, but it does point up an ironic danger to science inherent in its current political use. While politicians are drawn to science because of its reputation for objective purity, they can only undermine their opponents by attacking their science as somehow sullied and biased. It's impossible to predict what view of the overall scientific enterprise will emerge over time if science is repeatedly deployed as a political weapon rather than as a policy tool.

Interestingly, so far, none of the policy debates that revolve around science—and not even the political debate about the science of evolution—has had any impact on the debate over science policy. Funding for science, for example, still has widespread, even growing, support. But one cannot assume that this will be the case forever.

Scientists, policymakers, and concerned observers ought to be examining how science is employed in policy debates now, while science's reputation and funding are intact. And that means looking beyond charges and countercharges about the Bush administration to analyze how issues are being framed and how scientific certainty is being characterized more generally.

Rush Holt
Science and Citizenship

OUR CHALLENGE BEGINS WITH AMERICA'S AVERSION TO SCIENCE. I believe that this aversion began to emerge after the application of the National Defense Education Act, which was created in response to the Soviet Union's launch of the Sputnik satellite in 1957. Frightened by the prospect of being technically and scientifically outmatched by our rival, our government set about producing a generation of scientists and engineers the likes of which the world had never seen. And we succeeded, to our great benefit. But there was an unintended consequence. In encouraging the best and brightest students to pursue science and engineering and affording them opportunities to do so, we sent the other 80 percent of the population a message: "You are not among the best and brightest, so science and mathematics is not for you." It is as if there were a statement, perhaps in ink invisible to scientists, at the bottom of the every page in science books that read "Do not try this at home. This is meant only for experts."

The problem is, of course, that nonscientists *could* understand scientific thinking, and *would* understand it, if they were encouraged and expected to do so. Unintentionally, we created a situation where 80 percent of our population was not taught not to think scientifically. The result today is that we are at risk of losing what makes America great: our Yankee ingenuity or good old American know-how.

At one time, every shopkeeper, every farmer, every manufacturer was thinking about how things work, and how to make them better. They were thinking like scientists. Today our society is not illuminated by a scientific way of thinking. We are not asking questions in a way such that they can be answered empirically and verifiably. (I have not been able to come up with a better definition of science, by the way, for third graders or professional researchers, than this: science is a way of asking questions that can be answered empirically and verifiably—so that you avoid fooling yourself and others.) We have lost our scientific way of thinking as a society and the benefits that we reap from this way of thinking are depleting as well.

This problem is reflected in Congress, which is by design representative of America. Fewer than 1 percent of the Members of Congress are scientists, and as a result Members too have an aversion to science. By contrast, Members of Congress are not inhibited when it comes to speaking on other issues in which they have no special expertise. Members of Congress speak intelligently and constructively on international affairs, economics, education, and transportation. However, when it comes to science, they are unwilling to speak. They actively avoid talking about science. They, too, state that we need to leave science to the experts.

Though Members of Congress and their staff may avoid science, the institution itself cannot. In fact, it is more difficult to identify a topic that contains no scientific or no technical aspect than to identify topics that do. And, even when so inclined, Members of Congress and their staff lack the time to analyze scientific and technological points. But Congress moves forward anyway, voting on technical or scientific issues nevertheless.

Until the day comes when science is fully integrated into education for all, and even Members of Congress and congressional staff Members can deal with technical subjects, we will need special help for our legislation. Congress used to have an in-house professional office dedicated to providing technological assessment services known as the Office of Technology Assessment (OTA). From the OTA, Congress received regular reports in a legislatively relevant form on a myriad of subjects, including agriculture, arms control, banking, computer security and technology, economic development, education, energy efficiency, the fishing industry, health and health technology, international relations and technology transfer, natural disasters, oil, gas, and mineral resources, and many other areas. In 1995, in a move of overzealous cost cutting, the new congressional majority decided that it did not need an in-house body dedicated to technological assessment, and defunded the OTA.

What happened to Congress's scientific and technical assessment and advice after the demise of the OTA? Those calling for closing OTA said Congress could look to the Congressional Research Service, the Government Accountability Office, the National Academy of Sciences and its National Research Council, professional societies, universities, and their scientific constituents to fill in the gap. Despite excellent work, the aforementioned have been unable to meet fully the needs of Congress. This is in large measure because Congress in no way suffers from a lack of information. Just the opposite: we suffer from a lack of ability to digest the validity, credibility, and usefulness of the large amount of information and advice we receive every day. Also, the information and assessments received too often fail to be politically neutral, and they rarely are timely. In the end, the nation suffers as policy decisions are made without the scientific and technical analysis necessary to clarify the details and understand the consequences of the policy decision.

Congress still needs unbiased and timely technical and scientific assessments from experts who are familiar with the functions, language, and workings of Congress. We need a dedicated, in-house, permanently staffed organization. The management structure should be designed with responsiveness and quality in mind. Political neutrality must be protected. The experts should be physically close to Congress and the reports must be in time and in language that is accessible and relevant. As an author of legislation to create such an entity, I continue to work to see that this happens for the Congress.

Ensuring that good science informs and infuses good public policy requires scientists engage in the process of self-governance. This goes beyond merely voting. It requires organization, and participation. I know that scientists would prefer to stay above the fray of politics, which is often perceived as tainted and illogical when compared to scientific practice. However, when scientists do not engage with those who create public policy, policymakers quarrel over the facts instead of debating the merits of the policy choices before them.

Affecting public policy means investing in a working relationship with elected leaders and their staffs. Part of a successful relationship with elected officials is to learn to communicate in a way that is memorable and repeatable to a lay audience. Humans are much better adapted to remembering stories than statistics, for example. When discussing issues, a scientist must remember that she is not there to teach science, or to present her research, but rather to place the scientific work within the context of the politician's work. Science is a human endeavor, and it is the people and stories behind the results and its applications that move politicians to act for science.

Scientists must also serve as watchdogs for science. It is not enough to conduct science only; we all share a responsibility to blow the whistle on abuse of science publicly by writing op-eds and letters to the editor of local newspapers. Without such action, abuses of science can pass by without notice. Most scientific societies have a government affairs division aimed at following the work of the federal, state, and local governments, assessing the consequences for science, and informing their membership of opportunities to take action. Scientific organizations often take stands on controversial topics when there is a question of scientific fact or scientific analysis. The American Association for the Advancement of Science is an example of this, staying active in the evolution and intelligent design debate, where science and religious belief collide, as well as engaging in the stem cell research debate.

A scientifically literate society would be intolerant of demonstrations presented as tests of a flawed missile defense system. A scientifically literate society would not entertain teaching intelligent design in the science classroom, let alone elevate it to the state of a national debate. There is much work to be done to achieve a scientifically literate society, but it is fundamentally a question of instilling a scientific way of questioning from pre-kindergarten to the collegiate level. This includes addressing teaching methods, access to scientific equipment, up-to-date curricula, college affordability, and teacher training. Scientists can both support and participate in these endeavors on the local, regional, and national levels.

Science should not only be a tool of public policy, it should be its foundation. Like democracy, science is a self correcting entity when practiced properly. Our country has greatly benefited from science, its application, and its practitioners. Our quality of living, including our health, transportation, economy, and other aspects of our daily existence, have been improved by innovation derived from scientific understanding and creative thinking. We are currently the world leaders in science, technology, and innovation, but this status is not guaranteed. We cannot remain complacent. We must take action to maintain our place as a world leader in science, technology, and innovation.

With a scientifically literate society and public policy grounded in sound science, America can maintain its leadership in the emerging global knowledge economy. Without these, America will lose the very things that have fueled its greatness.

Ellis Rubinstein
Translating Good Science into Good Policy: The Us Factor

IN A WORLD OF CONTENTIOUS ASSERTIONS, HERE IS A STATEMENT THAT everyone can agree with: science has never been more important to the citizenry and to the body politic.

But instead of becoming better understood by the public and its representatives—something one might expect as this increasingly high-impact endeavor takes the center stage—polls indicate that science is as poorly understood as it was decades ago. In fact, science literacy is treading water . . . or worse.

In the United States, we have recently observed the renewed debates on the teaching of evolution, the lack of clarity about climate change despite the evidence, the battles over stem cell research, the public's reluctance in applying risk/benefit calculations to pharmaceutical products, and the general politicization of science in the current US administration (Specter, 2006: 58-69).

Is science literacy unacceptably sparse only here in the United States? The failure of sufficient numbers of European citizens to comprehend the basics about genetically modified organisms is leaving them as bystanders in a modern agricultural era. Far worse, their position has had devastating consequences for starving millions in the developing world.

To cite a stranger example out of Europe, Martin Enserink in *Science* (2005: 1394) reported that Holland's minister of science and education, Maria van der Hoeven, announced plans to "stimulate a debate about intelligent design." How could the science minister of a contemporary Western European nation take such a position? Van der Hoeven—a political appointee of the Christian Democratic Party and a practicing Catholic—seems to have thought that the "ID debate" would be a mechanism for achieving "common ground" among the Western religions at a time when religious extremism worries us all. Enserink reported that the minister wrote, in a blog she authors: "What unites Muslims, Jews and Christians is the notion that there is a creator. . . . If we succeed in connecting scientists from different religions, it might even be applied in schools and lessons."

American scientists and policymakers will immediately guess who was cheering that seemingly well-meaning statement. Enserink wrote: "Says Managing Director John Calvert of the Intelligent Design Network in Shawnee Mission [Kansas]: 'I think it's a dynamite idea.'"

This paper flows from a panel discussion that concluded the conference, "Politics and Science," held at the New School. The charge of the panel, in which I participated, was to address three questions: What needs to be done now, and by whom or by what institutions, to ensure that good science leads to good public policy that best serves the needs of the American public? How can we change the current situation so that scientists and scientific findings have more influence? And, how can we improve the policy decision-making process?"

This paper addresses those questions. But before turning to the challenge, I would like to cite one additional example of science illiteracy, occurring recently on a different continent. I refer to the hard-core Korean nationalists who have continued to support Hwang Woo Suk in the face of the most clear-cut evidence imaginable that he committed scientific misconduct on a massive scale and who reject the pronouncements of leading Koreans such at Seoul National University's research dean and the nation's public prosecutors.

So as we turn to a global problem—science illiteracy. Who is to blame, and what can be done?

THE BLAME GAME

Many commentators before me—politicians, sociologists, educators, and scientists themselves—have written extensively on this topic. And the candidates for blame are numerous: politicians who misuse science for their own partisan purposes; religious leaders who consider science in conflict with their belief systems; policymakers who fail to emerge from the halls of academe and power; publishers who distort science to sell copies; journalists who gloss over the complexities of science either to sell their stories to their editors or simply out of ignorance; industry that has misinterpreted science for its own interests; and even scientists themselves who are loathe—or unable—to convey their science to a general public.

All of these groups bear some blame. But this paper argues that, as the importance of science in our daily lives becomes ever clearer to the general public, the fickle finger of accusation needs to increasingly point inward—to all of us as individual citizens.

Why do I say this? First, I would like to assert that the citizenry in the developed world—and increasingly in developing countries—knows the economic value of science and technology. Whether in nations like China and India—which account for a substantial portion of the world's population and where science and technology are revered and viewed as a road out of poverty—or in the West, where it sometimes seems that every middling city is lusting for a biotech park, the connection of science and technology to prosperity is well recognized by the populace. So we should all be supporting science education as fiercely as the Chinese and Indians, shouldn't we?

And then there's our personal health. As science and technology have opened windows on the mechanisms of disease and as they have triggered dreams that one day we can avoid disease or live longer, healthier lives, more and more people learn the rudiments of biomedicine. Moreover, as the choices become more agonizing—to suffer chemotherapy despite the newest genetic indicator that it may not be effective or to trust in the efficacy of the latest pill to prevent your personalized form of cancer—families the world over are increasingly grappling with science, whether they like it or not.

Chemical spills, the new trade-offs on climate that have spurred discussions of nuclear energy, the debates over the ethics of mood enhancements and lifestyle drugs, the likelihood that a given autocrat or rogue state has weapons of mass destruction—all these are driving the adult citizenry to learn a great deal more about science and technology than they were taught in school. And that is where I come to my central point.

Where are the protests by the citizenry in Western nations over substandard science education in our schools?

ALTERNATIVE UNIVERSES

It's not that we aren't concerned at the deteriorating state of our public education in the major nations of the Western world. Whenever I travel, I encounter urban leaders—in London, Paris, virtually everywhere the world over—who bemoan the state of education in their school systems.

In my city—New York—the dynamic "businessman" mayor, Michael Bloomberg, announced early in his first term his determination to reform our schools, no matter how hard the job would be. To do that, he had to wrest control of the schools from local community boards. Because enough citizens were fed up with the weaknesses of the schools, he succeeded in establishing a constituency to do what his predecessors never had done.

Also, he hired an equally dynamic, totally dedicated chancellor who had never been in the school system in any capacity but who had led the US government antitrust suit against Microsoft. Was there a lesson there? Chancellor Joel Klein knows no fear of failure and is willing to wrestle octopi far larger than himself.

The results have included dramatic new programs—not all of which have yet proved to be successful—in reading and math reform. And, separately, the mayor has personally devoted hundreds of millions of his own dollars—usually anonymously—to support the city's cultural institutions and the efforts of hard-working private groups to bring arts and music back into our schools.

Great! But what happened to science?

Why had there been an outcry from everyone—private citizens, corporate leaders, politicians—to invest hundreds of millions of dollars in reading, math, and "culture," while the advocates for science remained isolated, treated for a couple of years almost as second-class citizens, receiving promises of reform in some second-stage process?

My academy is now working with the leaders of the major science museums to help the chancellor with science reform—and the chancellor has indicated that he supports an investment of funds equal to that for math. That's the good news here in New York. But cities throughout America haven't even gotten this far. I recently received a rueful report from a citizen of Seattle, home of Boeing and Microsoft. Now this is a manageable-sized city where the local billionaires are heavily in support of education reform. So if science in the schools is sleepless in Seattle, where is it awake and thriving?

The question in my mind is straightforward: with math and reading on everyone's agenda, why did science have to wait its turn? Is the public understanding of science in today's society less important than math literacy?

The problem is that science and technology, despite their palpable importance to the citizen of the twenty-first century, remain outside the tent—they are treated almost as an "alternative universe." How can one refer to culture today without referring to science? In what way is science not part of culture? But every definition of culture in a civic sense is limited to the arts and humanities. This is a symptom of the disease. And the disease is a virus rampant in lower and middle schools in the United States and virtually every country in the world except perhaps the "Confucian-influenced" meritocracies in Asia.

In our town, there are a handful of politicians and corporate leaders who are passionate about science in the schools. A similar group exists in your town. And everywhere, scientists and engineers will ring there hands and a very special subset will volunteer to try to bridge the divide between the so-called two cultures.

But until there is recognition that science is part and parcel of our single culture, and until there is a mass revolt over the failure of our education systems to identify, train, and reward science teachers on every level—and to provide students with uplifting facilities and role models, as well as psychic encouragement to pursue science—all the conferences in the world that are meant to address the need to improve the policy decision-making process will remain impotent in the struggle to create a true paradigm shift from public science illiteracy to public literacy.

REFERENCES

Enserink, Martin. "Evolution Politics: Is Holland Becoming the Kansas of Europe?" *Science* (June 3, 2005): 1394.

Specter, Michael. "Political Science." *The New Yorker* (March 13, 2006): 58-69.

Philip M. Smith
Creating a Broader Political Center for Science and Policy

AS HAS BEEN NOTED BY MANY DISTINGUISHED HISTORIANS OF SCIENCE, there was a comparatively great distance between science and government in the United States until the middle of the twentieth century. While government had supported some research in agriculture, geodetic surveying, geological and geographical exploration, meteorology, standards and testing, and military research (mostly during World War I), there was no consensus that federal funding should be directed to what we today call basic research. And there was little enthusiasm on the part of political leaders or the public for federal support of research conducted in universities. The importance of education had been recognized in laws such as the Land Grant College Act, but the large sums of federal funds that began to flow into university research following World War II did not exist previously. Moroever, science was not generally seen as useful in crafting policy beyond quite specific applications such as agriculture. Basic research depended largely on industrial funding that was largely conducted by industry in its own laboratories or by philanthropic support for university research from wealthy patrons, often through the foundations they established.

The relationship in the United States between science, government, and the public changed irrevocably in World War II. The massive research programs of the military services and the Office of Scientific Research and Development created a broad array of technologies and a large base of federally supported fundamental science—quite a bit of which was carried out by university research teams under contract, a new development in government-university relations. Technologies and products such as radar, the proximity fuse bomb, sulfa drugs, and the atomic bomb helped to win the war decisively. But there were three other major legacies. There was an acceptance by the public and political leaders of the importance of research and of government's support of it. That some wartime technologies would rather quickly be converted into useful consumer products—for example, penicillin, blood banking, greatly improved television screens, air traffic ground approach systems, microwave ovens, and the promise of electricity from nuclear power—made the benefits of research real to the public. Second, there was acceptance of a role for government in funding research at universities and finding the very best talent to carry it out, a case persuasively laid out in Vannevar Bush's 1945 report *Science: The Endless Frontier*. And, the federal institutions that support R&D that we know today were established or expanded. They include the military research organizations of each of the three services, a transformed and greatly expanded National Institutes of Health providing considerable university research support, the National Science Foundation, and the Atomic Energy Commission, the forerunner to the Department of Energy. (The National Aeronautics and Space Administration and the Defense Advanced Research Products Agency followed a decade or so later.)

Achieving political consensus for a larger federal research role during World War II was not easy even in the face of a wartime emergency that enjoyed broader political and public support than any war the nation has been engaged in since. Nor was it easy to create the political consensus for the postwar era of a greater federal role in support of research and research carried out in universities. There were many differences in views. Some congressional leaders wished for more specific congressional oversight, even to the approval of research projects. Others wanted federal research to include the social sciences and also initiatives that we would describe today as science-based social or societal assistance programs. In the executive branch, R&D leaders were zealous about retaining their decision-making prerogatives and insisted on peer review by scientists as the determinant for support of research at the project level. The public was enthusiastic about technology-based products but was less certain about basic research support (although there was an inherent public understanding that such support would put new inventions in the consumer product pipeline and cure major diseases).

Nonetheless, a political consensus for science support was achieved in World War II and in the postwar period. The importance of science for informed decision making was recognized. Over the ensuing decades there have been many examples of the ways that science informed policy for the direction and management of the scientific enterprise and to inform national policy. Let me mention a few spanning the decades. In terms of the direction of the scientific enterprise by administrations and the Congress, there are the many government science advisory panels that have helped guide directions of research and recommend levels of investment. The National Academies and the National Research Council have provided forward-looking decadal outlooks in different disciplines useful to leaders in both branches of government over the years. In the 1970s the Ford and Carter administrations, Congress, and scientists worked together—albeit at times with tensions—to craft federal guidelines for university-based recombinant DNA research; congressional committees such as the House Committee on Science and Space played important roles in insuring that basic research was not over-regulated. In the 1980s the scientific community helped inform the Reagan administration on appropriate levels of openness in research and where academic research was sensitive to national security.

In science-based policymaking, both branches of government and the science and engineering communities worked constructively to craft a response to Sputnik, one that guided national security policy and also investments in research, universities, and the training of scientists and engineers. The environmental legislation of the late 1960s and the early 1970s was informed by science and scientists were active in the crafting of those laws. Beyond its role in guiding defense research, the science community has been integral to the development of national security policy. The National Academy of Sciences and the Soviet Academy of Sciences created panels in the 1980s to discuss nuclear arms reductions, leading to responses from both the US and Russian governments to greatly reduce nuclear stockpiles. More recently the world academies have joined forces to create the Inter-Academy Panel and International Research Council to create science-based policy advice for world leaders. To be sure, through the decades there have been national policy areas such as energy where informed science has been less than successful in shaping policy.

Political consensus on federal funding for research and on the use of informed science to guide policymaking is still strong and bipartisan, as witnessed by the congressional response to recommendations in the National Academies' *Rising above the Gathering Storm* (Committee, 2005). But schisms and tensions affecting both the support of science and the use of science in policy have grown in the last two decades. I believe that today these divisions have reached a level unprecedented since World War II. Why is this? I would mention five interconnected reasons.

First is the rate of scientific discovery, which in all disciplines is proceeding at an astounding pace. The absorption of new knowledge into invention and products is becoming ever shorter. Science and technology, always disruptive to societal mores and religious beliefs, contributes to these tensions between science, government, and society. Genetic engineering for medical purposes or modified agricultural crops and stem cell research are examples. The rapid, socially disruptive pace of science itself creates political tensions that the scientific community too frequently fails to appreciate.

Second, there is a great polarization of the two political parties and of politics. The comity between political elected political leaders that existed for several decades after the Second World War has disappeared. Both parties, fueled by the money, lobbying machines, and ideologies among the lobbyists on the "K Street Corridor" have adopted an in-your face view of governance. It is too often my way or no way.

The nexus between money, energy development, and the oil and gas industries exacerbates the situation. While there is still a degree of an across the aisle good will, especially in the Senate, elected representatives are focused on partisanship and their reelection, not on the governance of the nation. Public opinion polling suggests that Washington may have a "tin ear" in this respect; the public is yearning for solutions, not polarization, in Washington.

Third, while we separate religion and government under the Constitution, the party presently in power has trafficked in blurring this separation and has pandered to an electoral base of Republicans who are religiously at the "far right" in terms of the religiosity of all Americans. The exploitation of issues that have been traditionally separated by the Constitution—for example, the teaching of evolution as science in the public schools—as a political issue is illustrative.

Fourth, the economy is not as robust as politicians and optimistic economists try to persuade. As a nation we are mired down in various Middle Eastern engagements that seemingly have no happy endpoints or outcomes. The war in Iraq and peacekeeping engagements elsewhere in the Middle East are financially draining. There seems to be no successful end in sight to the debt burden these international obligations have created. The now indisputable disparities between the incomes of the extremely wealthy on the one hand, and middle and lower income Americans on the other, show that the tax cuts enacted by the Bush administration after coming to office have not made life better for all Americans. Rising fuel costs add to consumer unease, even though by European standards, our energy costs for transportation and home heating are still not high. But these consumer and economic factors, taken together, show that there is voter disenchantment at this time.

The fifth contributing factor to the present relation between science and government—for the direction of research and the use of science in policymaking—is the devaluing of science and scientific advice by President George W. Bush's administration. Administration officials, including the director of the White House Office of Science and Technology Policy, deny this, but it is true. Many presidents have on occasion not accepted the advice of their science advisers because of other policy considerations. However, no administration from the Eisenhower presidency through Clinton has so disregarded science advice that could inform policy in the way the way present administration has. Even the Nixon presidency during the years leading to his resignation did not see appointments to scientific panels manipulated as they have been in this presidency. And Nixon embraced the science-based environmental legislation enacted by Congress during his time in office. The Bush administration has reached down into research agencies to place political appointees on advisory panels and acted in other unprecedented ways—for example, having a political "spin" added to research findings coming from government agencies and laboratories, and in other cases halting research papers or press releases. And in ways past presidents have not, Bush has inserted himself and his personal and religious views—on intelligent design, for example—into public school curriculum debates, further blurring the constitutional separation of government and religion.

These five factors—there are undoubtedly others—together create political gridlock in Washington. The gridlock affects all policy-making and also many issues of policy for the conduct of science and its federal support, and, the informed use of scientific knowledge to inform political decision-making. The effect of the present political gridlock in Washington on investment in science and science policy that informs government is no better illustrated than by the issues of stem cell research—basic research—and a national actionable response to climate change informed by science. While the biomedical community is culpable of overselling the promises of gene therapy and stem cell research, the promise is such that it has united an across the aisle coalition in both the House and the Senate. The commonality of views on stem cell research by a "center" in both the House of Representatives and the Senate is as of this writing insufficient to overcome the recent veto and prospective presidential vetoes by the president (who used his veto power for the first time), thus impeding nationally funded basic research in an area where the public believes science could potentially eradicate tragic and wasting genetically inherited and acquired end-of-life illnesses. Outside of the Washington beltway, most Americans—state legislators and governors, mayors, executives in most companies and the public—believe climate change is a reality. Climate warming affects day-to-day day decision making at the city or community level, states, institutions in the states, and federal policy. On this issue there is now a great disconnect between Washington and the rest of America. The multiyear drought in the Southwest and higher than average summer temperatures across the nation in 2006 have increased public concern.

So is there any way to move ahead? To move beyond the present gridlock that affects both the direction of federally sponsored research and development and the informed use of science to create national policy? Can the political center for the support of science and the informed use of science in policy be broadened?

I believe the center can be expanded but I also believe that the science community itself must take a vigorous leadership role in working to expand this center. We must seek new allies for research support and for the use of science in decision making. Our disciplines have been well supported over the years and we have perhaps become too accustomed to others (such as Congress) taking the lead on support for science and using science to inform policy. We have to work with our own professional societies and associations and groups like Research!America. While Washington is gridlocked on many issues, much is being done at other levels of government and by industry and nonprofit institutions. Governors and mayors across the nation have organized task forces on climate change and sustainability. These panels are state-level entry points for science policy. Industry is taking impressive steps to reduce their emissions and many companies seek outside advice from experts on these and other issues. State initiatives on stem cell research support provide another venue in which scientists can inform and explain and broaden a consensus on ethical stem cell research.

We have to engage groups that we are sometimes uncomfortable in working with. Too often our community finds fault with the media, saying they "don't get the stories right." By and large the print and electronic media do a remarkably good job in reporting. They will do an even better job if we work with reporters, not criticize them in public forums as we often do. There are others where we may be even more uncomfortable in opening a dialogue than we sometimes are with reporters. For example early in 2006 some 42 evangelical leaders expressed concerns about climate change and the plight of future generations. Without compromising our scientific principles, we ought to be able to find some common ground with these religious leaders and perhaps create a national consensus on global warming in the process.

Finally, I would say that is very important for us to connect with the young people of the nation and the world, not just budding scientists and engineers but all young people. They are interested in issues of science policy and we should reach out, explain, listen, and use their good suggestions and insights.

If we forge these and other alliances that enlarge the "center" for the support of science and informed use of science in policy, the stronger and wider array of voices stemming from the alliances will begin to make a difference in Washington.

REFERENCES

Committee on Prospering in the Global Economy of the Twenty-First Century: An Agenda for American Science and Technology, National Academy of Sciences, National Academy of Engineering, Institute of Medicine. *Rising Above the Gathering Storm: Energizing and Employing America for a Brighter Economic Future.* Washington, D.C.: The National Academy Press, 2005.

Ruth Wooden

The Principles of Public Engagement: At the Nexus of Science, Public Policy Influence, and Citizen Education

YOU CANNOT BE A SCIENTIST WITHOUT UNDERSTANDING AND ACCEPTING the core principles of the scientific method—the techniques for developing knowledge based on observable, empirical, and measurable evidence, and subject to laws of reasoning. The scientific method has an established, essential process involving the development of hypotheses, testing hypotheses, repetition to ensure dependable predictions of future results, and the development of theories to encompass whole domains of inquiry to bind together specific hypotheses. An understanding of the basics of the process—problem description, prediction, control, and understanding covariation of events, time-order relationships, and elimination of plausible relationships—is absolutely essential before getting started with any specific line of inquiry.

The same is true of engaging the public. Before one can answer the question, "What needs to be done now, and by whom or by what institutions, in order to ensure that good science leads to good public policy that best serves the needs of the American public?" we need to understand the basic principles guiding the stages of public opinion formation. Before we can answer, "How can we change the current situation so that scientists and scientific findings have more influence?" we need to accept the principle that the scientific community functions within society, not the other way around. The scientific community disregards the thinking of the public at its own peril.

From climate change to genetically modified organisms, from stem cells and cloning to bioterrorism—these are all scientific issues, but *non*scientists will be making big decisions about how they are addressed. All of these issues raise questions and values far beyond the laboratory that the public must evaluate. The question is: What can scientists do to make the most of public deliberation?

Good public policy should come by way of a political process where an engaged and knowledgeable public weighs in on policy, which in turn produces adequate funding for scientific research, high valuation of scientific research in the formulation of government policy, and appropriate regulations. It is not possible for the practice of science to be completely unfettered from public opinion since scientific research must be accountable to contemporary concerns about values and ethics.

Policymakers, the public, and the scientific community have mutual interests in working through the issues together, but at present real engagement is almost entirely lacking. The scientific community is forging ahead, hoping that it can avoid most, if not all, restrictions on its work and, until recently, assuming that its research would be accepted as the definitive word in policy formation. Policymakers are positioning themselves on politics and economics, and many give science short shrift or use it only when it suits their established positions. And the public remains seriously disengaged and largely uninformed.

Without a strong, informed public voice, decisionmakers are left rudderless—or worse, at the behest of special interests. The public has a right to come to judgment on the issues, but it also has an obligation to come to an understanding of them.

Scientists speak frequently about the "science literacy" problem. "If only people knew more about science, then that would take care of the problem." But the gap is not simply a "knowledge gap." The public may feel that, while scientists have facts and statistics, they themselves have knowledge, real-world experience and understanding, and, yes, even a personal connection to and faith in the unknowable that gives them a different—but not inferior—perspective.

The scientific community should take the lead in bridging the gaps. Only real dialogue can achieve the goal of sound public judgment on scientific issues. Scientists should begin to do this by framing issues in ways that acknowledge scientific content *and* social and political realities. By offering the public choices that show costs and benefits, advantages and drawbacks, scientists can provide information that will help Americans think, learn, and make informed choices.

PUBLIC ENGAGEMENT IS NOT PUBLIC RELATIONS

Campaigns aimed at "informing" the public often fail to have their intended impact because they don't take into account the Seven Stages of Public Opinion, developed by Public Agenda's founder, Daniel Yankelovich. Understanding the stages of public opinion is the first step in developing an effective public engagement process. What follows is a brief overview of the seven stages, presented specifically for the scientific community's needs.

People are not empty vessels just waiting to be filled up with scientific facts. They possess existing idea frameworks and dispositions that need to be taken into account. And public opinion as a whole, as well as individually, is not static. People's views about issues develop and change over time—usually starting at disconnected, poorly informed reactions to events to more thoughtful and considered conclusions. The whole of the public tends to move gradually from changeable public opinion to settled public judgment.

In Stage One, the public has "dawning awareness." People develop a general awareness of an issue as a problem, but no real urgency to deal with it. Americans are presented with a multitude of problems on a daily basis, but only a few rise to the top of their list of priorities. Some issues dwell forever in this realm of low awareness and lower priority.

In Stage Two, the public begins to feel "greater urgency." At this point, people are not thinking so much about specific solutions, but they do begin to think "we have to do something" about the issue because they see the impact it might have on their lives. It is in the next stage, "reaching for solutions," that the public begins to look at alternatives for dealing with issues, converting free-floating concern into calls for action. At this still relatively early formative stage, the public will often gravitate to one or more choices presented to them by experts or policymakers. But since people may not have come to fully understand the choices presented to them, Stage Three is a period Dan Yankelovich has characterized as "stunningly false endorsements." That is, the public expresses support for a proposal but backs down as soon as the costs and trade-offs begin to surface.

This is the stage when "expertism"—where the decision-making process is taken over by the jargon and agenda setting of elites—is also a real problem. The message that the public gets from that kind of "public discussion" is "I am not in this debate, no one is talking my language and no one thinks I'm qualified to be in this discussion." It is at this point that the public frequently checks out. This is such a common occurrence on science-related issues that it should not be a surprise when scientists seek public support, the public just is not there.

"Wishful thinking" is Stage Four. This is where the public's aversion to facing trade-offs is most pronounced. In part because they still do not have all the facts about how various aspects of the problem relate to one another and because they have not weighed various consequences against one another, the members of the public tend to think they can have things that are mutually exclusive or unrealistic based on available resources or other unchangeable conditions. Confronting the public with necessary trade-offs is essential to moving them into the next stage.

In Stage Five, the public begins "weighing the choices." It is at this point that the public does "choice work," weighing the pros and cons of alternatives for dealing with an issue. As people come to understand that easy, cost-free solutions are unlikely to work and that seemingly simple solutions may have down-sides, the public gives considerably more thought to the issue and proposals for addressing it. Stages Three,

Four, and Five can be grouped together under the general heading of "working through"—a term encompassing rational thought as well as feelings and ethical concerns. This is where the scientific community must become more open to give and take with the public and contribute to the "working through" process.

In Stage Six, the public takes a stand intellectually, but it is not until Stage Seven, that people fully integrate their new thinking about an issue into their lives and begin making responsible judgments about the issue, morally and emotionally. The intellectual, post-choicework resolution of Stage Six requires people to clarify fuzzy thinking, reconcile inconsistencies, consider relevant facts and new realties, and grasp the full consequences of choices. The emotional resolution of Stage Seven requires people to accommodate themselves to different situations, change their own thinking and behavior, and confront their own ambivalent feelings. The final two stages can be grouped together as the stages at which the public comes to resolution about an issue.

On so many public policy issues where science plays a major role, public opinion is still in the early stages of opinion formation. Even on issues where there has been a great deal of debate in the media and public policy circles, such as stem cells and climate change, the public is nowhere near the point of really thinking through the major dimensions and possible solutions to problems, let alone coming to settled public judgment about what should be done.

This presents great challenges and great opportunities for the science community. Public support for science in general is strong. Majorities believe that science and technology improve our health, make our lives better, and are important in maintaining US influence in the world. And yet, Americans do not really know very much about science and technology and have a natural tendency to fear the unknown.

But it is important for the science community to realize that the public engagement process is not a public relations exercise—it involves listening—and it certainly is not selling—it is two-way communications. Real public dialogue is not mass marketing. Neither is it a series of large forums (visualize your typical schoolboard meeting or a congressman's orchestrated "townhall" meeting) dominated or hijacked by advocates and the most strident voices. Nor is it a series of lectures from pontificating, jargon-spewing elites. Real public engagement involves laying out the major, plausible alternatives for addressing issues, identifying the pros, cons, and trade-offs of each, and providing substantial opportunities for average citizens to weigh the options and apply their own beliefs and experiences to the issues.

This kind of public engagement requires the dedication of time and resources just to get to the process of "working through." But once the larger public has understood the trade-offs associated with complex issues, leadership—in this case political and scientific leadership—will have invaluable insights into the public's most deeply held values and a view toward the policy options that best resonate with them.

What this process of true public engagement requires is a different kind of scientific leadership—one that is committed to breaking down the ambivalence between science and citizens and taking responsibility for a partnership of respect and working hard to build and keep trust with the American people that the scientific community is truly working in the larger public interest.

On a related note, recent Public Agenda research provides yet another indication that that the gap between the scientific community and the public is widening. In our *Reality Check 2006* series of public opinion research on public education, Public Agenda found education "consumers"—students and parents—to be indifferent to math and science education and mostly ignorant of the current policy concerns. While parents and students support the idea of more math and science education in general, they do not see the need for more of it themselves (as students, or parents for their children). In fact, a large portion of students said they would be quite unhappy in careers in science. So, while scientists may look back to the era of the space race when every kid wanted to be a scientist or an astronaut, those times are long gone and perceptions of science have changed. The inspiring vision has not emerged in recent years that would motivate legions of young people to recognize and consider the benefits of a career in science.

In the end, in order to answer the questions, "How can we [scientists] improve the policy decision-making process on scientific matters?" the science community must do some soul searching. It must encourage those scientists who are willing to step out of the relative safety of the lab and into communities to discuss the tough choices we face on so many science policy matters. Without a better understanding of what information the public needs to make fully informed choices, scientists will have to accept that they may well be subject to the decisions made by politicians who claim to speak on the public's behalf.

Understanding and employing the basic principles of public engagement is the first step in creating the conditions under which science and public opinion come together to produce good public policy. Many in the scientific community have begun to recognize that it is their responsibility to bring the public into the discussion of scientific matters. No major scientific policy can take hold or advance in society without public acceptance. It is therefore in the scientific community's own self-interest to reach out to the public to understand and educate—not with a dissertation but with true dialogue. But the scientific community needs to ignite this dialogue, and partnering with those institutions that exist to involve, educate, and engage the public are an important first step.

Notes on Contributors

ERIC COHEN is Director of the Biotechnology and American Democracy program at the Ethics and Public Policy Center and Editor of *The New Atlantis*.

KATAYOUN CHAMANY is a faculty member in the Science, Technology, and Society program of Eugene Lang College, The New School. She uses a sociopolitical approach to teach courses in the area of infectious diseases, cell biology, and genetics.

RITA COLWELL, Chairman of Canon U.S. Life Sciences, Inc., also serves as Distinguished University Professor at the University of Maryland, College Park, and on the faculty of the Johns Hopkins Bloomberg School of Public Health.

PAUL EHRLICH is President of the Center for Conservation Biology and the Bing Professor of Population Studies at Stanford University.

M. JOYCELYN ELDERS is Professor Emeritus at the University of Arkansas School of Medicine. She was appointed US Surgeon General by President Bill Clinton, and was the first women to hold that post.

IRA FLATOW is the host of *Talk of The Nation: Science Friday* on National Public Radio and the founder and President of Talking Science, a nonprofit company dedicated to creating radio, TV, and Internet projects that make science user-friendly.

ROBERT GEORGE is McCormick Professor of Jurisprudence and Director of the James Madison Program in American Ideals and Institutions at Princeton University. He is a member of the President's Council on Bioethics.

PAUL GILMAN is Director of the Oak Ridge National Laboratory Center for Advanced Studies. In 2002 he was appointed US EPA Science Adviser.

DAVID GOLDSTON is Chief of Staff of the House Committee on Science, which oversees most of the federal civilian research and development budget, including programs run by NASA, the NSF, the DOE, and the EPA.

KURT GOTTFRIED is Professor Emeritus of Physics at Cornell University and Co-founder and Chair of the Union of Concerned Scientists. He is a former Chair of the Division of Particles and Fields of the American Physical Society.

JAMES HANSEN is Director of the NASA Goddard Institute for Space Studies (GISS), a laboratory of the Earth-Sun Exploration Division of NASA's Goddard Space Flight Center and a unit of the Columbia University Earth Institute.

STEVEN HAYWARD is F. K. Weyerhaeuser Fellow at the American Enterprise Institute for Public Policy Research and a Senior Fellow at the Pacific Research Institute for Public Policy. He studies the environment, law, political economy, and the presidency.

MARTIN HOFFERT is Professor Emeritus of Physics at New York University. His research focuses on global environmental change, geophysical fluid dynamics, oceanography,